MW00667379

Alice Walker

WOMEN WRITERS OF COLOR

Alice Walker

A Woman for Our Times

Deborah G. Plant

Joanne M. Braxton, Series Editor

 PRAEGER™

An Imprint of ABC-CLIO, LLC
Santa Barbara, California • Denver, Colorado

Library of Congress Cataloging-in-Publication Data

Names: Plant, Deborah G., 1956– author.
Title: Alice Walker : a woman for our times / Deborah G. Plant.
Description: Santa Barbara, California : Praeger, 2017. | Series: Women writers
    of color | Includes bibliographical references and index.
Identifiers: LCCN 2017016395 (print) | LCCN 2017029393 (ebook) |
    ISBN 9780313377518 (ebook) | ISBN 9780313377501 (alk. paper)
Subjects: LCSH: Walker, Alice, 1944– | Authors, American—20th century—
    Biography. | African American women authors—Biography. | Civil rights
    workers—United States—Biography
Classification: LCC PS3573.A425 (ebook) | LCC PS3573.A425 Z85 2017 (print) |
    DDC 813/.54 [B]—dc23
LC record available at https://lccn.loc.gov/2017016395

ISBN: 978-0-313-37750-1
EISBN: 978-0-313-37751-8

21 20 19 18 17   1 2 3 4 5

This book is also available as an eBook.

Praeger
An Imprint of ABC-CLIO, LLC

ABC-CLIO, LLC
130 Cremona Drive, P.O. Box 1911
Santa Barbara, California 93116-1911
www.abc-clio.com

This book is printed on acid-free paper ∞

Manufactured in the United States of America

For
My Sister
Gloria Jean Plant Gilbert

Contents

viii   Contents

Series Foreword

DEBORAH G. PLANT, *ALICE WALKER: A WOMAN FOR OUR TIMES*

The Women Writers of Color series began in 2006 with books about two of the best loved women of color writers in the United States, *Lucille Clifton: Her Life and Letters* by Mary Jane Lupton and *June Jordan: Her Life and Letters*, by Valerie Kinloch. The next year Deborah G. Plant's *Zora Neale Hurston: A Biography of the Spirit* was published, followed by biographies of Sandra Cisneros, Louise Erdrich, Nikki Giovanni, and Toni Cade Bambara. For more than a decade, this series has offered enjoyable reading for an enlightened multi-ethnic audience that includes scholars and critics, poets and writers, librarians and young adults who read both critically and for entertainment and inspiration.

We are proud to present *Alice Walker: A Woman for Our Times* by Deborah G. Plant as the final volume in the series. Seer, sayer and doer, American novelist and poet Alice Walker has come a long way from being a young girl too traumatized to tell her parents about being shot in the eye by a BB gun. Plant is an English literature and Africana Studies scholar and literary critic whose special interest is the life and works of Zora Neale Hurston, who Alice Walker helped re-introduce to appreciative readers. Plant's books include

Every Tub Must Sit on Its Own Bottom: The Philosophy and Politics of Zora Neale Hurston (1995), *The Inside Light: New Critical Essays on Zora Neale Hurston,* editor (2010), and *Zora Neale Hurston: A Biography of the Spirit* (2007). She was instrumental in founding the University of South Florida Department of Africana Studies. She chaired that department for five years and was associate professor of Africana Studies there until being appointed associate professor of English in 2014. Plant currently resides in Tampa, Florida, and continues her research and writing as an independent scholar.

Alice Walker: A Woman for Our Times explores the philosophical thought that informs Walker's life, work, and activism. With exquisite attention, Plant takes us through the seasons of Walker's life and witnessing, from rural Georgia, to New York City, down to Mississippi, to Gaza, to East Africa and to many of the people and places that impacted Walker's intellectual and philosophical growth. What does it mean to be a woman for our times? Miraculously, Walker has endured from the civil rights era through the Black Arts movement to the present, often viewed as an outcast because of the things she chose to write about and the people she chose to love. Walker's career spans decades of embodied activism "at the intersection of creativity, peace, spirituality, and social change." We met her as a young woman in her first collection of poetry, *Once,* but today she speaks as an elder and a survivor, with an ever-deepening voice.

Walker's is a voice that is much needed today. The author of nearly 40 volumes to date, Alice Walker speaks out with a voice of salvific encouragement in titles like *Hard Times Require Furious Dancing* and *Anything We Love Can Be Saved.* She has been a voice for human rights, love for the earth, and love for every living thing. She advocates *Overcoming Speechlessness* as a form of self-healing, as she did after her 2008 trip to Gaza: "The one who stands and sees is also harmed, but not nearly so much as the one who stands and sees and says and does nothing."

Our country and indeed our world is in a very different place from where they were when the Women Writers of Color series was inaugurated. Two years after we began the series this nation witnessed the election of Barack Hussein Obama and the streets were filled with the dancing hope of America's young. They danced their dreams for a more inclusive America. Then came disillusionment, giving rise to Black Lives Matter and the Occupy movement. In 2017, as I write this foreword, some would say that our democracy is at risk, our democratic election process having been challenged by a cyber-attack from a foreign power. War rages in Syria, and global climate change makes refugees near and far. In a time such as this, the life and work of Alice Walker calls upon each of us to see and say and do. I believe that Zora Neale Hurston, June Jordan, Lucille Clifton, Toni Cade Bambara, and the other women whose lives are represented in this series would ask no less. May it be so.

Joanne M. Braxton
The College of William and Mary

Acknowledgments

I offer appreciation to Divine Grace for the publication of this work. It took me more years to complete it than I ever imagined and could not have anticipated. On the one hand, the depth and breadth of Alice Walker's work is truly amazing. On the other, I was riding the anaconda of CFIDS (chronic fatigue immune dysfunction syndrome). Yet I had set the intention to see the work through to completion. Even so, I know that integral to my ability to continue with the work was the continued support and encouragement of family, friends, neighbors, and the wise hearts and healing hands of healthcare practitioners who attended my health. I thank my editors, Joanne Braxton and Kim Kennedy White and my Project Manager Gordon Hammy Matchado for their support. And I wish to express my thanks and appreciation to all those who inspired me with their patient waiting and encouraged me with their expectations of one day reading this work. Because they were waiting for it, I had to deliver it.

I offer especial thanks and appreciation to Gloria Plant-Gilbert, Denise Plant, Dennis Plant, Dawn Plant, Kimberly Plant, Bobby Plant, Von Erick Plant, Tia Plant, Jaylen Gilbert, Phyllis McEwen, Laura Tohe, Kersuze Simeon, Cathy Daniels, Maria Basilieri, Judy Matheson, Felicia Kelley, Shekina Burson, Evelinda "Everlasting" Watkins, Jasmine Lankford, Malika Black, Kenya Gayle, Annisha Moses, Gurleen Grewal, Mary Wendelken, Mr. Henry Carter, Jr., Mrs. Roseann Carter, Gwendolyn Lucy Bailey Evans, Ms. Julie and Arlo, Ms. Charissa and Xander, Bobby and Bill, Bill and Mary, Joe and Wilco, Alberto Villoldo, Gomati Ishaya, Vasistha Ishaya, Dr. Shao, Reginald Eldridge, Kendra Nicole, Ms. Nina, Lisa Jemison, Valerie Boyd, and Evelyn C. White. I am also particularly appreciative of John Cochran, former associate dean at the University of South Florida. During my tenure there as chair of the Africana Studies Department, John revealed himself to be a person of integrity, a supportive administrator, and a compassionate human being. He was a true light for me. Thank you, John.

Introduction

Alice Walker is a woman for our times. She knows how to honor the difficult; for millions of people across the planet, life is difficult. She is a woman of courage who has been on the frontlines of every major and untold numbers of unpublicized "minor" social movements in America since the civil rights era, and she has traveled around the world to stand with people and to advocate for the planet. Courage is something we all can use in these times where fear is the cocktail of the day and the hate that goes by the name of domestic or international terrorism dares anyone to hope. She is a woman of vision who even as a child could see through lies and as a teenager and student activist could envision a life that defied her circumstances. As a 17-year-old daughter of Georgia sharecroppers and survivor of childhood trauma, Walker boarded a segregated Greyhound bus in her hometown of Eatonton, Georgia, en route to Atlanta where she would attend Spelman College. It was 1961. Though she was forced to sit at the back of the bus, she became a force to be reckoned with, as she committed to a struggle of creating a society that respected, protected, and valued all its citizens.

In a time where personal integrity too often takes a backseat to personal advancement and profit, and everything is commodified for exploitation—even the trust of the people—the character of Alice Walker invites exploration. Her honesty compels her to "tell the truth always" and to look for and appreciate ethical behavior in those around her. In every arena, the leadership in America is questionable, and most Americans, across demographics, simply despair of having a leadership that actually cares about their very complicated and stressed lives. Walker clearly and honestly states that "We are in peril and that there is no trustworthy leadership."[1] And at the same time, she knows that the only real power is internal—not external. When Alice Walker walked to the back of the Greyhound bus, with heavy feet and a heavy heart, she vowed to put an end to the South that permitted her humiliation. What she learned through her participation in the civil rights movement was that every effort toward change matters, that every thought, poem, dream, or choice made to bring about a world of peace and joy makes a difference.

And so the work of changing the world, of ushering in a time of balance, a time of peace and respectful relationships which includes a just regard for planet Earth—the only home in the galaxy that we know and that loves us—compels us all to action. "We have slumbered a long time believing the lies of those in power," says Walker. We all have been "morally and politically manipulated and tricked." And yet, Walker would have us consider our own contribution to the madness. "Consider your own part in this. . . . What have you learned about 'leaders' and 'facts' and your own willingness to believe, or disbelieve, what others tell you in a time of fear and, especially, of mourning."[2] Her statement was made in relation to the events of September 11, 2001, yet they apply to so many situations since, as well as before, that day. What she is telling us is that waiting for the right "leader" is futile and disempowering and that, in fact, "we are the ones we have been waiting for."[3] Nothing ends despair like action.

Having faced mobs, police dogs, and establishment officials on every level of government who insisted that separation, greed, and oppression was the ordained order of the day, Walker knows what it is to feel ineffectual, helpless, overpowered, and a victim. But the life she has lived has more than proved that not only are feelings of helplessness but passing illusions, but also that state-sanctioned injustice cannot stand forever. Walker's life and work as a writer-activist gives insight into how to move forward in a world that for many of us has become hostile and absurd. It encourages us to look to the light within one's self for direction. It urges us to do the work of coming into personal integrity in our own lives, and from there, to join hands with likeminded others and healing circles and councils that, together, can dispel the unconsciousness that clouds our reality and thereby transform our world.

Central to Alice Walker's writing and activism is a philosophical orientation that has kept her centered in mind, body, and spirit while she has done the dangerous work of speaking her truth. Her philosophy about life has been the wellspring of her extraordinary effort to end suffering wherever it arises on the planet. A personal, practical philosophy is essential if life is to have meaning and one's actions are to have integrity. Informed by philosophical reflection and reasoning, Alice Walker's life and work offer insight into what it means to live one's life fully and joyfully—even in the midst of difficult circumstances. Because I believe it is important that we, each of us, come to terms with our own personalities and personal politics and that we become empowered to live a large life of our own design, and because I believe that such a coming to terms is facilitated by a philosophical approach to life, I have written this philosophical biography of Alice Walker.

Philosophy helps us to understand our personal lives and our lives in relation to our society and the larger environment called life on planet Earth. Philosophy can help us to access the fortitude to face and move through challenges and crises. Importantly, philosophy can teach us to face and overcome the fear of death, which comes in a variety of guises beyond the fear of physical death—joblessness, homelessness, divorce, defamation, illness, inadequate healthcare, insufficient funds. Alice Walker's lifework is a meditation on facing and overcoming fear. Philosopher Ray Monk writes in his essay "Philosophical Biography: The Very Idea," that a subject for philosophical biography is "someone whose thought—whether expressed in poetry, music, painting, fiction or works of philosophy—it is important and interesting to understand."[4] It is important for us to understand how to live in bewildering and challenging times. It is important for us to know our power to transform these times. It is interesting to know that the sum of such engagement is joy. Therefore, Alice Walker is someone whose thought it is important and interesting for us to understand, someone whose life experiences and wisdom recommend her as a woman for our times. Her work situates us all in the healing circle of life, reminding us of our good, our light, our abiding connection to Earth and one another, and the power within us all that is love itself. She is Elder. She is Human Sunrise. She is the adventurer, the older sister, the philosopher, the sage who returns to light the pathway:

When life descends into the pit
I must become my own candle
willingly burning myself
to light up the darkness around me.[5]

SECTION I

Earth

Out of the primordial soup of darkness and hydrogen raindrops, condensed globules of matter, and explosive nebulae, "a small world of stone and iron" formed. A planet. Earth. From its undulating phases of condensation, eruption, and dispersion came soil, rocks, minerals, vegetation, animal and human bodies.[1] Earth sources and sustains all life forms. Radiating yellow-gold, Earth corresponds with north, the direction of growth, connectivity, solidity, and limits.[2]

Earth is Mother. Gaia. Terra Firma. Mother Nature. The womb of our physical expression. "Her living soil feeds us; her rocks make our bones; her minerals are in our life's blood."[3] Ever changing, always the same, out of Earth's constancy evolves a panoramic display of vibratory creations modulating from bush to towering tree, plains to peaks, desert to glacial realms. Earth is and contains all. It knows nothing of private property. Mountains inspire confidence and persistence and fixity and inertia. Shifting sand calls forth discernment and humility as firm ground engenders safety and security. The "deep matter of our existence," Earth teaches us our own holiness.[4]

Earth fashions the mortal garment of the human entity, "the little kshetra," and thus "stands for the perishable body."[5] Fruit of Undifferentiated and Unmanifested Nature, Earth also symbolizes potentiality and transcendent life—Spirit. The little kshetra—"the miniature embodiment of Nature"—reflects the attributes of Mother Nature.[6] With the Fire of Wisdom, humanity embraces the cycle of life, and aspires to unconditional love, boundless generosity, optimism, and beauty; realizing that in the galactic swirl of space and constellations, it is upon the Earth that the little kshetra walks, and it is as the salt of the Earth that it knows itself.

"There Are Bad Women Walking on the Planet Now" by Phyllis McEwen

The Earth
I know She is trembling, bleeding, smiling.
There is a Bad Woman
Walkin the Planet
Walkin til her toes touch Earth
Like a listening, like a
Nipple speaks to life
Like She never had any and needs it
needs it bad.

The Earth
She has been lonely
For my knowing Her like a Bad
Woman should.
She has been asking for me in
All Her secret places;
Wetting Herself ready to feel me
(This is so long overdue)
While She shakes out the magical menses and shouts about
rites of passage from good girl
To Bad Woman
OOOO Yeah.

I am passing out fear through my birth canal
Like something you might need to bury in the Earth
before you raise it
Until it blooms into a criminal female blossom;
I am passing fear
from a Bad Woman's birth canal.

Last night I dreamed Her green then blue
Then The Color Purple
When She touched me I burst bad:
This is my planet.
I am all over Her.
I am welcoming myself into places
Where some stupid body
Told me not to go.
I am checking things out.

Make sure that patriarchy knows
Make sure that hunger knows
Make sure that war knows:

There are some bad, Bad, Bad-Assed neck-twistin
shit-talkin, rainbow sistahs walkin on the planet now.

some sweet peach lovin
titty swingin
policy makin
purple wearin
rule breakin
poetry writin
baby catchin
high-heel steppin
bus drivin
cotton-pickin
bata playin

dreadlock growin
herb healin
boot sportiin
root workin
music makin

Bad Bad Women
Walkin on the Planet

NOW.

ONE

I Am the Earth. . . .

At the heart of Alice Walker's philosophical thought is the oneness of human nature and nonhuman nature. This foundational idea supports her belief in Earth as the sacred source of all life on the planet. "I'm from earth," she states. "I go back to earth. I'll always be here."[1] This philosophical orientation is Walker's guiding light. It informs her art and inspires her activism. Her appreciation of Earth as sacred and as source is an evolving personal and political philosophy that is apparent across the arch of her life-work and can be traced to her childhood roots in rural Georgia.

Alice Malsenior (Tallulah Kate) Walker is the youngest of eight children born to Willie Lee Walker (1909–1973) and Minnie Tallulah "Lou" Grant Walker (1912–1993). She was born at home in a sharecropper's shack in Wards Chapel near Eatonton, in Putnam County, Georgia. She was named for two maternal aunts. Both her parents were from families that were long established in Putnam County. Albert Walker, Willie Lee's grandfather and Alice Walker's great-grandfather, had inherited land from his Scottish slaveholding father. His cotton crop destroyed by boll weevils for several successive years, Albert Walker lost his land and social standing and became a tenant farmer to a local white family. His son, Henry Clay Walker (Willie Lee's father and Alice Walker's grandfather) would also become a tenant farmer.

Willie Lee and Minnie Lou married on June 1, 1930. Their future together was circumscribed by the white supremacist politics that reigned in the Jim Crow South. Their prospects became even more bleak with the onset of the Great Depression. The couple found employment as sharecroppers on the same

Marker welcoming visitors to Walker's hometown. (Gloria Jean Plant-Gilbert)

land worked by Willie Lee's father, Henry Clay Walker. The inequities inherent in the sharecropping system not only exploited the labor of African Americans but also routinely resulted in their being indebted to white farmers, promising a future of perpetual servitude. Alice Walker often describes herself as "a daughter of the rural peasantry."[2] This descriptive bespeaks the apparent and subtle similarities between the social and economic structure of rural Georgia and that of medieval Europe. The Walker family, like other African American families in the agricultural South, would be perceived and related to as peasants, just as their forebears were perceived and related to as slaves, as mere units of labor.

The life Willie Lee and Minnie Lou Walker faced in 1930 was not anomalous, and it did not represent a modern state of affairs. The ruling class of Georgia had decided over two centuries prior what the value and use of black life would be and then related to black people accordingly. The idea that the unpaid labor of African people was essential to the prosperity of Anglo-Europeans permeated colonial American society. Georgia, however, was poised to be the exception to this rule. On June 9, 1732, King George II signed the charter to establish the colony of Georgia in America. Most notable among the trustees charged with administering the new colony was James Edward Oglethorpe. The Georgia plan developed by the trustees of the new colony, and championed by Oglethorpe, forbade slavery. Oglethorpe strongly believed that the labor required to establish the colony should be provided by the "poor, the unemployed, and unemployable" of England and Europe. He believed that "through the medium of work," these dispossessed "wretches" and "drones" "would become useful and virtuous citizens."[3]

Discontent grew among the Georgia settlers as they observed the economic and material wealth accruing to their South Carolina neighbors whose economy was based on African slave labor, and they challenged Oglethorpe's authority in denying them the perceived advantage. The trustees successfully petitioned the British Parliament to pass the Act of 1734 that officially outlawed chattel slavery in the Georgia Province. Nevertheless, the settlers continued their demand for African labor: "'The one thing needful' for the success, if not the very survival, of Georgia," they proclaimed, "was black slave labor."[4] By 1742, enslaved Africans were being integrated into the Georgia Province. By 1750, proslavery proponents in Parliament and within Georgia, influenced and encouraged by those in South Carolina, defeated Oglethorpe's decree, and, in 1751, elected to officially permit African slave labor into the Georgia economy. Alice Walker's progenitors would be numbered among those sold into bondage in Georgia.

Walker traces her ancestral line through the early 1800s back to May Poole, her great-great-great-great paternal grandmother. Sold on the auction block in Virginia, Mary "May" Poole then "walked to Eatonton with a baby straddled on each hip."[5] She was held in bondage throughout the nineteenth century. For three-quarters of a century, she was servant to a white woman "to whom she'd been given as a wedding gift." May Poole's "attitude and courage" gave her the capacity to endure and live, and to "attend the funerals of almost everyone who'd ever owned her." She lived to be 125 years of age. Walker's father was 11 years old when she died.[6]

This kind of strength and tenaciousness sustained Willie Lee and Minnie Lou Walker who eked out a living tilling the soil and working as laborer and domestic to their white neighbors. The limited prospects of sharecropping compelled Willie Lee Walker to seek more profitable employment as a laborer, although he would again and again have to return to either sharecropping or tenant farming to feed his family. Though the Walkers survived the Great Depression, making a living continued to be a struggle. By 1944 when Alice Walker was born, the family's annual

Sign for Alice Walker's childhood home. (Gloria Jean Plant-Gilbert)

income ranged between $200 and $300. Given the economic challenges of the time for most Americans, even this income felt significant, as the Walkers managed to have hard currency on hand to pay Miss Fannie, the midwife, for her services during Alice's birth. Mrs. Walker's pride in being able to do so is evidenced in the poem Alice Walker wrote, "Three Dollars Cash," which commemorated the event. Rather than allowing Miss Fannie to make a selection from a litter of pigs, as she had done when she assisted at the birth of one of Alice's brothers, Mrs. Walker was able to pay the midwife "Three dollars cash." "'We wasn't so country then,' says Mom."[7]

While her father was en route to get Miss Fannie, baby Alice, unassisted, pushed her way into a world peopled by family and community. Among the surprised and welcoming smiles were her elder sister Mamie's and, her paternal grandmother "Ma-Ma" Rachel Walker's. Later would arrive Miss Birda Reynolds, the local schoolteacher, bringing Alice her first set of clothing. Reynolds observed, "Alice was a very alert baby, and we could all tell, by the way her eyes took in everything, that she was going to be special." The community of Wards Chapel embraced and doted on Alice Malsenior. Before she made her first birthday, they bestowed on her the first place award in a fund-raising contest that sought "the cutest baby." Her parents fussed over her and were proud of this baby who, having begun to crawl, "would back herself up against a wall and pretend to read the Sears and Roebuck catalog" and write with a twig into the margins of the pages.[8]

When Mrs. Walker returned to the "six-hundred-acre farm" to pick cotton alongside her husband, she took newborn Alice with her. When she could walk, Alice would "trail along behind her as she chopped cotton." Sometimes, Walker recollected, "I'd fall asleep out at the edge of the field where she couldn't really look after me because she had to work."[9] Born under the influence of Aquarian stars and compelled to explore the wonders of the agrarian terrain into which she was born, young Alice would wander off. Mrs. Walker had neither the luxury of remaining home to take care of her youngest daughter, nor had the family the financial means to hire a sitter. Though Ruth, six years older than Alice, was eager to watch over her baby sister after school, Alice required more consistent attention and adult supervision.

As was typical of schoolteachers in sharecropping communities, Miss Reynolds supported the Walkers by accepting Alice as a student at four years of age. She was attentive and studious, Reynolds recalled, "a smart and extremely focused little girl." Whereas the minds of other children strayed while Miss Reynolds read to them, "Alice would be looking right back at me scrunching up her little brow like she was trying to make a mental picture of what I was reading." She could spell better than children older than she and when reciting rhymes or lines of poetry, she did so with precision and self-assurance. "A lot of children passed my way," reminisced Miss Reynolds, "but Alice Walker was the smartest one I ever had."[10]

Continuously engaged in the demands of survival, their employment dictated by the firmly entrenched caste system of the rural South that divided

along the lines of race, class, and sex, Willie Lee and Minnie Lou Walker were
bent on forging better options for their children. In this endeavor, education
was uppermost: they "worshipped education" and they "worshipped reading."
Newspapers were readily available, and they "always had books in the house."
The Walkers would retrieve books thrown onto trash piles by their white
employers. They would bring the books home and read them to their children.
For most African Americans, education was perceived as the key to economic
viability and to social respectability and acceptance, so they worked to provide
that possibility for their children. Whether that education was of an industrial
nature as advocated by Booker T. Washington or of a liberal arts nature as
advocated by W.E.B. Du Bois, education was foundational. A white plantation
owner had chided Mrs. Walker for sending her children to school. It was his
belief that black folks had "no need for education." Mrs. Walker's rebuttal was
legendary: "You might *have* some black children somewhere . . . but they don't
live in this house. Don't you ever come around here again talking about how
my children don't need to learn how to read and write."[11]

Formal schooling for Mr. Walker ended at the fifth grade. Mrs. Walker
went as far as the fourth-grade level. In spite of their abbreviated educational
careers, they recognized the value of education not only for their own children,
but also for those children in their community and surrounding areas. When
the all-white members of the Board of Education refused to repair or replace
the leaking and worn-out separate-but-unequal school buildings in which
African American children were to be schooled, local farmers gathered their
scarce resources to buy and convert an old barracks into a schoolhouse. Willie
Lee Walker spearheaded and organized their efforts. A Walker family member donated land for the premises, and community members held contests to
raise money for the project. In June 1948, East Putnam Consolidated primary
school opened. Alice was among its inaugurating student body. "Running in
and out of the lantern-lit rooms, what I felt, I think," Alice Walker reflects,
"was simply the warmth and generosity of the grownups as they ate, danced
and played after their labor. . . . There was such security in knowing they were
building a place for us."[12]

Even as all the Walker children would learn to read and write and attend
school, they were also compelled to contribute to the family economy with
odd jobs or by assisting their parents in the fields. Alice, too, would help. At
five years of age, Alice no longer trailed her mother in the field but worked
the field as well. "We had these huge fields to . . . clear, and plant, and poison cotton," Walker recounts. "I remember being out there five years old
with my little dipstick and my bucket. You have to do that to kill the boll
weevils."[13]

As landowners exhausted the land by planting the same cash crops year
after year, the sharecropping and tenant farming systems exhausted those who
toiled in the fields. Their labor and need discounted, no amount of tilling the
land could raise them above subsistence level. The work was relentless, dispir-
iting, and unrewarded. "We worked *so* hard," states Walker. And though they

"had plenty food," they were poor. A family of 10, they "lived in very small, substandard houses" that Mrs. Walker would transform into habitable homes. Their committed and hard work proved to be no guarantee as the family, after a year or so, was often driven out of the shacks and off the land by the landlord, "who exploited the labor of the entire family."[14]

The 1896 *Plessy v. Ferguson* U.S. Supreme Court decision sanctioned the Jim Crow system. The ruling officially and constitutionally upheld the doctrine of separate-but-equal, separating the races in public spheres and effectively casting whites as supreme and privileged and African Americans as inferior, subhuman, noncitizen, and unworthy. The social segregation of the races extended to the economic spheres of American society as well. As a function of Jim Crow policy, African Americans would be subjected to the most onerous kind of work, in the most challenging of environments, with the least compensation. They would not only be separated from the full fruits of their labor, but because the majority of white society had deemed them not-quite-human interlopers, the purveyors of the cult of white supremacy in America would attempt to also separate them from the land itself. As farmers and farmhands, African Americans in the rural South lived close to the soil and felt themselves one with nature. They worked the land, but it wasn't their prerogative to own it. Their labor exploited, they rarely owned their own homes and were callously evicted from the shacks they inhabited. They walked the land but were made to feel as though they weren't worthy of doing so.

Because of their official status, initially as slaves and then later as peasants and pariahs, African Americans would be cast at the bottom of the economic well and would be treated as "environmental others"; they were physically and psychologically circumscribed to certain places and spaces within both the human social environment and the natural American landscape. Nevertheless, the fundamental attitude of African Americans was one that recognized their status as human beings who perceived the beauty and wisdom in nature and understood themselves to be an integral part of the natural environment.

Thus, in spite of schemes and campaigns, of one sort or another, to render African Americans as environmental others, on the whole, African Americans retained their sense of "ecological belonging."[15] Alice Walker lived and observed this environmental struggle as endured by black folk in the rural South. Over time, the indignities and economic hardship would undermine the stamina of her parents, as they would factor into the flight of her siblings who, one by one, fled Putnam County, Georgia. Yet, Walker extols her Southern roots and the natural beauty of the South, and the humanity that evolved from it inspires her works.

The Walkers, like others in their environs, experienced what Kim Ruffin describes as the "'ecological burden-and-beauty paradox,' which pinpoints the dynamic influence of the natural and social order on African American experience and outlook." As Ruffin explains, "An ecological burden is placed on those who are racialized negatively and they therefore suffer economically and environmentally because of their degraded states."[16] Kibibi Tyehimba captures a sense of the onerous nature of an ecological burden as he recounts the experiences of blacks from emancipation to the postbellum wage-labor market:

> After reaping the benefits of free labor, in 1865 the federal government freed 4 million Blacks in January, no less, to wander the countryside, one of the coldest months of the winter, without a dime, with no property, and largely illiterate, leaving few choices for the freed African peoples other than to exist in virtual slavery locked in place by Black Codes, convict lease, peonage, and cleverly crafted share cropping schemes.[17]

America's history of genocide, slavery, lynching, *de jure* segregation, and the continuation of virulent racism had not only resulted in the physical displacement of blacks and their exploitation but for many, it had also resulted in their actual and psychological disconnection from natural resources. Notwithstanding the alienating forces of social and economic oppression, the greater majority of African Americans yet maintained a sense of "ecological agency" which allowed them to negotiate both "*the human and nonhuman social systems that determine survival.*" As African Americans managed ecological burdens, they simultaneously experienced the ecological beauty that "results from individual and collective attitudes toward nature that undercut the experience of racism and its related evils."[18]

Reverence for the Earth, for the beauty of the natural, organic environment into which Alice Walker was born was nourished in her by her mother's example: "I grew up with a woman who was so connected to life and so much in sync with the source of all that there is. It was just wonderful watching her exist in the world, and this was true even though we were poor and we had to deal with people who hated us or couldn't really see us."[19] Mrs. Walker brightened the shacks they lived in with "ambitious gardens" that mitigated the impoverished conditions of their lives.

"Before she left home for the fields, she watered her flowers, chopped up the grass, and laid out new beds. When she returned from the fields she might divide clumps of bulbs, dig a cold pit, uproot and replant roses or prune branches from her tallest bushes or trees—until night came and it was too dark to see." Young Alice was moved by the splendor of her mother's "magic." She observed that just as her mother transformed their environs with her flower gardens, work among her flowers and plants nurtured and transformed her mother: "I notice that it is only when my mother is working in her flowers that she is radiant, almost to the point of being invisible—except as Creator: hand and eye. She is involved in work her soul must have. Ordering the universe in the image of her personal conception of Beauty."[20]

Walker sees her mother as "goddess," "the most sincere worshipper of nature. I know that," proclaims Walker, "because I am also."[21] As did her mother, and the "ecological ancestors" before her, Alice Walker, too, would find consolation in nature's refuge as she negotiated the burdens of her life.

TWO

For Six Years I Do Not Look Up

The beauty of Putnam County enthralled Alice. The "small rounded hills easily walked over," poplar leaves and the wafting scent of pine were home and haven.[1] She had an easy assurance when meandering through both human and natural environments. As an "itty-bitty little girl," Alice would walk through town, past jook joints and their rowdy customers, to the undertaker's parlor where she would sell eggs she collected to earn money. She was equally comfortable in the hush of bush and tree. Where her childhood friend Doris Reid would be apprehensive about "snakes and spiders," "Alice never seemed to be afraid of the outdoors. She'd cross her arms under the back of her head, stare up into the sky, and start talking about the clouds and the trees."[2]

Her relationship with nature surpassed fascination to manifest as an intimacy that spoke of friendship, trust, mutual understanding, and mutual support. She claimed one tree in particular, a noble "old-growth pine," as her "dearest companion," and "earliest love." When this tree was struck by lightning and cut down to be used as firewood, her "crushed spirit . . . ran in circles." The loss of this tree that had given shelter to her father when he was a schoolboy and stood sentinel-like on a hill above their "tiny, overcrowded house" pained Alice who "grieved as if it had been a person." In Wards Chapel were the first trees Alice beheld, the first hills she climbed, the first rivers she "dreamed [herself] across," the first pebbles—sun-warmed—that she felt on her tongue. The idyllic landscape of her birth that stirred her little girl's heart was also the bosom upon which Alice placed her "unbearable cares."[3]

Though born into a large family and doted upon by kith and kin, Alice felt alone and "in some ways neglected."⁴ Both parents worked and were very much partners in all they did. Her siblings, too, were either at work or in school. While this "neglect" was inadvert, Alice nonetheless felt herself alone, an outsider. Being the youngest of eight children created an inherent distance between Alice and her older siblings. Once her siblings began to leave home, the distance in age was exacerbated by the distance in space and time. Eldest sister Mamie would leave home before Alice was two years of age. There was no Negro high school in Putnam County; thus, Mamie attended school in Macon, Georgia. Subsequently she would move to Atlanta and attend Morris Brown College.

When Mamie returned to the family fold during summer breaks, she would fill the humble living space of her family with the excited happenings of the world beyond. "When she came to visit us in Georgia," Walker reminisces, "it was . . . like having Christmas with us all during her vacation. She loved to read and tell stories; she taught me African songs and dances; she cooked fanciful dishes that looked like anything but plain old sharecropper food." Exhausted from their labors over the years, Willie Lee and Minnie Lou no longer read to their children. So Alice delighted in Mamie's visits. "You know the song 'God Bless Mother Africa?'" Walker queried. "When I was six or seven years old, my sister taught me that song." The visits became infrequent, and Mamie eventually "drifted away."⁵

Walker captures the impression of her sister's presence and the sense of her abandoning absence in her signature poem "For My Sister Molly Who in the Fifties." The poem is at once a praise song and a swansong. It brims with affection and delight for the sister whose creativity was magic, whose talk about faraway places was mystical, and whose sophistication about the world was formidable. It resonates with quiet heartbreak, as this mythical sister becomes more and more a part of the world she talked about and less and less a part of the world of the gentlefolk she only visited—until, imperceptibly, she "Left us."⁶

Along with the gaps in age between her and her siblings and the racially circumscribed barriers to black success in education and employment that compelled her sister to leave Putnam County, gender was also a factor in Alice's sense of aloneness. Being female placed Alice beyond the pale of her father's sense of fairness and equality as it related to gender. In the outset of his domestic life, Willie Lee Walker demonstrated an egalitarian sensibility. As Minnie Lou Walker worked alongside her husband in the fields and on dairy farms, Mr. Walker assumed the role, at home, of a tender helpmeet, bathing his children and nurturing them even more than his wife did. However, by the time Alice came along, "he had become very narrow." The line he drew in the division of family labor reflected typical double standards inflected with sexist ideology. The females in the family would participate in labor outside the home, but labor in the home became "women's work." Mr. Walker "would not let his sons sweep a floor or wash a dish." Alice Walker recalled that she was "not happy" with the roles and rules her father established in their home. She experienced the situation as unjust, "a kind of oppression": "Needless to say, we fought."[7]

The traditional notions of masculinity professed by her father were reflected in the behavior of her brothers whom Walker described as "very brutal in some of their ways . . . they were brought up not to be gentle with animals or younger siblings."[8] Perhaps loneliness and the sense of being in an oppressive family environment were among the "unbearable cares" Alice shared with the meadows, trees, and clouds. Yet among her childhood playmates were her brothers Curtis, who was two years older, and Robert ("Bobby"), who was four years older than she. Together, in their games of cowboys and Indians, they rustled cattle, became outlaws, and rescued distressed damsels. Like her brothers, she dressed in a cowboy hat, checkered shirts, and pants and boots.

Their otherwise-equal playing field was upturned when their parents bought BB guns for the boys. "Because I am a girl," writes Walker, "I do not get a gun. Instantly I am relegated to the position of Indian." Not only do the guns introduce a decided and gendered distance between the siblings but they also become instruments of a life-changing accident. "One day while I am standing on top of our makeshift 'garage' . . . holding my bow and arrow and looking out toward the fields, I feel an incredible blow in my right eye. I look down just in time to see my brother lower his gun." The brothers rush to Alice's rescue. They were at a loss to stop her tears and ease her pain. Sensing the situation to be a grave one, the three agree they were not to tell the truth of what happened. "'If you tell' they say, 'we will get a whipping. You don't want that to happen, do you?'" Alice complies, as she doesn't want her brothers to be beaten, and she also fears what might happen if she doesn't comply: "I know my brothers will find ways to make me wish I had." They therefore concoct a lie: "Here is a piece of wire," brother Bobby instructs, "say you stepped on one end of it and the other flew up and hit you."[9]

The force of the copper BB pellet was traumatic. The damage done to Alice's right eye caused her body to go into shock. She experienced chills and fever and sharp, shooting pains that caused severe headaches. Alice's father and brother Jimmy walked to the highway in hopes that a driver would stop and assist them in getting Alice to a doctor. William "Bill" Henry, one year older than Jimmy, had use of the only car the family had. He was a mechanic at Stribling's garage in Eatonton, 20 miles from the sharecropper's shack they had moved to in Milledgeville, in Baldwin County. The one driver Mr. Walker and Jimmy flagged down refused to help: "'It was this white man, and Daddy said, "My little girl's been hurt and I need to take her to the doctor." The man gave Daddy a dirty look and just drove off.'"[10] The cold compresses, home remedies, and tender care the family gave did little to relieve Alice's pain or prevent the cataract from spreading over her right eye.

After about a week, with no signs of improvement and in fear of infection, relatives urged the Walkers to take Alice to the white doctor in Macon, Georgia, who agreed to perform whatever operation was necessary. The charge was $250, more money than the Walkers earned annually. Bill managed to borrow the money from his employer so his parents could make the trip to Macon. "Why did you wait so long to come?" the doctor queried. He looked at the wounded eye and then made a pronouncement: "Eyes are sympathetic. If one is blind, the other will likely become blind too."[11] The Walkers were hopeful that the doctor would remove the scar tissue from the injured eye, allowing Alice to see again. But vision in the right eye had already been lost. The doctor did nothing to treat the cataract. He made the declaration, prescribed eye drops, and pocketed the $250.

Though the truth had been revealed that brother Curtis shot his sister with the BB gun, the circumstances around the event remained debated into the adult years of the siblings. Was Alice also shooting a BB gun? Was she on the tin roof of the carport alone with bow and arrow? Was brother Bobby on the roof with her, helping her to shoot his gun? Was the shooting *accidental*? When Alice Walker writes about the incident for the first time, decades later in "Beauty, When the Other Dancer Is the Self," she draws attention to the term *accident* by placing it within quotation marks. "A week after the 'accident' they take me to see a doctor." The doubt she felt made her hesitant in responding to the questions asked by her schoolmates: " 'What's the matter with your eye?' they ask, critically. When I don't answer (I cannot decide whether it was an 'accident' or not), they shove me, insist on a fight."[12]

The *how* and the *why* of the incident varied in accordance with the perspective and the memory of those present, but the *what* of it—the BB pellet shot into Alice's right eye—was inarguable and the effect was devastating. With her sight now impaired, her freedom to run through "sunny meadows and shaded woods" was curtailed. Like the last tree her right eye would behold, the landscape that received and relieved Alice's childhood burdens became dimmed and distant: "There is a tree growing from underneath the porch that climbs past the railing to the roof. It is the last thing my right eye sees. I watch as its trunk, its branches, and then its leaves are blotted out by the rising blood."[13]

She has not the comfort of enfolding nature. And because the family had just moved from Wards Chapel to Milledgeville, she has not the comfort of familiar human nature, her community. "We do not know any of the people around us," Walker relates. When she returns to school in Milledgeville—not a school that her father helped to build, but a converted former state prison that still bears the circular imprint of an electric chair—children she does not know scorn and bully her. Her grades suffer. Her delight in school is gravely diminished. To shield her from the torment, her parents move her back to Wards Chapel where she stays with her paternal grandparents. She is enrolled again at her old school, East Putnam Consolidated. Miss Reynolds is there. "It is she who makes life bearable." In familiar surroundings again, Alice is around people who know her and care for her. The teasing and ridicule from other students lessen, with the notable exception of one student who insists on calling her a "one-eyed bitch." On familiar ground and emboldened by Miss Reynolds's presence, Alice defends herself. "One day I simply grab him by his coat and beat him until I am satisfied."[14]

Though very much happy to be again with the one teacher who loved her most, Alice did not know how to be without her parents and the one person she loved most—her mother. The separation was profound. Not understanding why she was sent away, Alice felt she was being punished. "My parents didn't explain why, what, when, or anything. . . . It was decided and off I went." In the absence of any explanation, eight-year-old Alice concluded that she was being blamed for what had happened to her. "At the time of the injury everyone referred to it not only as 'an accident,' but as 'my accident'—thereby absolving my brothers of any blame."[15] Not only was she removed from the family hearth, her brothers were allowed to keep their guns.

The family would also return to Wards Chapel within the year. But by that time, Alice had developed a sense of herself as "an outsider" within her family and her community. She believed the "glob of whitish scar tissue" to be unsightly and shameful. Where she once dared to stare into the eyes of others, she now feared that "they will stare back. Not at the 'cute' little girl, but at her scar." "For six years I do not stare at anyone, because I do not raise my head."[16] Her father, who, before the accident, would take her anywhere with him because she was "the prettiest!," no longer chooses her. "I consider that day the last time my father, with his sweet home remedy of cool lily leaves, chose me, and that I suffered and raged inside because of this."[17]

She became shy and withdrawn. Insular. When relatives visited, she hid in her room. She felt ugly, shameful, betrayed, and abandoned. Irreconcilable to the loss of being cute and the easy rapport it allowed her, Alice's grief and rage turned inward. She railed against and blamed her eye, which never cleared up. Her night prayers were for beauty. Her daydreams were "not of fairy tales but of falling on swords, of putting guns to my heart or head, and of slashing my wrists with a razor." Where she was wont to seek solace and an inspired sense of self in the world of trees and grass and lakes and sky, Alice began to take comfort in books and in writing. Feeling old and "unpleasant to look at" and afraid to freely run over the rounded hills of Putnam County, Georgia, she "retreated into solitude, and read stories and began to write poems."[18]

THREE

Everything Changed

Alice had begun to feel herself as one who was on the outside of life, peering in. From this position, "the position of an outcast," she began to develop the power of observation, the ability to note and the astuteness to follow the complexity of thought, feeling, and motive in others. She had begun to really see people and their situations, "to really notice relationships and to learn to be patient enough to care about how they turned out."[1] She had begun to develop and hone the sensibility of a writer. It was during this time, also, that she had begun to keep a notebook, "because," Walker explains, "my life has had its trials."[2]

The childhood trials Alice experienced left her downcast and forlorn. Older brother Bill felt deeply the change in his pensive youngest sister. For Bill, Alice was the ice cream and the cake. For Alice, Bill was this "amazing brother." Of her five brothers, Bill was her favorite. There was always "a strong bond between us," writes Walker.[3] By 1955, Bill Walker had repaid Dickie Stribling, dollar by dollar, the $250 he had borrowed to help his parents get medical attention for Alice's injury. Once "Paid" was stamped on the receipt of his last installment, Bill, too, left the South.

Bill and wife Gaynell moved to Boston, Massachusetts, near relatives who had also relocated there. The bond between Bill and Alice remained strong in spite of the distance that separated them. Letters from home informed Bill that though Alice was doing well in school, she was still crestfallen. He was empathetic: "It hurt me that Alice didn't have a lot of friends. The older children had left home. Bobby and Curtis were standoffish because they felt guilty. It just seemed to me that Alice was more alone than she'd ever been."[4]

In 1958, Bill and his wife invited Alice to spend the summer with them, to assist with the care of the couple's infant son Billy. The invitation was a ruse. In reality, Bill wanted to make another effort at having Alice's eye treated. The subterfuge was out of concern for his sister's feelings: "We didn't want to tell her the plan right off," says Bill, "because we knew she'd get all excited. She'd been through so much already with the doctors in Georgia that we didn't want her to be disappointed if things didn't work out." Once she was there, Bill casually asked Alice one morning to go with him to the hospital. "What for?" Alice asked. "They're just gonna look at your eye and see if they can do anything about that white spot," Bill answered. "OK," was the reply.[5]

Ophthalmologist Dr. Morriss M. Henry examined the wounded eye. He readily concluded that vision had been permanently lost. He could, however, remove the scar tissue. Thus, Alice was admitted to Massachusetts General Hospital on August 6, 1958. At 9:20 that morning, Dr. Henry performed an extracapsular cataract extraction. The procedure was successful. Dr. Henry skillfully removed the "unsightly" milky film that made Alice feel ugly and had her looking down for six years. The procedure did not just change the way the injured eye looked, it transformed Alice's outlook.

"There is still a small bluish crater where the scar tissue was," Walker writes in "Beauty," "but the ugly white stuff is gone. Almost immediately I become a different person from the girl who does not raise her head. . . . Now that I've raised my head I win the boyfriend of my dreams." His name was Porter Sanford III, a student at Butler-Baker High School where Alice was also a student. He was two years her senior and had been enamored of Alice since she was in fifth grade. When Alice returned from summer vacation in Boston, the two spent more time together, attending school events, dances, and going to the movies. Eventually they become an item.[6]

"Now that I've raised my head I have plenty of friends." Because she has raised her head, Alice could then see the friends who had always been there. As her childhood companion Doris Reid and boyfriend Porter Sanford attested, her friends were never put off by the appearance of the injured eye. "Alice had so many attractive qualities," said Sanford, "that most people didn't even pay any attention to her eye either before or after she had the operation." Though her head may have been bowed in self-castigation, Alice's friends and peers respected her perspectives, mused Sanford. "She was conscious of the injustices long before the rest of us recognized them and started to fight."[7] Her introversion and taciturnity notwithstanding, Alice could be outspoken about racial injustices and impatient with those inclined to acquiesce to the status quo.

Sanford and their mutual friend and classmate, Bobby Baines, would take note of just how "serious" Alice could be about such matters. As the three conversed one day on their way to work at Rock Eagle, A 4-H center, Alice declaimed against the racial inequities they experienced in their everyday lives in South Georgia: School buses were available to white students, but blacks had to walk. Wages were higher for white workers, even when blacks and whites performed the same job. Whites could gather at Rock Eagle and participate in recreational activities, but blacks could only work there, and then, only in menial positions. Alice worked there herself as a "salad girl."

Whereas Alice found such conditions unconscionable, untenable, and unacceptable, Sanford thought blacks "had to accept it and there was no use in complaining." Infuriated by his attitude, Alice demanded that Porter stop the car and let her out. She rallied Baines to her point of view "telling him he should be ashamed to ride with [Porter]." Alice and Baines walked the remainder of the distance to Rock Eagle. Years later Bobby Baines would contemplate the long walk and the radical perspective of his companion who "never accepted the lowly station of blacks in the South" and possessed "a tremendous amount of rebellion in her personality that made her a real force in our community."[8]

The pow wow on the way to Rock Eagle proved to be prescient. A center that symbolized the segregation of the races and the domination and exploitation of one group by another, Rock Eagle was also a symbol of Native American genocide, a theme Alice Walker would address again and again in her writings and activism. She would capture both dignity and doom in "Eagle Rock," a poem of foreboding that resurrects memories of the Cherokee who were forced to walk a trail of tears. The poem describes a mound of stones which, only from an eight-foot observation tower, is transformed into the figure of "An eagle widespread." Tourists photograph the grounds and the Eagle Rock. Annually, student members of the Future Farmers of America come before the rock as innocent "paleface warriors" and "Jolly conquerors." But the narrative voice in the poem warns that this Rock Eagle, raised by the now "silenced" Cherokee, "*Lives* and is bound" to bind within its wings the innocent warriors of the 4-H Club.[9]

"Now that I've raised my head class work comes from my lips as faultlessly as Easter speeches did, and I leave high school as valedictorian, most popular student, and *queen*, hardly believing my luck."[10] Walker's civic concerns and academic aspirations merged as she brought her feelings for the plight of oppressed peoples, in general, and African Americans, in particular, into her schoolwork. During her last semester at Butler-Baker, she staged excerpts from *Imitation of Life*, the 1933 novel written by Fannie Hurst. She won the first place award in the statewide drama competition for her direction of the excerpts. Alice's selections highlighted the story of Peola, the very light-skinned daughter of a black domestic who attempts to pass for white, that is, to live as a white woman. In the process, Peola disowns her mother and her African American heritage. Alice cast her friend Doris Reid as Peola. Reid would later reflect on the significance of the script and Alice's efforts. "When [Alice] had me say, as the daughter, that I wanted to be white, it was to show how black people, as a consequence of constantly being degraded, had learned to hate themselves."[11]

Reid described her friend's theatrical insights and efforts as "very powerful." By her early teens, Alice had memorized "most of *Hamlet*, *Romeo and Juliet*, and *Macbeth* by heart." She was enthralled with *Oedipus Rex*. Bobby Baines introduced Alice to the play and the two discussed it when Baines was on break from Morris Brown. *Oedipus Rex* was for Alice "profound to-the-bone literature."[12] As a young artist, Alice was able to infuse her literary interests with her developing power of observation both as an outsider within her own family and as "an exile in [her] own town."[13] Her directional debut hinted at her growing ability to see past the dance of form into the inner emotional and psychological lives of the people around her, and to have her reader, her audience, see what she saw and feel what she felt. "Alice forced you to look at the ugly stuff, the stuff nobody wanted to face."[14]

Even as she excelled in her senior-year studies, Alice's accomplishments would not significantly increase her academic or occupational options in Putnam County, Georgia. By virtue of the social and economic system of the place of her birth, Alice Walker's future had long been circumscribed. Her first aspiration was to become a pianist. But 50 cents per lesson was more than her parents could afford. "I tried very hard," Walker says looking back, "but I couldn't raise it every week." Though she wasn't "that good" at drawing, she considered a career as an artist.[15] But art supplies were costly as well. In the aftermath of the injury to her eye and the surgery that cleared away the cataracts, Alice thought about becoming a research scientist. However, the Jim Crow schools of her adolescent years would never deliver a curriculum to support that dream.

Like several states in the former Confederacy, Georgia defied Supreme Court rulings that struck down the nation's "Separate-but-Equal" doctrine. In 1954, *Brown v. Board of Education* declared segregation in public schools unconstitutional. In 1956, *Browder v. Gayle* outlawed segregation on buses operating within state boundaries. A few years later in 1960, *Boynton v. Virginia* forbade discrimination in interstate passenger transportation. Though civil rights gains had been made legally, much remained the same, as these rights, generally, were neither enforced nor protected. Civil rights activists therefore protested the continuation of discriminatory practices. The ensuing conflagration and violence against African Americans and civil rights workers would ignite the moral outrage of the country.

Alice watched the drama of racial hate and the struggle for freedom and equality play out on the used television set her mother managed to purchase in 1960, on her maid's salary. She watched as Hamilton Holmes and Charlayne Hunter (Gault) faced down racist white students, their parents, and the white city fathers who would prevent them from integrating the University of Georgia. Although Eatonton, Georgia, was still structurally and officially a Jim Crow town, the spirit of the civil rights movement found its way into the Walkers' living room and into Alice's heart. It came in the image of Martin Luther King, Jr., "the sober and determined face of the Movement," a Southern Baptist preacher who "dared to claim his rights as a native son." He appeared with a calmness, confidence, and serenity that mesmerized the 16-year-old Alice and stirred her soul. "At the moment I saw his resistance I knew I would never be able to live in this country without resisting everything that sought to disinherit me, and I would never be forced away from the land of my birth without a fight."[16]

The civil rights movement and the vision of Martin King's arrest—as he was handcuffed and pushed into a police van for participating in a sit-in, in a downtown Atlanta department store—heartened Alice and filled her with enthusiasm for her future and a future that was possible for black people. King was the hero for whom she had unwittingly waited. The televised events she witnessed and the trust King's "pattern of strength and sincerity" inspired in her, awakened her faith in the human spirit, and called her to life.

Alice felt deeply the direct and indirect impact of racial injustice in Eatonton. She saw it manifested in the weathered and pained bodies of her parents and in their loss of spirit and resilience over time. It registered in the loss of family members who could not bear the daily indignities suffered when one chose to remain home. "I watched my brothers, one by one, leave our home and leave the South. I watched my sisters do the same." And it registered in her very life: "I awoke to the bitter knowledge that in order just to continue to love the land of my birth, I was expected to leave it." In contemplating her future she saw herself confronted with the same dilemmas as her siblings. She, too, would be required to leave or take "the risk that others could not bear."[17] But Alice "would not be a maid, and could not be a 'girl,' or a frightened half-citizen, or any of the things my brothers and sisters had already refused to be."[18] To stay would be to subject herself to the rule of Jim Crow and a mean and barely tolerated existence.

Alice would leave home, but she would not leave the South. She enrolled in Spelman College in Atlanta, Georgia, and accepted a "rehabilitation" scholarship available to her because of the visual impairment resulting from the eye injury. The May 1961 *Butler-Baker News* announced that upon completion of her studies at Spelman, Alice Walker's goal was to "strive for excellence in the arts." So in August 1961, Mr. Willie Lee Walker drove his daughter to the Greyhound bus station in Eatonton. Community members gave her a departing gift of $75. Her mother gave her "three things she never owned herself": "a typewriter, a sewing machine, and a suitcase."[19]

In the manner of Rosa Parks, whose refusal to give up her seat on a Montgomery city bus catalyzed the Montgomery Bus Boycott of 1955, Alice sat in the front section of the bus. Although she had every constitutional right to do so, she was still in Eatonton. The complaint of a white passenger compelled the driver to have her move to the back of the bus:

A white woman (may her fingernails now be dust!) complained to the driver, and he ordered me to move. But even as I moved, in confusion and tears, I knew he had not seen the last of me. In those seconds of moving, everything changed. I was eager to bring an end to the South that permitted my humiliation.[20]

Those seconds of changing seats steeled Alice's determination to be a change-agent. As she wrote about the incident later, she was leaving home, but not abandoning her homeland, her birthplace, or her heritage. In the seconds of moving, she had resolved to respond to life's call and join the civil right's freedom movement. She would not be forced away from her home without a fight.

FOUR

A Spelman Girl

THE SOUTHERN REVOLUTION

When Alice Walker arrived in Atlanta, Georgia, in the fall of 1961, she stepped into a city pregnant with possibility and imminent change. Several years of planned and spontaneous confrontations by a demoralized black citizenry against racial segregation were coalescing into a movement to dismantle Jim Crow and to champion the civil rights of African Americans. Inspired by the Montgomery Bus Boycott victory of December 1956, a group of ministers engaged in "sit-down" actions on the trolleys and buses of Atlanta, in January 1957, challenging Georgia's segregation policy on intrastate public transportation. Also in January 1957, student members of the Social Science Club at Spelman College and their faculty advisor Howard Zinn sat in the white section of the gallery of the state capitol. Their original intention was only to observe the proceedings of the Georgia General Assembly. But upon finding the gallery divided into a main section for whites and a "colored" section, the students made an impromptu decision to sit in the section reserved for whites. Zinn joined them.

Once the speaker of the House perceived the impropriety, he bellowed through the microphone, "You nigras get over to where you belong!" He then reminded them, "We got segregation in the state of Georgia!" The students moved, and Zinn, a Jewish American professor of history and chair of the history and social science departments of Spelman, sat with the students in the "colored" section. Once the impropriety had been satisfactorily corrected, the speaker welcomed the visitors: "The members of the Georgia state legislature would like to extend a warm welcome to the visiting delegation from Spelman College." The students and their professor would return to the capitol the following year, staging a silent protest. In January 1963, the state capitol, along with other state facilities, was desegregated.[1] Student members of Spelman's Social Science Club were also instrumental in bringing an end to the segregationist policies of Atlanta's public library system.

Like Eatonton, Atlanta was a racially segregated city, "as rigidly segregated as Johannesburg, South Africa." Unlike Eatonton, the status quo in Atlanta was being challenged. This challenge was taken up not only by the established, adult leadership in the city, but the youth as well, particularly the students who would eventually become the vanguard of the civil rights movement in Atlanta. So when Alice Walker arrived at Spelman College, she stepped into the halls of an institution whose student body was as restless as she. Perhaps as a matter of their coming of age in a modern world, perhaps as a consequence of their vital participation in an accelerating freedom movement, or perhaps as a combination of both, students at Spelman—as well as the other colleges within the Atlanta University Center—questioned the authority of white society as they also defied the authority of their college administrators. Thus Walker became part of an institution that was initiating change in the nation even as it was itself undergoing internal change.

Heretofore viewed as a finishing school for the middle-class black female, Spelman was evolving into a progressive, student-driven institution with a global perspective. Albert Manley was president of Spelman during Walker's matriculation. His administration spanned the years from 1953 to 1976. As the first African American and the first male to be inaugurated as president of the college, Manley, himself, was a symbol of internal, institutional change. Enhancement of curricular offerings, increased enrollment, and establishment of the Merrill Foreign Travel-Study Program were aspects of Manley's vision for the school. Even as Manley sought to expand the experience of Spelman's students and extend the mission of the college, he also closely guarded "the cult of true womanhood" established by his predecessors.

Fundamental to Spelman's mission was the fashioning of a moral, Christian character within its students and the transformation of the students into proper "young ladies." Howard Zinn observed that the alumni and friends of the college boasted, "*You can always tell a Spelman girl*": she was well-spoken, morally upright, and socially sophisticated. "*If intellect and talent and social consciousness happened to develop also, they were, to an alarming extent, by-products.*" So in spite of its academic advancement and national and global outlook, "Spelman College in the 1950s was in many ways a parochial and conservative place."[2]

Spelman College began as Atlanta Baptist Female Seminary in 1881. "Our whole school for Christ" was its motto. Its founders, Sophia Packard and Harriet Giles, were members of the Women's American Baptist Home Mission Society of Boston, Massachusetts. The school was infused with the missionary and pragmatic zeal of its founders. Its curriculum was designed to produce literate and religious graduates skilled in homemaking, proselytizing, and racial uplift. The graduates would become wives, teachers, missionaries, and "Race Women." In ensuing years and under successive administrations, the Atlanta Baptist Female Seminary transformed into the Spelman Baptist Seminary. In 1924, the institution would be granted collegiate status and become Spelman College, a leading liberal arts institution in the South among black colleges.

At Spelman, then, Alice Walker was indeed poised to "excel in the arts." Along with the objectives of expanding her reading materials and honing her writing skills, Walker was committed to deepening her knowledge and understanding of the world—the world she wanted to change. For as much as Walker was intent on developing her scholastic aptitude, she would not forget her vow to bring an end to the South that permitted her humiliation. The intention of a liberal arts education at Spelman was to prepare students to be a part of the "talented tenth"; however, that intention did not include student participation in a civil rights movement. Yet Spelman's students and the faculty who dared to do so were engaged in civil rights activities on campus, in the city, and across the South. "For the first time in the eighty-plus years of Spelman's existence, the students and the faculty who participated in the movement took actions that directly challenged the injustices of the social and political status quo."[3]

Spelman administrators, from the founders to President Manley, assumed a nonpolitical stance to all matters beyond its walls. Rather than directly engage the issue of racial injustice as it was expressed in mid-20th-century America, the Manley administration encouraged students to avoid or ignore places and situations wherein they might be subject to indignities. As students grew less tolerant of racial injustices, Albert Manley, along with a majority of the Atlanta University Center (AUC) presidents, sought to dissuade students from expressing their protest through direct action. Yet they could not stem the rising tide of resistance to the status quo. On February 1, 1960, Franklin McCain, Ezell Blair, Joseph McNeil, and David Richmond, four black students at North Carolina A & T College in Greensboro, North Carolina, sat at a whites-only lunch counter in a local Woolworth's department store and refused to move. The incident made national headlines, sparking similar sit in demonstrations in several Southern states, effectively launching the sit in phase of the civil rights movement.

The Southern Revolution was underway, and in Atlanta, "Spelman girls" were to be found in the midst of it. Ignited by a fire that promised to burn away "a lifetime of suppressed indignation," Spelmanites joined with students from the other AUC schools as leaders and foot soldiers in an ever-advancing student movement toward social justice. Members of the student organization Committee on the Appeal for Human Rights (COAHR) published its manifesto, "Appeal for Human Rights," in the March 9, 1960, issue of the *Atlanta Journal*, the *Atlanta Constitution*, and the *Atlanta Daily World*. The "Appeal" stated: "*we plan to use every legal and nonviolent means at our disposal to secure full citizenship rights as members of this great democracy of ours.*"[4] They declared their intent to gain the respect and dignity due to them as Americans and as human beings. They pledged their support of student activists across the nation and their unwillingness to wait any longer for the already long-awaited rights and privileges that were legally and morally theirs.

Six days later, on March 15, about 200 students participated in sit in demonstrations throughout downtown Atlanta. They sat in at restaurants and cafeterias in city and county courthouses, federal buildings, and bus and train terminals. Among the 77 students arrested, 14 were Spelman "girls." The students' campaign for a just society would permeate "every aspect of life." They organized kneel-ins at churches, lie-ins at hotels and hospitals, boycotts and pickets at supermarkets. They continued their sit ins at downtown Atlanta businesses, and in the fall of 1960, targeted Rich's department store, the "flagship of the Atlanta business community."

Morehouse senior Lonnie King and Spelmanite Hershelle Sullivan, cochairs of the COAHR, invited Dr. Martin Luther King, Jr., to participate in the demonstration. On October 19, King joined the students at Rich's. After being refused service at a snack bar, Dr. King and several students sat in at the Magnolia Tea Room, Rich's "most elegant restaurant." Dr. King and the students with him were arrested for trespassing. The unfolding of these events moved across the TV screen that sat in the living room of Alice Walker's home back in Eatonton, Georgia. It was Reverend Dr. Martin Luther King, Jr.'s, face that had captured Alice's restive attention. And it was the student movement at Spelman College that would honor her spirit of resistance and become a means through which she would express her will to change the world.

Like many of her Spelman sisters before her, Alice Walker would participate in the Saturday morning demonstrations in downtown Atlanta. And like many participants in the civil rights movement, she would come to see sociopolitical and economic justice for African Americans as an integral aspect of a comprehensive human rights agenda that envisioned world peace. Thus in the spring of her first year at Spelman, Walker would be counted among the 18 students and one faculty member—Staughton Lynd—from Spelman College to join the February 15, 1962, peace demonstration in Washington, D.C. The delegation from Atlanta was the "only group from the South" to attend the demonstration. "Several students carried signs saying 'Atlanta Center Students Support a Turn Toward Peace.'"[5] Alice Walker was one among the 6,000 student activists supporting the cause for world peace.

ENGAGED WITH THE WORLD

In the summer of 1962, Walker journeyed to Helsinki, Finland. She was selected as a delegate to the World Festival of Youth and Students, an event that signaled her growing commitment to political activism and her growing awareness of and interest in international affairs. This first trip abroad was funded by the "remarkably generous women of Atlanta's black churches."

They supported Walker and another Spelman student in their desire "to see the world from another continent and demonstrate—after the United States resumed nuclear testing in 1961—our commitment to world peace."[6] From July 28 to August 6 1962, youth from around the world gathered in Helsinki. Freedom was afoot. In the swirl of talk, song, cultural performances, and sober awareness, the world's youth shared information, exchanged ideas, laughed, cried, and danced in the face of ongoing social, political, and economic oppression and the promise of and potential for global peace. Budding activist Angela Davis was among the youth gathered in Helsinki, as was Gloria Steinem.

Walker would not recall meeting Davis or Steinem at the festival, but both would, in time, become associates and friends. Walker, like Davis, was impressed by the dramatic performance of the Cuban delegation. Their presentation "conveyed a fiercely compelling spirit of revolution," chronicling the attempted overthrow of the Castro regime by the United States and the United States' invasion of Cuba at the Bay of Pigs in 1961.[7] The performance concluded with a spirited conga dance. Davis joined the line that snaked out of the building and into the streets. Equally captivated by this infectious spirit, Walker, too, formed part of this undulating movement through Helsinki streets.

Walker knew little of the oppressive conditions in the world beyond the suffering of African Americans in the South. At Helsinki, she would begin to conceptualize "the international nature of oppression." Heretofore, she had not believed poor people could win against stubborn and entrenched oppressive forces. The Cuban Revolution, however, proved otherwise: "By making their revolution, the Cubans proved that oppression needn't last always. . . . This was profoundly important to me," Walker writes. "I think part of my 'illogical' despair had been due to my sense of political powerlessness, caused to some extent by a lack of living models. I believed poor people could not win. . . . But here at last was a revolutionary people I could respect, and they made it quite clear they did not intend to lose."[8]

She breathed in the heady perfume of hope. She drank in the potent images and metaphors of the revolutionary Russian poet Yevgeny Yevtushenko. His stirring recitations at the festival captivated her imagination as a writer and an activist. With the events of Helsinki still strong in her mind, she traveled to the Soviet Union in the company of Julius Coles, an upper-classman at Morehouse College whom Walker had met at a social-mixer when she first arrived at Spelman. As they both were interested in international affairs and exhilarated by the possibilities of the future, their train ride across the intervening region alternated between singing rum-inspired choruses of "songs about 'the revolution'" and conversations about the world.[9] In the "tiny, wood-paneled compartment" of the winding train, Walker stilled time to read Castro's *History Will Absolve Me*, a gift from a Cuban she had befriended. "I read and cried, cried and read, as I recognized the essence of a struggle already familiar to me."[10]

Walker's experiences in Helsinki and in Russia awakened her to the depth and breadth of what she did not know. She would write later, "Indeed, I was so ignorant of history and politics, that when I left the festival, went to Moscow and was taken on a stroll across Red Square, I could not fathom for the longest time *who* the Russians were queuing up to view in Lenin's tomb."[11] These experiences only deepened her yearning to know. In the fall of 1962, Walker enrolled in "Revolution and Response," an interdisciplinary course on Russian history, taught by Howard Zinn. He had assigned Gogol, Chekhov, Dostoevsky, Tolstoy, Gorky, Turgenev.

Walker read all the Russian authors she could find. "I read them as if they were a delicious cake."[12] Hearing the absence of the female voice, she searched out the works of counterrevolutionary poet Anna Akhmatova, a contemporary of Yevshenko. Zinn observed that "Alice didn't say much in class."[13] What Walker did not say in class, she expressed in her essay assignments. Zinn was taken aback by her penetrating insights and eloquence. "I read with wonderment the [essay] by Alice Walker on Dostoevsky and Tolstoy. Not only had I never read a paper by an undergraduate written with such critical intelligence, but I had rarely read a literary essay of such grace and style by anyone. And she was nineteen, from a farm family in Eatonton, Georgia."[14]

Walker's political activity would also continue unabated, keeping pace with her academic progress. In the spring of 1963, Alice Walker would stand with other students in front of the Trevor-Arnett Library on the Atlanta University campus and listen to leaders of the Student Non-Violent Coordinating Committee. "John Lewis was there, and so was Julian bond—thin, well starched and ironed in light-colored jeans, he looked (with his cropped hair that still tried to curl) like a poet (which he was). Everyone was beautiful, because everyone (and I think now of Ruby Doris Robinson, who since died) was conquering fear by holding the hands of the persons next to them." It was springtime. The cherry trees were abloom. The air "a green sea" of pollen. The very earth spoke of life while the students, "young and bursting with fear and determination to change our world, thought, beyond our fervid singing, of death."[15]

In the tradition of the new Spelman girl, Alice Walker would take her place on the picket lines and brave the reactions of those who stood for the status quo and against change. Though Walker was still introverted and shy, her social life kept par with her academic and political life. Indeed, there were no lines of demarcation between the spheres of her life, as each informed and enhanced the other. As she had concluded from her experience in Helsinki, world peace hinged on a mutual understanding and valuing of one another: "I believed my *job* at that point (being powerless to do much else) was to see other peoples not as strangers but as kin."[16]

This attitude would become foundational to Walker's character and would guide her interpersonal relationships. Her roommate, Constance Nabwire of Uganda, appreciated Walker's openness to the world beyond the one with which she was familiar: "Alice was informed, political, and had an international perspective." Nabwire described Walker as "someone who was intellectually stimulating and engaged with the world."[17] That same spirit of openness and discovery would guide Walker into the dancing arms of David DeMoss, a white exchange student from Bowdoin College, in Brunswick, Maine. DeMoss and Walker met at a social event at Morehouse College in March 1963. They had mutual interests and were intrigued with each other. During her summer respite in Boston, the two began dating.

That DeMoss "really cared about the struggle" was important to Walker. Northern whites often visited the South only to cast a disapproving eye, then leave. DeMoss, Walker observed, expressed and demonstrated a keener interest. "He'd grown up poor, so he understood how the system kept people down. Still, he was so hopeful and full of optimism." He was connected to the world and "connected to his emotions." Moreover, he was enamored of Alice and "a wonderful lover." "We were together all the time," DeMoss recalled, "I guess you could call it a torrid summer romance."[18]

BURIED ALIVE

The "torrid summer romance" of Walker and DeMoss was also the "sweltering summer of the Negro's legitimate discontent." The momentum of years of nonviolent resistance to racial injustice and human indignity culminated in "the greatest demonstration for freedom in the history of our nation"—The March on Washington for Jobs and Freedom.[19] Initiated by A. Philip Randolph, "the dean of Negro leaders," the march would bring attention to and express support for pending civil rights legislation, and would also focus the consciousness of America on the unendurable plight of a people whose full American citizenship was long overdue. Walker and DeMoss were among the sea of over 250,000 demonstrators. An array of nationally and internationally renowned figures were present. Dr. Martin Luther King, Jr., would deliver the keynote speech: "I Have a Dream."

King had not only inspired hope in Alice Walker but he also gave her a *raison d'etre* and a plan. But her soul had risen with the crescendo of King's oration only to sink again when she returned to Spelman in the fall and faced the absence of her cherished teacher, Professor Howard Zinn. Albert Manley had unceremoniously fired Zinn at the end of the spring 1963 semester. Manley saw Zinn "as an instigator rather than simply a supporter of the protests," Zinn writes.[20] Manley's firing of Zinn was met by an outpouring of support for Zinn and rancor against the administration. Alice Walker expressed her outcry in a letter to the editor of Spelman's newspaper, *The Spotlight*, questioning the reason for Zinn's "abrupt" dismissal, highlighting Zinn's contribution to the "modern and progressive character" of the school, and bemoaning the lack of freedom of expression at the college.[21]

That Spelman administrators and trustees would fire "a dedicated American" such as Zinn who was a model of civil, nonviolent resistance, Walker conceived as unconscionable and hypocritical. Zinn's dismissal reinforced Walker's perception of Spelman as an unjust system enmeshed in colonialist politics. Noncooperation, a component of nonviolent resistance, was one means by which people could resist repressive authority. Walker enacted this principle when she refused a $2,000 Merrill fellowship to study abroad in Paris. "They offered no support whatsoever for the black students who were putting their lives on the line trying to bring down Jim Crow. Yet, there was money to send us off to Europe . . . the 'cradle of civilization.'" Walker's rejection of the fellowship "was unprecedented in the history of Spelman."[22]

"Apprised that she was the daughter of struggling tenant farmers," Morehouse College trustee Charles Merrill was flummoxed by Walker's decision. He questioned her about her wisdom in turning down the fellowship while also questioning her aptitude for becoming a writer. Merrill's patronizing and condescending attitude was emblematic of much of Walker's experience with administrators at Spelman. Walker was disheartened. She continued as president of the Social Science Club, but she felt "sort of lost" without Zinn around as advisor. She learned too that Staughton Lynd, the only other professor Walker liked at Spelman, was resigning. A colleague and a friend to Howard Zinn, Lynd was also outraged by Manley's firing of Zinn. As Lynd tendered his letter of resignation, he conveyed to Zinn his intention to help Walker transfer to another school "as her letter in *The Spotlight* will be the end."[23]

Walker was a student in Lynd's American history class. Like Zinn, Staughton Lynd was impressed with Walker's intellect and writing style. He was also impressed with Walker's bravery and "applauded her willingness to confront Manley."[24] Yet he was mindful that the administration could be vindictive with students, as well as faculty. In any case, Walker had concluded that she could not remain at Spelman. "There is nothing really here for me—it is almost like being buried alive. It seems almost a matter of getting away or losing myself—*my self*—in this strange, unreal place."[25]

FIVE

On My Own Terms

I t was, indeed, the *self* that was central to the visionary founders of Sarah
Lawrence College where Alice Walker enrolled in the spring of 1964.
Staughton Lynd made good his promise to assist Walker in transferring
from Spelman. He had written his mother, Helen Merrell Lynd, about his talented and brave former student and inquired about the possibility of Walker
continuing her studies at Sarah Lawrence. Helen Lynd was a renowned social
philosopher who had been on the faculty of the college for 40 years. Having reviewed Walker's records and assessed her activist-oriented community
work, Lynd assisted in arranging Walker's admission to Sarah Lawrence with
full scholarship support.

Founded in 1926, Sarah Lawrence College was the vision of William Van
Duzer Lawrence, a wealthy and philanthropic pharmaceutical and real estate
mogul. Lawrence named the school in memory of his wife, Sarah Bates Lawrence who was an advocate of education and social justice. Like Spelman College, Sarah Lawrence was a private, women's college. As Spelman students
were largely of the black middle class, the students of Sarah Lawrence were
drawn from the upper class of white society. Although Sarah Lawrence was
originally conceived as an elite institution, exclusive to white, Protestant,
"well-to-do girls," the school would evolve to become more diverse in terms of
the social and economic demographics of its student body.

A political and social conservative, William Lawrence intended to establish an educational institution for young women that reflected his conservative politics and Victorian principles. And as "Racial uplift" was an aspect of

Spelman's mission, a species of racial uplift was integral to Lawrence's social philosophy. An adherent of the Cult of Domesticity or the Cult of True Womanhood, Lawrence believed that "there is a woman's sphere of activities and a man's sphere of activities in the world." The school he envisioned would make clear the lines distinguishing the spheres and would "educate its girls to become able and influential leaders in this woman's world, accomplished in all arts and sciences that tend to elevate and strengthen the race and extend the influence of her sex and to this end a new curriculum should be established by this college, having this end in view."[1]

Lawrence, however, allowed himself to be influenced by his more liberal-minded friend Henry Noble MacCracken, president of Vassar College for women from 1915 to 1946. MacCracken aspired to the progressive ideals of philosopher, psychologist, and educator John Dewey who believed that schools were fundamentally social institutions and were, therefore, critical to social reform. Education, then, needed to cultivate the individual, as "a progressive society counts individual variations as precious since it finds in them the means of its own growth." Amenable to the guidance of his friend, Lawrence resolved that "their institution would uphold the individual as the central focus of its educational ideology." Thus, rather than a finishing school, Sarah Lawrence would become a bona fide academic educational institution. Rather than a traditional liberal arts college, it would offer "an innovative curriculum that would include fine arts, drama, and music as formal courses rather than extracurricular activities."[2]

William Lawrence, however, would not live to see the full expression of his vision. Lawrence died on May 16, 1927, but he had early on laid the financial foundation for his vision, which included his twelve-acre estate home in Bronxville, New York. Under the presidency of progressive educator Marion Coats, the Sarah Lawrence College opened its doors to 210 students on October 1, 1928. They would follow an innovative curriculum that would reflect the main tenets of a progressive education: "responsibility for one's own education, freedom to learn at one's own pace, and encouragement to develop one's individuality."[3] They would determine and follow their individual course of study through the don tutorial system rather than the conventional selection of majors and minors. And they would submit weekly written reports on their studies and receive written assessments of their work from their don, or advisor, rather than grades.

Constance Warren would assume the presidency of Sarah Lawrence in the following year. During her sixteen-year tenure, Warren would further develop Sarah Lawrence's progressive curriculum and its don system of student advising. Warren and her faculty would be encouraging and would emphasize an interdisciplinary approach in formulating their classes so that students might "gain a 'more realistic understanding of the complexities of our world.'" Warren revised Sarah Lawrence's admissions policy: "She revamped the admissions process and initiated a financial aid program to create a student body that would more closely reflect the heterogeneous nature of society."[4] And in 1931, Warren successfully petitioned the Regents of the University of the State of New York for a permanent charter as a four-year collegiate institution, with the capacity to offer a bachelor of arts degree.

Though both were liberal arts colleges for women, Spelman and Sarah Lawrence were a study in contrasts. Nevertheless, each school's curricular and extracurricular offerings corresponded, to a certain degree, with Walker's own direction, growth, and intellectual and personal evolution. At Spelman and through her activities as a student there, Walker had begun to explore the world beyond Putnam County, Georgia, and continued to develop the intellectual tools to investigate, understand, and respond to that world. She had begun to attain an appreciation of the social constructions of gender, race, class, and nationality and how these intersecting ideologies informed and shaped one's self-concept. As she had refused to be nobody's "girl," in Eatonton, she had learned to "be nobody's darlin" at Spelman. Dismissed by Albert Manley as "one we tried to help, but she refused it," Walker was not interested in conforming to the status quo. An idealist whose personal and social philosophy continued to evolve, she was not inclined to cooperate with individuals or institutions that would, in any way, undermine her sense of self and her freedom to be self-expressed in the world.

An independent thinker, writer, and activist who believed in personal autonomy, Alice Walker would find Sarah Lawrence to be a nourishing environment. It was, as she would write later, what she was looking for, as she was free to come and go as she pleased. Compelled to surrender her room in the French House at Spelman and the dogwoods she could see from her window, Walker embraced the New England clime with its maples, tulip trees, and evergreens. For the first year of her matriculation at Sarah Lawrence, she settled into room 27 of MacCracken Hall. Helen Lynd would become her don and assist in fashioning a program of study and selection of courses that supported Walker's interests and direction. As her don, Lynd would support Walker's ongoing academic progress and give personal guidance. "In keeping with Sarah Lawrence's founding principles," students would explore each course "intensively in small seminars and private conferences with their professors. In addition to several courses in writing, Alice, guided by Lynd, would turn her attention to studies in theory building, Western Europe in the twentieth century, comedy, and a rigorous examination of Cicero and Petrarch."[5]

Walker was now in an environment that recognized her as a writer and was committed to the education of her whole, autonomous self. The "*self*" she feared losing at Spelman flourished at Sarah Lawrence. She and her talents as a writer would be taken seriously: "I had written at Spelman, but very few people seemed to care. For the most part, writing was considered decorative. At Sarah Lawrence everybody understood that writing was about your heart and your soul and you did it because you had to. Students of dance, danced. Musicians made music. Writers wrote and painters painted." Focused on her studies and her art, Walker spent little time worrying about her appearance "because unlike at Spelman, nobody cared about what you wore or if your hair was done the right way. I was consumed by my work. It was wonderful."[6]

Poet Jane Cooper would remember Alice Walker as a student who was truly outstanding. Cooper was a faculty member at Sarah Lawrence from 1950 to 1987. She taught a fiction writing class that Alice attended. Cooper noted Walker's confidence in her work and in herself as a writer. "'She'd written a story in which she described the land as being red, so when she came to conference, I told her she had the color of the earth wrong,' Cooper remembered. 'Alice looked me dead in the eye and said, "No, you've got it wrong. The land is red where I come from. And that's the way it's going to be in this story. Period."'" By the time Walker reached Sarah Lawrence, she had been involved in the civil rights movement, Cooper noted, and so "was very clear about where she stood." Walker possessed an "integrity and strength of character" that she was able to transfer to the page.[7]

"The Suicide of an American Girl," said Cooper, was an example of such attributes. Walker's story explores the consciousness of African American Ann "Ana" Harriman. An independent-minded and sensitive soul, Ana is a civil rights activist and artist who paints on Sundays and writes poems of requited love during the summers. But Ana's life is full of an unrelieved despair, for in every situation wherein she has expressed love and desires to share it, her feeling is never reciprocated. The father she adores stops talking to her once she turns 13. The country in which she lives despises her very existence. The African homeland to which she flees respects her as an American, but does not love her as a "returning daughter."

After a 10-year sojourn in Ghana, Ana decides to return to America. En route, she stays at the International House in London where she meets the Ghanaian Djin Jdin. The two engage in spirited conversation in which Ana feels herself, more often than not, in a defensive posture. One African American, another African, both away from home, they spar around issues of cultural identity, displacement, racial politics, racial allegiance, political doctrine, social history, belonging, and the sense of home. Like two pugilists returning to their corners, Ana and Djin bade each other good night and return to their rooms in the house. He is impressed with her, but she is not an African woman and could never assume an African ethos. She admires him and believes divides are meant to be crossed, but she also feels his half-hearted rejection of her. When he returns to her room that night, their embrace is fraught with all the contention of their verbal sparring. "She now knew fully the uselessness of love which can never be understood, . . . she fell, quickly to sleep."[8]

As a matter of course the writing faculty and senior writing students would gather to discuss exceptional work. They gathered to discuss "Suicide of an American Girl." "Well," said Cooper, "everybody was completely bowled over by Alice's story. It was a complex, extremely prescient piece. . . ." Although Walker "still had many of the formalities of fiction that she needed to learn, . . .

what she was doing as a student was remarkable," Cooper observed. "She wrote with a daring and force that separated her from the rest." "She had a wild intelligence that she refused to hold back."[9]

This daring and force Walker spied in Muriel Rukeyser with whom she studied poetry, contemporary writers, and the South. "What I learned from Muriel," wrote Walker, "is that poetry, done well, is always about the truth; that it is subversive; that you can't shut it up and that it stays. . . . More than any specifics about structure or technique, she taught me that it was possible to be passionate about writing and to live in the world on my own terms."[10] "Afraid of little, intimidated by none," it was "Muriel Rukeyser the Poet and Muriel Rukeyser the Prophet-person, the Truth-doer" whom Walker would later credit for inspiring her determination to move in the world on her own terms. "If it had not been for her I might never have found the courage, to leave not just Sarah Lawrence, but later the New York City Welfare Department, on my way to becoming a writer."[11]

Rukeyser was equally impressed with her student. Like Cooper, Rukeyser recognized and was struck by Walker's literary gifts and her singular personality: "Many times this semester," writes Rukeyser in an end-of-term assessment, "this student was valuable to the entire class—through clear description, penetrating analysis, candor, and grace . . . and she has not hesitated to make the personal application of her findings. . . . A student of remarkable capacities."[12] Whereas at Spelman Walker was instructed to focus only on style, at Sarah Lawrence, she could engage in substance.

Walker was resentful about a term paper written for a speech and drama class while at Spelman. The paper was to be based on a lecture given by Dr. King. The students were not allowed to contemplate what King said, but only how he said it. "'I am not interested in his politics,' he warned, 'only in his speech.'" To her dismay, her resulting paper reflected the assignment: "Martin Luther King, Jr. is a surprisingly effective orator, although *terribly* under the influence of the Baptist church so that his utterances sound overdramatic and too weighty to be taken seriously." She included comments about his facial features and the quality of his "gray sharkskin suit."[13] Upon hearing King speak at the March on Washington, she was bowled over and felt outdone by this teacher whose instruction had her produce such shallow and vacuous work.

In addition to her earnest dedication to her calling, it was the content of Walker's work, infused with the passion of her experiences that had her teachers at Sarah Lawrence recognize her as an extraordinarily talented individual. With the exception of Rukeyser, who in 1931 spent time in an Alabama jail while she was reporting on the trial of the Scottsboro Boys, neither Walker's teachers nor her classmates had any intimate knowledge of the South or the Southern Revolution. And what information they had was not from the perspective of those who were compelled to rebel against the status quo. Through her writing and her interactions with faculty and students, Walker brought her knowledge and experiences of the South, North.

Helen Berggruen attested to the impact Alice Walker had on her peers. Self-described as "rich, white, northern, naïve, and sheltered," Berggruen, like the majority of Sarah Lawrence students, was unaware of "the *real* America." Her conversations with Walker empowered her to act rather than feel guilty about the injustices. "She talked to me one-on-one," mused Berggruen, "with a calmness and clarity that helped me understand how I could get involved in the movement." Enlightened and inspired, Berggruen joined Walker in a summer 1964 stint of civil rights activities in Alabama. "And when I got to Alabama, I truly felt welcomed. Nobody cared about my background. Their attitude was, 'Hey little sister, glad you came. Now make yourself useful.'"[14]

During the school term, Walker would miss her involvement in civil rights campaigns. She would stay present to their spirit in her work and relations and anticipate the summers when she would return to the South and to direct participation in the movement. The summer of 1965 would find Alice Walker, in Liberty County, Georgia, about 200 miles northeast of Eatonton where her parents then resided. She was engaged in registering rural blacks to vote. With neither community support nor police protection, Walker was wary of her vulnerability. "As those rocks and bottles whizzed past my head, I realized I could easily lose the sight in my other eye. . . . There was no support for us in the community and I wasn't ready to be a martyr just then. I had a fall back position, so I quit."[15] She elected to travel abroad with the Experiment in International Living, a study group organized in 1932 with an agenda of peace and global citizenship.

Walker's program took her to the pineapple plantations of Kenya. The Experiment in Living program was designed to facilitate a poetic comparative analysis of the effects of social segregation and European colonialism in Africa. Walker would also make her own comparative analysis of the effects of social segregation in America and in Africa. As African Americans struggled for personhood in the South, Africans strove for personhood and nationhood in Africa. Her trip to Kenya would bring her face to face with both struggles. "Of course, I was happy to be in Africa, to connect with my roots and to see the people still fighting for survival. But it was very hard."[16]

From Kenya, Walker traveled to Uganda, homeland of her Spelman friend and roommate Constance Nabwire. There, in a village a short distance from Kampala, the capitol, Walker was surprised with a visit from David DeMoss, who was working with the Peace Corps in nearby Tanzania. Though their romance had ended, they remained friends and kept in touch. Caught up in the excitement and passion, they were sexually intimate. Neither was prepared for the occasion. DeMoss's visit was "a total surprise," conveyed Walker who, without anticipation of sexual involvement, had not continued to take oral contraceptives. "The pill had just become available and there were still lots of questions about side effects, so I figured why take it, unless I really needed it."[17] In the fall of 1965, Walker returned to Sarah Lawrence College "healthy and brown, and loaded down with sculptures and orange fabric—and pregnant."[18]

SECTION II
Fire

*T*he vibrating energy of protons, neutrons, and atoms radiate the grosser
light of fire, the cosmic life force of universal structure. The grosser light
of fire sources the sun and its sister stars and the moon's reflected light.[1]
Fire blazes a luminous red and "corresponds with South, the direction of energy,
passion, courage, will, expansion."[2]
    Fire is power. Creativity and destruction dance in its flames. It gives birth; it
consumes. It consumes; it gives birth. It transmutes and transforms. Fire ignites
passion—excitement, enthusiasm, sexual desire. It gives rise to joy and bliss and
to anger and rage. Wild and untamed, fire burns. At home in the hearth, it warms
and inspires.[3] Fire cleanses and purifies: "as enkindled flame converts firewood
into ashes, so does the fire of wisdom consume to ashes all karma."[4] A "radiant lamp," fire is a true teacher. Fire teaches awareness, individual responsibility,
interdependence, and community, as well as nonattachment.[5]
    Creative power and cosmic life force, fire is the light of Spirit and Cosmic Con-
sciousness. Fire, "The light of intelligent life energy, the Word, is the first mani-
festation of cosmic consciousness in creation." Its light is associated with truth,
wisdom, and freedom. **Truth** (satya) is the foundation stone of the universe. 'The
worlds are built on truth.'"[6] The discriminating awareness that fire teaches guides
one to true knowledge—of self and of creation. Perseverance in philosophical
contemplation and in the pursuit of Self-knowledge is essential to gaining control
of one's life force. True knowledge unveils the mysterious, and wisdom is gained
thereby. "[W]isdom . . . **banishes the darkness that is born of ignorance**," and
wisdom's flame lights the path of freedom.[7]

"A Message to Younger Sisters: Be Whole"
by Phyllis McEwen

Young girls
With peach firm bodies
Long pussy—cat painted nails
and voices like champagne:
Beware of these years when you are beautiful and dear.
They will not always love you for these things.

Look often in the mirror and go beyond
the cherry grape lips and jaguar eyes.
Think of the power packs stored in your words.
The visions set strong in your sights like stars.
The mind that makes calculations for those things
you're going to build.

Look often at your legs.
See them as seal skin smooth, pecan brown,
Unveined and clear
But also and again
As strong and trees running for you in races
Sure to win first place.

Young sisters
with peach firm bodies
sweet cherry lips and Black cat eyes:

Look quietly at yourself
And memorize each gift.
The world will not always be so gracious with you.

You must learn to be all things to survive:
A Whole and Free Earth woman
Completely determined to live.

SIX

I Would Only Be the Philosopher

PHILOSOPHY, THOU GUIDE OF LIFE

Alice Walker was engulfed in a sea of despair when she learned she was pregnant. The actuality brought her to the point of planning suicide in response to a future she refused. It was an abortion or suicide. "One or the other of us was not going to survive," Walker resolved. As she had withdrawn into solitude and immersed herself in literature and writing when she suffered the injury to her eye, she now consoled herself with philosophy. "I made myself acquainted with every philosopher's position on suicide, because by that time it did not seem frightening or even odd—but only inevitable."[1] But Walker survived what felt to her to be an impossible situation. And more and more she would explore philosophy as a means through which to understand her world.

Walker began a formal study of philosophy during her sophomore year at Spelman College when she enrolled in an introduction to philosophy course. In her academic essays, she endeavored to use philosophy as an interpretive filter and as a venue wherein she would express and test her own philosophical thought. In "Comments On: *The Year of Protest (1956)*," for example, an essay written in the Russian literature course she took with Howard Zinn, Walker assesses the collected works of post-Stalinist Russian writers. In her critique of "A Trip Home," a short story by Nikolay Zhdanov, she weaves the wisdom of Socrates into her commentary on Zhdanov's "new class" of privileged Russians who become oblivious of the workers who create the country's wealth: "Perhaps Socrates was right after all. Maybe man would be better off without a body because then he would not be able to sell his soul for physical comforts."[2]

Later, at Sarah Lawrence College, Walker would take several courses that would broaden her overall understanding of philosophy while intensifying her appreciation of particular thinkers. Her coursework included the writing of précis, which were opportunities to not only examine the ideas of various philosophers and writers, but to also posit her own philosophical perspectives in response. During the 1964–1965 academic year, Walker studied the works of ancient, medieval, and modern humanist philosophers. In the fall of 1964, she wrote a 20-page essay on Marcus Tullius Cicero in which she admiringly and sympathetically chronicles Cicero's rise as a central figure in Roman politics and explores his ability to find meaning in a life filled as much with challenges and disappointment as it was with achievements and honors.

"There were two Ciceros," her paper began. "The man, and the philosopher. All his life he made an effort to unite the two. That he did not completely succeed in fact I think we can estimate from his letters. That he did succeed in his effort we can determine from his letters, from his philosophical treatises, and from his life."[3] Walker found Cicero, the man, extraordinary in his capacity to rise from his humble beginnings as the son of a gentleman farmer to become Consul of the Senate, a prestigious position within the most powerful political body in Roman government at that time. She found Cicero, the philosopher, to be something of a Platonist with stoical tendencies. But because Cicero was attuned to the day-to-day affairs of the republic rather than the formulation of "plans for future governments based on his 'ideas' as Plato did," Walker considered Cicero "far beyond both Platonism and Stoicism."[4]

Toward the latter part of his life, when the Rome that he knew was no more and he had "lost his 'place' in Roman politics," Cicero had turned to philosophy for comfort and for meaning in the midst of chaos and evanescence.[5] "What he learned he put into his own soul and in this way strengthened himself against whatever else was to come," writes Walker, "I cannot imagine how the study of Philosophy could be put to better use."[6] Walker attests that for Cicero, philosophy was more than "mere contemplation." In the same sense, philosophy was more to Alice Walker than an academic exercise.

Like Cicero, Walker, too, faced the task of "wringing order out of chaos." Her study of Cicero gave her more of an understanding about abstract ideas such as truth, justice, and reality. Given her commitment to social change in a tumultuous America, she was compelled by Cicero's ideas on duty. Accordingly, Cicero believed humans to be, first and foremost, social animals, and therefore, naturally directed toward the formation of societies. Once a society is formed, "our first duty is to the maintenance of this human society, all other duties to family, friends, etc., are of necessity secondary." Although Cicero saw duty to society as paramount, this duty, did not conflict with the duty to one's self: "Our primary duty to ourselves is not to go against the bias of our natures (neither in emotional intrigues, nor in choosing our life's work), lest we live to regret it. And regret, in addition to being painful, is a waste of time."

Predisposed to being good, honest, and sociable, humankind had only to reinforce these virtues with wisdom. "This," Walker writes, "he learns from intercourse with his fellow men, from contemplation upon philosophical truths, and from acting in the affairs of society."[7] As a kind of coda to her essay on Cicero, Walker wrote, "We live in a world of which we can never be sure—and then if we are lucky, or wise, or a philosopher, maybe we discover that the meaning of the world is to be searched for within ourselves. Once discovered, we put our knowledge into use—as Cicero did, at the risk that probably cost his life, his writing of the *Phillipic Orations*."[8]

In the postscript to her essay, Walker wrote against the backdrop of societal structures in America and the Soviet Union. She decried both as failed systems that were anathema to the sovereign dignity of the individual. "For we are today, no less than in Cicero's age, ruled mainly by our emotions, subject to the instinct and whim of the herd, disregardful of reason, suspicious of intellect; and, in a word, 2000 years older as a civilization and not much wiser." She concluded, however, that failures can never justify our not trying to construct just and democratic societies, social structures that are not based on color, class, caste, and categories of citizenship. Walker proclaims her personal sovereignty, her right to live a life that is not circumscribed by the state. And for her part, even in "a philosopher-king ruled country, I would not feel that I should be anything but the philosopher."[9]

ENGAGÉ

Having become familiar with the classical humanist tradition, Alice Walker could easily perceive its expression in the works and life of 14th-century Renaissance humanist Francis Petrarch, whom she describes as "a sort of combination of Augustine and Cicero."[10] In her paper titled "Francis Petrarch: Prototype of the Modern Student," Petrarch is depicted as a light among medieval philosophers and Christian scholars who were thralls of the methodology of scholasticism and dialectical reasoning, and who, having made Aristotle "the last word in philosophy . . . left themselves no where to go."[11] Petrarch turned to the ancients, Walker explains in her essay, adapting the oratorical and rhetorical skill of Cicero and the introspective sensibility and candor of Augustine.

As he believed philosophers of antiquity to be superior to those of his age, Petrarch set about reviving the work of the ancient Greeks. And this, Walker writes, was the beginning of Petrarch's philosophy and the inspiration for his literary endeavors. In the tradition of the humanists he admired, Petrarch sought to recover his cultural past. He therefore penned *Africanus*, an epic poem chronicling the defeat of Hannibal by the Roman military general Scipio Africanus. Africanus had also been the subject of a novel by Cicero.

Walker asserts that Petrarch's epic spoke to the importance of honoring historical figures and their legacies or "hidden treasures." She dubbed *Africanus* a *magnum opus* of great historical import, as it was conceived of and written "when the historical awareness of mankind was anything but keen."[12] Perhaps *Africanus* and Petrarch's commitment to it were the ideological seeds inspiring Walker's interest in the hidden treasures of her ancestors and literary foremothers.

It is as a student that Alice Walker felt most deeply a kinship with Petrarch. "Not only is this feeling relevant because Petrarch was so ostentatiously a student—in the academic and social sense of the word—but he was also *engagé* in the perpetual struggle which makes all of us students": the constant battle between individual will and the impersonal force of the universe.[13] What Walker liked most about Francis Petrarch was his willingness to assess and appreciate the uniqueness of his own nature and his willingness to concede that others were also uniquely endowed. She admired "his determination to live and do his work in his own, if seemingly, irregular, way," and she appreciated "his sense of being in the mainstream of recorded life and history." She felt "obscurely honored" that modern scholars were "very much like him. Or at least we try to be."[14]

As Walker studied the schools of philosophy and their practitioners, she studied philosophical fiction as well. Her course selections for the 1965–1966 term included topics on the philosophical aspects of the modern novel. Given her sociological and philosophical interests, Walker was wont to give more attention to the biographical and intellectual aspects of an author's work and less to a specifically literary analysis. Even in courses that were specifically literary in scope, Walker brought the speculative lens of philosophy. Ultimately, in consistently taking a philosophical approach in the writing of her class papers at Sarah Lawrence, Alice Walker was exercising and honing her own philosophical sensibilities and developing her own philosophical orientation.

The philosophers and writers she studied, in turn, influenced her thought and creativity as a private person, a public citizen, and as a writer. Philosophy, for Alice Walker, was never merely academic. It would become the intellectual lens through which she would interpret an otherwise senseless, violent, and indifferent society; an absurd reality wherein—based on arbitrary social and cultural prejudices—she could be robbed of her humanity and disinherited from the very soil on which she was born.

PHILOSOPHY: THE ART OF LIVING IN TIMES OF CATASTROPHE

"A *good* paper" punctuated the summary assessment Helen Lynd penned in neat, precise longhand at the end of Alice Walker's 28-page thesis, "Albert Camus: The Development of His Philosophical Position as Reflected in His Novels and Plays." The senior thesis was the last requirement Walker had to fulfill for her bachelor of arts degree. "I think you got a great deal from doing this paper," Lynd wrote, "I got a great deal from reading it. You combine well the pertinent analysis of detail and the major trends in his thought." Lynd was particularly impressed with the way Walker used "recognition of the absurd as a basis for human solidarity and a preparation for rebellion" in Camus's writing.[15] Walker had, indeed, gotten a great deal from doing the paper. In a postscript to her study, she wrote, "There comes a time in one's life—perhaps many times in everyone's life—when what one learns about another's life and ideas amounts to a revelation. Camus' life and work present just such a discovery of another way of looking at life and the world; and offer as well an immense reservoir of strength."[16]

Walker had a vague familiarity with the work of Albert Camus from her days at Spelman. Student participants in the civil rights movement and members of the Student Non-Violent Coordinating Committee were well versed in revolutionary ideologies and literatures of resistance. Camus's writings, which questioned the sociopolitical and cultural status quo in Europe, were integral to their thought. Nonetheless, as she later acknowledged in her thesis, Walker had casually dismissed Camus with a facile comparison to Jean-Paul Sartre "without knowing really what either of them was about." Through her research and writing at Sarah Lawrence College, Walker discovered Albert Camus to be an extraordinary figure "whose giant philosophical contributions to the world make him uniquely unequatable [sic] with anyone."[17]

Having "plunged" into Camus's work, Walker read and explored his writings in accordance with the three established phases of his oeuvre: The absurd, revolt, and collective guilt and responsible means.[18] During the weeks she read the novel and plays of the absurd—The Stranger (The Outsider), The Misunderstanding (Cross Purposes), and Caligula—Walker felt "absolutely hopeless." Buoyed up by The Myth of Sisyphus, the expository component of the first phase, she felt "a glimmer of hope" for herself and the world. Enthralled with The Myth, Walker imagined herself as Sisyphus: "at every rough spot in my own day-to-day life I got into the habit of imagining that I was a real Sisyphusian heroine actually, only nobody knew it but me, naturally."[19]

The works of the revolt period—"The Plague, State of Siege, etc."—inspired her spirit of resistance and her sense of collective consciousness: "I began to see myself working with others . . . 'conscious' and 'lucid' in the face of destiny and death rather than resigned and foggy." In The Fall and The Just Assassins (Les Justes)—works Walker categorized as the literature of collective guilt and responsibility—she felt her own innocence, culpability, and sense of social responsibility. These works, Walker states, "makes the reader aware that he too has something to confess. He too, is guilty. He too must realize his role and responsibility for the condition of the world as it is."[20]

In her thesis, Walker described Camus's idea of the absurd as the "awareness of the futility and senselessness of the effort of one's life." She then traced the "progression in Camus' writing from the Absurd experience as an individual, solitary phenomenon to a collective revolt of political and social action based on solidarity and the use of responsible means to reach desired ends."[21] In context of Camus's thought, Walker writes that an indifferent universe becomes a hostile and decidedly cruel and treacherous place in which humans are essentially alone and at the mercy of chance. The one thing unifying other-wise isolated humanity is the inevitability of death. However, the fact of death, of finality, could not be conceived as a justification for limitless individual freedom as Camus demonstrated in *Caligula*.

Walker believed that in order to understand Camus's absurdist standpoint, it was necessary that she "first take a look into Camus' own life": "what inter-ests me most about Camus' early years are 1) his poverty, and 2) his recur-rent attacks of tuberculosis."[22] Camus's paternal grandparents migrated from France to Mondovi, Algeria, in 1870. His father, an agricultural worker, was killed at war, when Camus was a boy of three. His mother worked as a char-woman. They lived in a two-room apartment with his maternal grandmother, an uncle, and an elder brother. These circumstances likely reminded Walker of her own humble beginnings in the cramped sharecroppers' shacks of her childhood in rural Georgia.

Walker recounts that Camus was academically talented and was encour-aged in his studies by a primary school teacher who assisted him in acquiring a scholarship to the lycée. He continued his studies at the University of Algiers in 1933, eventually obtaining a master's degree in philosophy in 1936. Earlier on in 1930 at the age of 17, Camus was forced to drop out of school because of the onset of tuberculosis. Walker perceived Camus's physical condition as the key factor in his "experiment" in the philosophy and literature of the absurd. She conjectures that upon discovering his illness, Camus "felt as if life, which he loved so much, had betrayed him."[23]

Walker had had her own dance with despair. The event of the injury to her eye not only interrupted her early school years, but also resulted in a sense of isolation. As a college student in 1965, Walker would be engulfed in despair over an unwanted pregnancy. She had suffered the angst of contemplating an illegal abortion, for *Roe v. Wade* would not be decided until 1973. And she had slept with a razor blade under her pillow, with the intent to cut her wrists, should an abortion prove unattainable. She, too, spoke of feeling betrayed—by her own body and by life in general. There was much in Walker's experi-ence that would have her sympathize with Albert Camus's social and economic challenges and personal struggles. That she commiserated with Camus is evi-dent in the compassionate tone that infuses comments she makes regarding Camus's illness: "What the direct confrontation of the constancy and inevi-tability and mercilessness of death did to young Camus can only be surmised from what he says in his work. How he must have felt. He who loved life so much!"[24]

As Walker saw Camus's illness as key to the literature of the absurd, she saw his response to the absurd—to his illness—as key to the literature of revolt and of collective guilt and responsibility. Rather than acquiesce before the natural indifference of the universe and the injustice in human society, Camus resolved to struggle for the dignity of the individual and the freedom of oppressed communities. In 1938, Camus wrote for the socialist newspaper *Alger républicain*. His articles defended the rights of Arabs while probing the conditions in which they lived. Walker read Camus's stance as a reflection of his revolutionary commitment and growth as an activist-writer. As she quotes him, "There always comes a time when one must choose between contemplation and action. This is called becoming a man."[25]

Walker's biographical profile follows Camus to Paris where, in 1943, he joined the French Resistance movement against German occupation. He eventually becomes editor-in-chief of *Combat*, the movement's underground newspaper, writing editorials initially supporting the punishment of French collaborators with Nazi occupation and later questioning "revolutionary justice." Walker saw Camus's participation in the Resistance movement as a momentous "decision to fight against the nihilism of his age": "conscious that I cannot stand aloof from my time, I have decided to be an integral part in it." Her biographical sketch concludes with summary remarks on Camus's acceptance speech for the 1957 Nobel Prize in literature. She was moved by Camus's recognition of men like himself, born during the First World War who faced unstinting social and political chaos, death, continuation of war, and destruction. And she, too, grieved for those who had to "bring their children and their works to maturity in a world threatened with nuclear destruction."[26]

Even as such a world would not easily lend itself to optimism as Camus had stated, Walker spied the optimism in Camus's unwavering determination to resist those who were consumed by "the death instinct" while insisting, also, on maintaining compassion for the perpetrators of injustice: "I even go so far as to feel that, without ceasing to struggle against those who through an excess of despair insisted upon their right to dishonor and hurled themselves into the current nihilism, we must understand their error."[27] Camus's thought, expression, and sentiment here must have recalled for Walker the attitude of Dr. King who also insisted on loving the "enemy" and meeting physical force with soul force.

In his creative and nonviolent response to the existentialism and nihilism of his time, Camus's life and work were a revelation to Walker. An artist may require solitude, but need not assume herself an isolated, unconnected island. And the artist's creativity could be a profound contribution to society, transforming both the individual artist and the world of which she is a part. Camus declared as much in a passage from *The Myth of Sisyphus* that Walker quotes in the epigraph to her thesis. Though the path of an artist is perceived to be solitary, Camus states that "this is not true." The artist abides "in the midst of all, in the same rank, neither higher nor lower, with all those who are working and struggling." The very vocation of the artist, "in the face of opposition, is to open the prisons and to give a voice to the sorrows of all. This is where art, against its enemies, justifies itself by proving precisely that it is no one's enemy."[28] Walker writes that in fashioning for himself "an art of living in times of catastrophe," Albert Camus "sought to give the world a new way out through his literature."[29]

SEVEN

Changing the World

"Your job, when you leave here—as it was the job of educated women before you—is to change the world. Nothing less or easier than that." With these words, Alice Walker sought to inspire and guide the 1972 graduating class of Sarah Lawrence. Leaving Eatonton in 1961, Walker had vowed an end to the South that permitted her humiliation. This South was the microcosm of a larger world in need of amelioration. Thus she impressed upon her audience that "the world is not good enough; we must make it better."[1]

Leaving Sarah Lawrence, Alice Walker's initial effort toward this end was as a caseworker with New York City's welfare department, assisting welfare recipients who were being treated at Bellevue Hospital. It became apparent to Walker that the administrators of Bellevue were willing to address the symptoms of the patients with medication, but they were not willing to address the conditions of their lives. Her work therefore became an endeavor of "trying to personally save the walking wounded," an effort that undermined her creative energies. In the interim after leaving this job, Walker accepted a study abroad fellowship proffered by Charles Merrill, whom she had kept in touch with since their confrontation at Spelman. "Because the award was no longer tied to me being a student at Spelman," Walker reasoned, "I didn't feel that I was compromising my morals or integrity."[2]

But even as she packed, Walker questioned the point of immersing herself in Senegalese culture when the culture of poverty and violence continued to be the nightmare that African Americans all over the South suffered every day. So the summer of 1966 found Alice Walker in Mississippi. There was something visceral in her decision to join the Mississippi Freedom Movement. Her quest for the respect due to all Americans was intimately conjoined with the need to live unafraid. "All my life," Walker asserted, "Mississippi had been the epitome of evil for black people. I knew that if I wanted to be able to live at all in America, I needed to be able to live unafraid, anywhere. I had to face up to the system that had almost done me in and so many of my people." Mississippi was infamous for the 1955 lynching of 14-year-old Emmet Till; the 1963 slaying of NAACP field secretary Medgar Evers and the murder of civil rights activists Andrew Goodman, James Earl Chaney, and Michael Schwerner during the Mississippi Freedom Summer project of 1964. "Mississippi was the test."[3]

Walker joined forces with the NAACP Legal Defense Fund, under the direction of Marian Wright (later Edelman). Appreciative of Walker's "gifts and talents as a writer," Edelman gave Walker the task of taking depositions from rural blacks who had been evicted from their homes as retribution for registering to vote.[4] The testimonies Walker recorded documented Mississippi's defiance of the 1964 Civil Rights Act and the 1965 Voting Rights Act. Walker was paired with Melvin ("Mel") Leventhal, a New York University Law School student whose main endeavor was to draft and file lawsuits against the state of Mississippi. Depositions such as those collected by Walker would support the lawsuits that would be filed.

Edelman had assigned Walker and Leventhal to Greenwood, Mississippi. They spent a scary night in a local motel where civil rights workers were not welcome. They held a vigil through the night in each other's presence. The danger they expected in the night came as an unveiled threat in broad daylight during their lunch break at a local restaurant: "Don't let the sun set on you in Greenwood," was the warning.[5] Yet by the time Walker and Leventhal had combed the backwoods searching out the dispossessed poor for their testimonies, the sun had set and they were being followed. However, the pickup truck that trailed them had crashed with another vehicle, giving them an opportunity to get out of town safely and then to Jackson. They learned the next day that the "accident" had been arranged by local NAACP members who had been informed of the threat made.

Frightened but undeterred, Walker and Leventhal continued their activities. The challenging situations that ensued allowed Walker a glimpse into Leventhal's character. She was impressed and in love. "I loved Mel because he was passionate about justice and he was genuinely passionate about me. He was soulful, expressive, and didn't hold back any of his feelings. It was so obvious he enjoyed every moment we were together."[6] When they returned to New York, Walker moved in with Leventhal. He worked toward the completion of his law degree. She completed a prize-winning essay, "The Civil Rights Movement, What Good Was It," and received a MacDowell Colony fellowship to complete the manuscript that would later be published as *The Third Life of Grange Copeland*.

The couple planned to return to Mississippi once Leventhal was graduated, and Walker set the terms of their return: "If we were going back to Mississippi, then we'd be going as husband and wife." Walker expounded, "There was a long tradition of white men having black mistresses in the South. That was not going to be my path. So I proposed to Mel, and he happily obliged."[7] They were wedded in a civil ceremony in a New York City courthouse, on March 17, 1967. The marriage surprised some members of Walker's family and upset others. Friends and associates questioned Walker's loyalty to black men and to black solidarity. Miriam Leventhal had judged her son's bride "a *schvartse* (the pejorative Yiddish term for a black person), [and] sat shiva, mourning him for dead."[8]

Others questioned the judiciousness of the couple's intent to live in a state where their marriage was officially construed as illegal. In defiance of Mississippi law, Walker and Leventhal established themselves in Jackson. "We intended to stand our ground," Walker had avowed. "We came to Mississippi to kill the fear it engendered as a place where black life was terrifyingly hard, pitifully cheap."[9] Her poem, "While Love is Unfashionable," a poem dedicated "to Mel," spurned the very notion of miscegenation laws and the prerogative of a state to impose them. Walker and Leventhal would face down the political and social aspects of racial segregation. And they would do so together, "under fire."

Melvin Leventhal, absolute in his insistence on social justice and equal opportunity in Mississippi, concentrated his efforts on school desegregation. "We will," he proclaimed, "have quality education for every child."[10] While Leventhal held forth in the courtroom, Walker was immersed in the community. She would give herself to the project of observing Mississippi and of recording "the consciousness of a people."[11] Walker's insights into the human condition as expressed in the lives of impoverished rural blacks were deepened and expanded by her work as a consultant to the Friends of the Children of Mississippi Headstart program. Her work entailed creating a black history curriculum for teachers in the program and conducting pedagogical workshops.

Even as 1968 began hopefully enough with the anticipation of their first child, the hope inspired by new life was overshadowed by the April 4 assassination of Dr. King. The extent to which Walker's soul had been stirred by the heroic visage of King years ago, was the extent to which her soul would experience another dark night. Walker and Leventhal joined the procession that trailed the mule-drawn coffin in Atlanta on April 9. The sound of footsteps in a march of sorrow echoed in the hollow regions of their lives when they returned to Jackson. The week following the four-mile walk across Atlanta, Walker miscarried. "I lost the child I had been carrying. I did not even care. It seemed to me, at the time, that if 'he' (it was weeks before my tongue could form his name) must die no one deserved to live, not even my own child."[12]

She who had completely identified with the steady calm of Martin King wrestled with the absurdity of "a nonviolent, pacifist philosophy in a violent, nonpacifist society," and engaged in fantasies of retaliatory violence.[13] Into this doleful cavern appeared the countenance of Coretta Scott King expressing her grief and proclaiming that her faith "in the redemptive will of God is stronger today than ever before." In the light of Coretta King's clarity and strength, Walker's demeanor of grief paled as "self-pity," and her voice, recalled Walker, "pulled me to my feet, as her husband had done in a different way."[14]

As she questioned this knight whom she once followed "unquestioningly," Walker also questioned the value of her work as a writer whose efforts were one with the movement. For in the wake of King's death, it seemed that the oppressor needed murdering rather than manuscripts. She felt that art, her art in particular, was without value and incapable of effecting change. Coretta King's words, however, forced Walker to acknowledge a debt, "not only to her husband's memory but also to the living continuation of his work."[15]

SUICIDE OR REVOLT

The continuation of King's work entailed honoring the philosophical and moral tenets of nonviolent resistance and the commitment to the envisioned "beloved community." As a writer informed by this philosophy and vision, Alice Walker would bear witness in her writing to the unfolding drama of the struggle for justice and lay bare the conditions of brutality and beauty of a people "under continuous pressures."[16] In her first novel, *The Third Life of Grange Copeland*, she would work the soil of her progenitors and analyze the milieu in which they were forced to live. Walker's exploration is grounded in both the Christian morality of nonviolent direct action and the sensitivity of Albert Camus's philosophy of the absurd. She holds forth the vision of the beloved community over and against the absurd and violent world of rural Georgia.

The novel opens a door into the stagnant, wishful, and resigned lives of the Copelands, sharecroppers who eke out a living in Green County, Georgia. Margaret pulled baits all day, while Grange planted, chopped, poisoned, and picked cotton. Their son Brownfield scraped cotton in the children's section of the same cotton fields. *The Third Life of Grange Copeland* assesses their world in absurd terms: the world is inimical and indifferent to the survival, the hopes, the dreams, and the suffering of those who must contend with it. Absurd reasoning dictates that given such a world, one must then decide whether it is worth one's effort to live in it.

This question, this "one truly serious philosophical problem," is raised at the critical juncture in the novel when Star is born.[17] Star was not the shining hope his name implied. He was the gray-eyed, red-haired, ignored bastard of Margaret and Shipley, the man who owned the fields in which Grange labored. Determined to match Grange in his Saturday night ritual of drunken debauchery, Margaret had consoled herself "in the transient embraces of strangers."[18] But rather than exacerbate the tensions in the Copeland family home, Star forced them to face the fundamental question: Was the microcosm of misery that was their world worth the effort required to contend with it?

Each member of the Copeland family rendered a judgment and each one's consequent decision reflected options outlined in *The Myth of Sisyphus*: suicide or revolt. In the philosophy of the absurd, resignation is a species of suicide, and both represent a "No" to life, a confession "that life is too much for you or that you do not understand it."[19] This is Margaret's judgment. And one month after Grange's desertion, she poisons herself and Star and walks out into the night. Brownfield discovers them the next morning. Like a disenchanted Madonna, Margaret "was curled up in a lonely sort of way, away from her child, as if she had spent the last moments on her knees."[20]

Brownfield, the absurd antihero of the novel, had chosen a half-hearted rebellion. After the burial of his mother and half-brother, he headed "up Norse," presumably to find his father. But Brownfield was confounded by his own lack of direction. "To gaze hopefully at the sky was in his blood, but nothing came of it."[21] Unlike his forebears, he had no wisdom about the North Star. Brownfield made it as far as the Dew Drop Inn in Baker County, the haunt frequented by his father. And like his father, he became ensnared in the wiles of "Fat Josie," proprietor of the inn. But when he met Josie's niece Mem, a quiet, plump, "cherry brown," schoolteacher, he saw his saving grace and conceived of his marriage to her as a guarantor of his freedom and success.

The fifth year of Brownfield's marriage "was a year when endless sunup to sundown work on fifty rich bottom acres of cotton land and a good crop brought them two diseased shoats for winter meat, some dried potatoes and apples from his boss's cellar, and some cast-off clothes for his children from his boss's family."[22] He clearly saw his nightmare: the reproduction of his father's life. This was Brownfield's moment of "lucidity": A consciousness of "the vast repetition" that negates one's aliveness and dreams and the subsequent rising passion to revolt against it. "What follows is the gradual return into the chain or it is the definitive awakening. At the end of the awakening comes, in time, the consequence: suicide or recovery."[23]

Though Brownfield becomes conscious of the impossible conditions of his life, he does not probe deeply enough to reach an understanding that inspires recovery. For as much as he resented the Captain Davis's and the Mr. J. L.'s of the world who treated him and his wife like a string of horses to be swapped for farm equipment or to be handed off from one family member to another, he could not summon the fortitude to defy them. Yet he was impelled to revolt against a reality he knew to be absurd. Powerless to destroy his white gods, Brownfield remade himself in their image and unleashed his rage and anger on those around him. Giddy with his power to desecrate and destroy, Brownfield mutates into a version of Caius Caligula, the tyrant emperor in Camus's play *Caligula*, who delights in turning his empire topsy-turvy.

After the death of his beloved sister-mistress Drusilla, Caligula becomes conscious of life as "intolerable." He awakens to this truth: "Men die; and they are not happy." He rebels against this fate and resolves to liberate himself from it by rendering possible the impossible: He will have the moon.[24] Caligula flouts law and convention, scorns the gods, and permits himself everything, including mayhem and murder. His logic leads him to proclaim everyone as guilty and therefore condemned.

With the same logic, Brownfield destroys his fiefdom. He plots Mem's "come down" and drags his family from one sharecropper's shack to the next. He weakens Mem with a series of pregnancies and kills the one child to come to term. In the fashion of Caligula, Brownfield "was enjoying himself in a sort of lunatic way."[25] As the murder of his mistress Caesonia signaled Caligula's apotheosis, the murder of Mem signals Brownfield's. On Christmas Eve, standing in the circle of porch light that surrounded him like a halo, Brownfield awaited Mem's approach to the house and raised his shotgun "with drunken accuracy right into her face and fired."[26]

Caius Caligula argued that any man can harden his heart and become a god. But he also saw that god-men were blind souls whose logic inevitably led to a blind alley. In the end, he averred that he "had chosen a wrong path, a path that leads to nothing."[27] Brownfield came to the same conclusion and "ground his teeth under the pressure of his error." Like a weak candescence that capitulates to impregnable darkness, Brownfield's momentary thought that he could make a different choice was whelmed by the "rigidity of his belief in misery, knowing he could never renew or change himself, for his changelessness was now all he had."[28] The logic of their nihilistic thought led both Caligula and Brownfield to a "superior suicide," as each one "does what is necessary to arm against him those who will eventually kill him."[29]

In Brownfield's world, as in Caligula's, "nobody is innocent."[30] In Grange Copeland's third life, innocence is everything and is to be protected. Grange, the novel's hero, comes slowly to this understanding through self-reflection and examination of his first and second lives. He had struggled against the absurd reality of a black sharecropper. He had experienced the weariness and numbness of a mechanical existence. And he admitted that in reaction to his circumstances he had done a lot of things with which, in his third life, he did not agree. Grange's rebellion took him North, and there he was embraced by a cold indifference to his very being.

His existential crisis was exacerbated by the acrimony with which a pregnant white woman in Central Park rejected his help. In her effort to avoid touching him, she had fallen into an icy pond. "She reached up and out with a small white hand that grabbed his hand but let go when she felt it was *his* hand. . . . She called him 'nigger' with her last disgusted breath." His choosing to allow her and her child to sink to a chilling death was his moment of lucidity and his revolt against any feeling of human compassion for white people. His refusal to help the woman was a death sentence, and therefore, "simple murder."[31] Grange felt this "murder" to be his liberatory act against an absurd reality, initiating him into his second life.

Just as his son had discovered, Grange, the father, discovered that by taking a life, he could reinvigorate his own and regain, on some level, his suppressed manhood. Whereas the son would sacrifice the lives of his family members, the father would sacrifice an entire group of people: "They must kill their

oppressors."[32] Grange refuted the morality of Christian love in which "enemies" were to be forgiven. He declared that the biblical gospel was useless
in changing the hearts of whites or in ameliorating the conditions of blacks:
"Man is alone—in his life as in his death—without any God but himself (and
the world)."[33]

Grange Copeland thenceforth claimed full responsibility for himself and
permitted himself the right to unleash his pent-up aggression "in the real hostile world," wherein—in the name of Margaret and Brownfield and his own
beleaguered life—he indiscriminately fought the "blue-eyed devils" at every
opportunity that presented itself.[34] Weary from his campaign, he returned to
the South to reestablish himself in complete independence and isolation from
them. He resolved to spread his revolutionary gospel and to free from white
oppression his people and "every other of the downtrod, especially if he's a
man of color."[35] Grange came to realize that in order to initiate his granddaughter Ruth into his hate-based faith, he would risk corrupting the mind
and spirit of the one somebody that he loved. It was a risk he was not willing
to take.

Grange's character is a composite of Prince Dmitri Nekhlyudov in Leo
Tolstoy's *Resurrection* and Ivan "Yanek" Kaliayev, "The Poet," in Albert
Camus's *The Just Assassins*. Nekhlyudov seeks redemption for his reprobate
soul by petitioning the courts for a pardon on behalf of Katerina "Katyusha"
Maslova, a servant girl whom he raped and abandoned to a life of prostitu-
tion and subsequent imprisonment. Her pardon would be his: "I seduced
her, and got her into the situation she is now in. If she hadn't become what
I turned her into, she wouldn't have been on a charge like that."[36] Like Nekhlyudov, Grange Copeland acknowledges his moral turpitude and seeks to
atone for his misdeeds even to the point of assuming moral responsibility
for Brownfield's destruction of Mem. Over time Katyusha would open to
Nekhlyudov's attempt to make amends, but Brownfield's heart would remain
hard against his father.

Grange could not save his son from the dragnet of the poor, but he refused
to abandon Ruth to the same fate. In securing her welfare, he was prepared to
kill his son and sacrifice his own life. In this, Grange is like Yanek Kaliayev, the
just assassin who volunteers to throw the bomb that will kill the Grand Duke
of Russia. Yanek and his comrades have committed their lives to ending the
despotic rule of Russian people. "When we kill, we're killing so as to build up
a world in which there will be no more killing," says Kaliayev. "We consent
to being criminals so that at last the innocents, and only they, will inherit the
earth."[37] Grange's third life was the paradoxical life of the just assassin who
kills and sacrifices his own life for the greater good of others, but who simultaneously finds murder indefensible. So when Grange took Brownfield's life in
order to secure Ruth's present innocence and future possibility, he knew he
could not keep his own life.

The first path Grange Copeland trod in his third life was one that would
eventually have led to "the gradual return into the chain" since Grange's desire

for freedom and independence was being built on hate. As his consciousness began to shift, his obstinacy to the possibility of social change and a beloved community that did not fence off whites also became a possibility, albeit a remote one. This possibility was reflected in Grange's treatment of the black and white civil rights workers who came to his farm to register voters.

Grange is thus initiated into the second phase of his third life. In this phase, he frets whether what he had done to secure Ruth's well-being was "*human*" of him or not. The more he speculates over his own condition as a human being, the more he contemplates how he could protect her full humanity. "Survival was not everything. *He* had survived. But to survive *whole* was what he wanted for Ruth."[38] He felt it was too late for him, but Ruth Copeland would be his fourth life. She would be the recovery he could not achieve.

EIGHT

Meridian: Coming of Age in Mississippi

STAND YOUR GROUND

Walker and Leventhal had committed to gathering blossoms under fire in one of the meanest states in the country. Together, they wrought social and political change that would allow the next generation to move more freely about the state, the country, and their lives. Their work in courtrooms and classrooms, movie theaters and bowling alleys, in the mass media and in literary journals, and books of poetry and fiction moved a nation. Yet on the morning they moved and left their home for good, Walker writes, "I was so tired of it that, at the end of the street, when the car stopped for a final farewell, I could not, would not, look back. I did not expect ever to set foot in Mississippi again."

Everybody knew about Mississippi, but Alice Walker lived there. "It was a period of constant revelation, when mysteries not understood during my Southern childhood came naked to me to be embraced. I grew to adulthood in Mississippi."[1] Walker's season in Mississippi steeped her in the knowledge of her ancestral heritage and provided fertile ground for her writer's imagination. These gifts bequeathed her, however, exacted a price: Anxiety. Depression. Suicidal thoughts. Listening for a husband's footsteps. Such exactions brought Walker to "the brink of spiritual collapse."[2]

The strides Walker and Leventhal made in concert with the Mississippi Movement made the difference. "Whites Only" and "Colored" signs came down; schools were integrated; African Americans were granted access to public facilities; employment opportunities expanded; and voting rights were being upheld, yielding a number of black elected officials. These changes were conceded grudgingly as civil rights workers "tested" the state's compliance with federal law. "One afternoon each week," Walker writes, "I drive to downtown Jackson to have lunch with my husband at one of Jackson's finest motels."[3] They would do so to "test" the quality of service in the motel's restaurant and to see, through the glass window, whether black people could swim the pool without incident. By year seven, they could.

By year seven, Walker and her husband could eat a meal without concern "that a hostile waitress will spit in our soup." She no longer worried whether her husband would return home; he had "become a celebrity to the same extent that he had earlier been 'an outside agitator' and a pariah."[4] Yet there was no ignoring the impact of having endured the years that were rife with Mississippi's birth pangs. "For us," Walker wrote, "every day of our lives here has been a 'test.'"[5] A politically active black woman in an illegal marriage, and mother of a "mixed-race" daughter, Alice Walker lived in a state of hypervigilance. By year seven, she would seek psychiatric therapy. By year seven she would seek, also, a less absurd environment.

In the meantime, Alice Walker, inspired by the example of Margaret Walker, would keep the sense of art alive in the students she taught at Jackson State University during Margaret Walker's sabbatical. As guest lecturer at Tougaloo College in 1970, she would encourage and support students in their creative expression. To keep art alive in herself, she applied for and received a Radcliffe Institute writing fellowship. In September 1971, Walker traveled to Cambridge, Massachusetts, with daughter Rebecca to begin her residency and work on her second novel, tentatively titled "Atonement and Release." Her ambitions, however, were frustrated when she and Rebecca had succumbed to a flu epidemic.

Walker made little progress on the manuscript, but was able to complete a second volume of poetry, *Revolutionary Petunias & Other Poems*, published in 1973. She had also been appointed as lecturer at the University of Massachusetts and at Wellesley College, in 1972, where she created and taught the first course in the American academy on black women writers. Daughter Rebecca remained in Jackson in the warmer climate when Walker resumed her residency at Radcliffe. She made progress on her manuscript while also seeing the 1973 publication of her first collection of short stories, *In Love and Trouble: Stories of Black Women.*

Success with her art, however, could not lessen the depression Walker felt while living in even a changed Mississippi. Because of the changes, Melvin Leventhal wanted to remain in Mississippi, indefinitely. In spite of the changes, Alice Walker could not stay: "Mel, it's our marriage or Mississippi."[6] In 1974, the family relocated to New York City where Leventhal continued work with the NAACP Legal Defense Fund, and Walker began a stint as contributing editor to *Ms.* magazine while continuing her literary endeavors.

BLACK-EYED SUSANS AND MIDNIGHT BIRDS

Walker polished her manuscript at the 1975 Yaddo Writer's retreat in Saratoga Springs, New York. It was published the following year, as *Meridian*. The novel documents the waning years of the civil rights movement and the nationalistic fervor of the emerging Black Power Movement. The novel's protagonist, Meridian Hill, is inspired by the life of Spelman student-activist Ruby Doris Smith-Robinson and pays homage to student-activists across the South.[7] Multivalent and multilayered *Meridian* functions on many levels. As the novel dramatizes the actual lives of black female activists who came of age during the civil rights era, the narrative is at once biography and bildungsroman. As it recalls key events of the Southern Revolution and the student movement that catalyzed it, *Meridian* is history. As it examines the hearts and minds of a people in the midst of revolutionary social change, *Meridian* is national memoir. And as it offers a vision of individual and societal harmony and explores transformative possibilities, it is social philosophy and myth.

The influence of Camus's philosophy of the absurd is apparent in the ethical questions posed in the outset of the novel: "Will you kill for the revolution?" It is the litmus test question to which Meridian could give no definitive answer; for, "the question of killing did not impress her as rhetorical at all."[8] Who would she become if she shed the blood of another human being? What would happen to her soul? She would have to renounce that part of her cultural past that spoke of Christian love, compassion, and nonviolence—the part of her past of which the revolutionaries made her feel ashamed.

Murder as a tool of social change and its consequent effect on the personality are questions that frame the novel and are concerns that permeate Meridian's thought and action. In addressing these issues, Alice Walker also draws on the ideas and methods of social philosopher Helen Merrell Lynd, Walker's mentor at Sarah Lawrence College. In her work *On Shame and the Search for Identity*, Lynd sees shame as an emotion unique in its ability to reveal the nature of both the individual and the individual's social environment. However, Lynd states that shame is typically overlooked in understanding human personality and identity.

In *On Shame*, Lynd draws on the disciplines of psychology and the social sciences to investigate what are essentially questions of philosophy or social philosophy. "Who am I? Where do I belong?" are the constants in human history, says Lynd. "Times of swift change and social dislocation bring them to the fore, against the background of whatever personal hopes and social harmonies an earlier period has cultivated."[9] The advent of the civil rights movement was just such a period of swift change which Walker examines in *Meridian*, through the lens of one individual—Meridian Hill.

Like the main characters in *The Third Life of Grange Copeland*, Meridian Hill discovered her society and surrounding world to be indifferent to her existence and inimical in their neglect. The outcome was Meridian's pregnancy at sixteen, expulsion from high school, and a husband named Eddie. Meridian perceived Eddie, Jr., as "a ball and chain" and compared caring for him with being in slavery. "Rebelling, she began to dream each night, just before her baby sent out his cries, of ways to murder him."[10] Frightened by this, she entertained ways of killing herself.

Unable to envision a future filled with anything but monotony, Meridian withdrew into "a fog of unconcern." Her listlessness was pierced by a news report of a firebombing in her neighborhood, killing several civil rights activists. "And so it was that one day in the middle of April in 1960 Meridian Hill became aware of the past and present of the larger world."[11] She took pause to reflect on her life. She had "slipped up." Self-sacrifice was deemed the just punishment. She was expected to acquiesce to social roles in a manner that acknowledged her guilt, conceded her shame, and demonstrated her agreement to do penance.

In her revolt, Meridian joined the civil rights movement, gave her baby away, and accepted a scholarship to Saxon College in Atlanta. She responded to her absurd reality with a "Yes" that negated the life to which she could not adjust. In her disidentification from prescribed social roles, Meridian initiated a journey to discover who she was and where she belonged. "The kind of answer one gives to the question Who am I?" Lynd points out, "depends in part upon how one answers the question What is this society—and this world—in which I live?"[12] In the environs of Saxon College and through her activities in the movement, Meridian begins to fathom the society and the world in which she lives. She contemplates her sense of belonging, and she does so from the singular standpoint of a black female.

Guilt and shame were the time-honored machinations utilized to force Meridian and other young women into social conformity. Meridian, however, refused to be shamed into rearing Eddie, Jr., and abandoning her opportunity to return to school. Mrs. Hill, who never wanted any of her six children, charged Meridian with "selfishness" and declared, "You ought to hang your head in shame." Meridian did not hang her head in shame, but she did find herself weighed down in a bog of guilt. "On some deeper level than she had anticipated or even been aware of, she felt condemned, confined to penitence, for life."[13]

In scrutinizing her anguish, Meridian realized that giving her son away—a fate she believed to be far better than a murder-suicide—figured as a transgression of historical and mythic proportion: Not wanting to keep her child flew in the face of the "maternal history" of black women who, during the period of slavery, had not the right nor the choice to claim their children as their own. Women like her mother, Meridian thought, were worthy of this maternal history. She, considered herself "as belonging to an unworthy minority, for which there was no precedent and of which she was, as far as she knew, the only member."[14]

Neither the new and lush environment of Saxon College nor the intensity of her studies could silence the voice in her head: "Why don't you die? Why not kill yourself?" Meridian's suicidal inclinations were sublimated into courageous acts in the streets of Atlanta. Her participation in demonstrations was as much a ritual of purgation as it was a stride for justice. So in the midst of being clubbed and beaten, she felt free and blithe. "Only once was she beaten into unconsciousness, and it was not the damage done to her body that she remembered when she woke up, but her feeling of yearning, of heartsick longing for forgiveness."[15]

Meridian's sense of guilt was exacerbated by the death of Wild Child and the harm suffered by Anne, the young girl Meridian invited to join her in the demonstrations. Meridian felt responsible for both of them. Meridian Hill's identity was oriented along what Helen Lynd describes as the guilt-righteousness axis of personality development. In this schema, guilt for wrong acts could be surmounted through culturally sanctioned means that would lead to the restoration of one's sense of righteousness. But Meridian never felt right.

THERE IS CONFUSION

Fueled initially by wonder, then by guilt, Meridian's political activism, was subsequently inspired by shame, re-orienting her identity along the shame-freedom axis of personality development. Lynd explained that the emotion of shame was subsumed or overshadowed by a focus on guilt, and that shame, typically associated with females, might likely have been overlooked with gendered indifference. Both guilt and shame may arise in a person's experience of a stressful situation, but the two emotions express distinct aspects of personality. Lynd defines "guilt" as "a culturally defined wrong act, a part of oneself that is separable, segmented, and redeemable."[16] It involves a specific act or sin that violates or transgresses expressed or tacit rules, laws, or agreements. As it is specific, a wrong act carries a correlative and specific payment, penalty, or punishment.

Whereas a guilty act is often executed with forethought and intentionality, shame has the distinction of unexpectedness. It is characterized by "the impossibility of ordered behavior, the sudden sense of exposure, of being unable to deal with what is happening." Shame is self-reflexive and reveals some hidden, vulnerable aspect of oneself. It may disclose a "wounding of one's self-ideal and disgrace in the eyes of others"; however, "the deepest shame is exposure to oneself even though no one else may pay any attention to or even know of it."[17]

In her romantic dealings with movement activist Truman Held, Meridian experienced this deepest kind of shame. She imagined herself Truman's equal and likely companion. But Truman preferred the white exchange students who were also active in the movement. "It was strange and unfair," Meridian thought, "but the fact that he dated them—and so obviously because their color made them interesting—made *her* ashamed, as if she were less."[18] After having seduced her into a night of sex, Truman left Meridian alone and pregnant. In a flash, she saw her lack of worth in his eyes when, en route to abort their baby, she spied him driving across campus with Lynne Rabinowitz.

Meridian never disclosed to Truman her pregnancy and abortion, nor how what turned out to be a one-night stand broke her heart and upturned her world. It was her private shame. The situation caused her to question everything, as Truman's choice of "the white girl," "went against everything she had been taught to expect."[19] Meridian searched her life for meaning. "[I]t seemed something *understood*: that while white men would climb on black women old enough to be their mothers—'for the experience'—white women were considered sexless, contemptible and ridiculous by all." No one in her hometown would want one.[20]

Such beliefs informed Meridian's self-ideal, and they informed her identity as a movement activist. She struggled for full citizenship for blacks and the recognition of their full humanity, but Meridian did not recognize the humanity of "the white girls" alongside whom she struggled, and those, like Lynne, whom she actually liked. Shame exposed Meridian's fragile sense of self and its attending hypocrisy, and it uncovered her unconscious expectations of black male-female relationships in the movement. She could hide her shame from Truman, but she was compelled to witness her own presumptions and assumed privilege as a black woman activist. In her own eyes, she was undone.

Shame is all-encompassing "because one's whole life has been a preparation for putting one in this situation."[21] As shame is an experience that involves the whole self, a shameful experience requires a holistic response. In self-exposure—the tension between expectation and actuality—one makes this discovery: "I am ashamed of what I am."[22] Meridian's situation mirrored her fears—that she was foolish, worthless, unlovable, and even in the world of black revolution, she was not valued. Her ideal self—configured by black bourgeois ideology and the politics of black empowerment—was shattered, and along with it, her sense of place in both worlds. Then she lost her mind, the part that worried about such things, and was set adrift from her social and cultural moorings.

Truman Held was no less governed by contradicting and self-limiting attitudes and beliefs. He vacillated in his personal life and his revolutionary politics. He married white and chaste Lynne Rabinowitz, but pined for "used up" Meridian Hill. He painted and sculpted black women and masterful images of black life, but was embarrassed by the unsophisticated nature of black folk. He believed in equality and freedom of political expression for the black oppressed, but conceded to the silencing of white voices in the movement. When black became beautiful, he despised his white wife whom he referred to as "you people."[23] As he hid his art from his wife, he hid his own sense of guilt and shame from himself.

Lynne Rabinowitz, too, was similarly conflicted. She worked on behalf of the humanity of black folk while perceiving them as art. Thinking them to be lacking in emotional complexity, and therefore harmless, she snapped their pictures. "'I will pay for this' she often warned herself. 'It is probably a sin to think of a people as Art.'"[24] Identified with the empowered white majority,

Lynne felt responsible for the impoverishment of blacks. She would atone by utilizing her intellect, passion, and the power of her American, white and female body—"everything" she had—on behalf of the movement.[25]

Mistaking Lynne's guilt-inspired kindnesses as sexual wantonness, activist Tommy Odds rapes her. He rationalizes his assault as vengeance against Lynne's crime of whiteness and an attack on all whites. Where Tommy is filled with hate and self-loathing, Lynne is left in fear and is overtaken by shame. The incongruity between what she believed and what she experienced had her, too, doubt everything. Incongruity, Helen Lynd writes, is an essential aspect of shame: "We have acted on the assumption of being one kind of person living in one kind of surroundings, and unexpectedly, violently, we discover that these assumptions are false. We had thought that we were able to see around certain situations and, instead, discover in a moment that it is we who are exposed; alien people in an alien situation can see around us."[26]

CHAIN CHAIN CHANGE

Like the generation of youth who came of age in the heat of the civil rights movement with its decentering and destabilizing force, the major characters in *Meridian* are compelled to come to new terms within the understanding of their identities and the societies that forged them. In Walker's novel, the experience of shame becomes the alchemical agent which brings them to a questioning of all they knew or understood theretofore. The power of shame is that it "interrupts any unquestioning, unaware sense of oneself." It unmasks, uncovers, exposes, and brings to light both unconscious perspectives and latent capacities to see anew. "Fully faced, shame may become not primarily something to be covered, but a positive experience of revelation."[27]

In fully facing her feelings of shame, Meridian shattered the identity that gave rise to her breakdown. "Guilt can be expiated," Lynd explains, "Shame, short of a transformation of the self, is retained. This transformation means, in Plato's words, a turning of the whole soul toward the light."[28] Meridian's "blue spells" represent such a transformation. During these spells everything Meridian saw was awash in a bluish light. The blue spells became black, then blindness, then a state of ecstasy: "she felt as if a warm, strong light bore her up and that she was a beloved part of the universe; that she was innocent even as the rocks are innocent, and unpolluted as the first waters."[29] Roommate Anne-Marion saw something of a halo about Meridian while in her ecstatic state.

With the shattering of one's identity, there is the possibility for self-renewal or self-creation. There is the possibility to enlarge one's views beyond prescribed roles, beyond social or state-sanctioned niches, and beyond the current expression of history. Rather than die or be resigned, there is the possibility to live and to discover the authentic terms of one's living. In falling through the looking glass, Meridian shattered the image in the mirror and thereby acquired the capacity to construct her own narrative, rewrite her story, and to not so much discover who she is as to create the self she desires to be.

Helen Lynd posits that "the feeling of shame for the values of one's society, and the transcending of personal shame, would depend upon having some perspective, some standards of significance, against which one can call into question the codes of one's immediate culture."[30] These perspectives and standards emanate from transcultural, universal human desires, decencies, and values. Further, Lynd states that the individual has a latent capacity to appeal to this realm of wider human identity and dignity. Whereas the end of guilt is condemnation or atonement and the reconciliation between the individual and society, situations of shame can explode perceptual limitations and become the means by which one accesses the potentiality for expansion and transcendence.

This latent potentiality in the human personality is symbolized in the novel by the bar of gold Meridian discovers when a child. She files through its encrusted layers to the brilliant yellow gold within. No one in her family is impressed with her boon, so she puts it in a box and buries it under a magnolia tree. "About once a week she dug it up to look at it. Then she dug it up less and less . . . until finally she forgot to dig it up. Her mind turned to other things."[31] In *The Hero with a Thousand Faces*, Joseph Campbell describes gold as the symbol of immortality, "the mysterious creative energy of God."[32] Gold also symbolizes Christ consciousness, reflecting the innocence intrinsic to humanity. In *Meridian*, human innocence, like Meridian's bar of gold, is encrusted with limiting and repressive societal conventions and traditions, like so many layers of sediment covering and silencing an individual's unique and eternal spark.

Meridian comes to realize and recognize as her value an innocence that is primordial and mystical. She glimpsed this in her son whom she baptized as "Rundi, after no person, I hope, who has ever lived."[33] And it is this immortal purity radiating through the human form that she spies and protects in the Southern black folk among whom she lives. Meridian had taken herself off the cross of guilt and shame, and being one with them, she wanted for them the same sense of freedom and possibility.

Meridian knew it was no small feat for a people to move beyond inherited fear. Her own experiences taught her the consequences of defying the "threshold guardians" of tradition. But defy them she must, as she must also assist others in getting to their feet and stepping beyond the known world. Joseph Campbell explains that guardians of the threshold, of the gateway beyond, symbolize both protective forces and, if challenged, forces of annihilation. They keep the individual bound to the status quo and discourage entry into the realm of the unknown; for, "the crossing of the threshold is the first step into the sacred zone of the universal source."[34] It is in this realm, as Helen Lynd suggests, that one discovers values, attitudes, and ideals beyond one's immediate sphere and life horizon.

Having survived and transcended her own experiences of guilt and shame, Meridian is not repulsed by "the child who killed her child," nor the bloated and putrid body of the five-year-old boy she lays upon the mayor's desk, nor is she disheartened by the seeming foot-dragging of a people under siege who balk at registering to vote. Rather, she is heartened by the crystal stone of their innocence. Her unconditional love for them and her faith in them transform "the rock of mother and god" into the stone of hope King promised to hew out of the mountain of despair. Like Camus's Sisyphus who rolls the boulder up the mountain again and yet again, Meridian's struggle "teaches the higher fidelity that negates the gods and raises rocks."[35] Out of the valley of the shadows of unconscious fears and fixations, Meridian Hill rolls the stone of hope, "the crystal stone of our innocence," to the summit of a mountain no longer hidden in clouds of despair, but a mountain whose peak intersects with the sun at its meridian, causing "the brilliance of the jewel beneath the stone" to shine.[36]

NO MORE TIME ON THE CROSS

In her recurring dream, Meridian was a character in a novel whose ending required her death. This dream signaled the initiatory death of the ego, igniting the flame of Meridian's renewal and re-creation. Her life then takes on an epic dimension, and her journey parallels the classic path of the hero: "*separation—initiation—return.*" "The hero," writes Campbell, "is the man or woman who has been able to battle past her personal and local historical limitations to the generally valid, normally human forms. Such a one's visions, ideas, inspirations come pristine from the primary springs of human life and thought, . . . the unquenched source through which society is reborn."[37]

Through a series of trials and victories, Meridian as warrior-hero and culture-hero, engages the mythic process of continuous regeneration. "Only birth can conquer death—the birth, not of the old thing again, but of something new. Within the soul, within the body social, there must be—if we are to experience long survival—a continuous 'recurrence of birth' (*palingenesia*) to nullify the unremitting recurrences of death."[38]

In *Meridian*, experiences of guilt and shame expose hidden expectations, beliefs, and fears, but, more importantly, as suggested in Campbell's work, such experiences reveal "all the life-potentialities that we never managed to bring to adult realization, those other portions of ourself, are there; for such golden seeds do not die." Campbell writes further that "if we could dredge up something forgotten not only by ourselves but by our whole generation or our entire civilization, we should become indeed the boon-bringer, the culture hero of the day—a personage of not only local but world historical moment."[39]

It mattered not that Meridian no longer remembered to dig up her gold bar. Over time, her life had become, itself, a crucible, a holy grail, enabling her to see through the baseness of life to the immortal golden seeds resonant in everyone and everything. Meridian remembered her innocence and her intrinsic worth. And she had learned "that the respect she owed her life was to continue, against whatever obstacles, to live it, and not to give up any particle of it without a fight to the death, preferably *not* her own. And that this existence extended beyond herself to those around her." She therefore, as warrior-hero, developed the capacity to contemplate "retaliatory murder."[40] To be unable to kill, she reasoned, was to be complicit with the forces of oppression. Nevertheless, she had not the will to act on this new capacity. For she understood, too, that to be a revolutionary was to live with ambiguity. And she resolved to be a revolutionary on her own terms.

The opening chapter of *Meridian* is titled "the Last Return," indicating that Meridian, as culture-hero, had made a series of returns—to one small town or another, teaching, protesting, registering voters, stoking the fire of the golden seeds. She was told that voting was useless. "It may be useless," Meridian responded, "Or maybe it can be the beginning of the use of your voice. You have to get used to using your voice, you know. You start on simple things." And she made them promise that "they would learn, as their smallest resistance to the murder of their children, to use the vote."[41] The use of the vote was a social and political act. But it was also a moral and spiritual act that could be transformative.

"The only new thing now," Meridian thought to herself as she turned down a muddy lane, "would be the refusal of Christ to accept crucifixion. King . . . should have refused. Malcolm, too, should have refused. All those characters in all those novels that require death to end the book should refuse. All saints should walk away. Do their bit, then—just walk away."[42] And so she did, leaving her sleeping bag and visor to Truman, Anne-Marion, and the rest of them.

NINE

Thought at the Meridian

SLAVERY, BY ANY OTHER NAME

Thought at the meridian is "solar thought," writes Albert Camus. It is thought that is elevated as high as the sun at its zenith over earth. It is thought infused with an all-embracing "strange form of love" that encompasses all and excludes none. It recognizes the unity of humankind, the "We are" collective experience inherent in the fact of human existence.[1] It elucidates the significance of intercommunication as a fundamental aspect of humanity and the bedrock of a society of equals. It is mindful of the human condition—the indifference of the universe, the inevitability of death, and the abiding tendency in the human breast toward excess—and so it denies "servitude, falsehood, and terror" and speaks of "a philosophy of limits."[2]

Alice Walker's novel, *Meridian*, is at the meridian of thought. The title of the novel and the protagonist's name evoke Meridian Hill Park, a historical site which commemorates the location of one of four prime meridians that marked the area where the United States Capitol was to be constructed. The Capitol Meridian, situated at Meridian Hill, was just north of the White House.[3] That Walker prefaces the novel with several definitions of "meridian" and chooses Meridian Hill as the name of a character engaged in civil rights activism and the pursuit of her own individual liberty is telling.

At the meridian of thought, from the highest point of human consciousness, the character Meridian Hill envisioned an egalitarian society wherein the beauty and power inherent in all life is cherished and protected. She knew the worth of her own life and that existence has its own value. As civil rights activist and warrior-hero, her efforts contributed to the restoration of a sense of worth to a people.

As culture-hero, Meridian understood the cultural history of black Americans—those aspects that enslaved the mind and body, as well as those that freed the soul. She understood their sense of outcast, of being just beyond the pale of society and contained within an isolationism enforced by legislated and *de facto* practices of discrimination. She knew the vote would not undo this calamity, but it would initiate a people's movement toward expression and toward establishing a relationship of equals in a society of Americans and an elevation of their esteem in the realm of collective humanity.

Albert Camus writes that authentic revolutionary action coheres with its origins and is faithful to the human condition. In realizing its objectives of equality, freedom, and justice, revolutionary action recognizes limitations to its own relative power. There can be no inconsistencies between means and ends. Thus revolutionary action recognizes the common bond of existence and allows the absolute freedom of speech which respects and preserves this condition. For, "There is no justice in society without natural or civil rights as its basis. There are no rights without expression of those rights."[4]

Meridian saw the right to vote as a reclamation of civil rights, and the exercise of that right as the *sine qua non* of self-expression in American society. More than an act of political will, exercising the right to vote was an act expressive of the individual will to be and the rejection of a diminished and humiliated existence. It impeached the assumed deification of conceited mortals and reasserted equality as a fact of life. "To remain silent," reasoned Camus, would be "to give the impression that one has no opinions, that one wants nothing." But the least of any rebellious act "tacitly invokes a value," and "[w]ith rebellion, awareness is born." Intimated in the action of the rebel, the voter, is the knowledge that human life is the only necessary good and freedom to live it is sacrosanct.[5]

From Meridian's perspective, the attempt of the state to abrogate the black vote was an attempt to extinguish the spark of life inherent in the individual. It was an attempt to continue slavery and imprison a people in a state of shame. Helen Lynd writes that given the fact that shame isolates and induces feelings of inferiority, finding ways to share and communicate this experience "can bring about particular closeness with other persons and with other groups. This can become the situation with minority groups or with minority positions in a particular historical situation. What is directed against a group as a label of shame can be converted into a mark of honor, and the group itself gains in strength."[6]

Civil rights leaders committed to overcoming injustice through nonviolence, sang, litigated, prayed, and spoke from pulpits and mountaintops. They were the organs of expression of the millions who had learned to mourn in hushed cadences, for the "*decade marked by death*" had silenced them again.[7] Yet, they would have to learn again to speak—of their inalienable right to justice, dignity, and freedom. Registering them to vote was Meridian's way of empowering them with a means to break the silence that isolates and enslaves. This move toward articulation was imperative. Albert Camus emphasized the relationship between the freedom of expression and a just and democratic society:

> There is, in fact, nothing in common between a master and a slave; it is impossible to speak and communicate with a person who has been reduced to servitude. Instead of the implicit and untrammeled dialogue through which we come to recognize our similarity and consecrate our destiny, servitude gives sway to the most terrible of silences.[8]

Meridian explores the meaning of expression as a faculty of human existence and dignified living. As it delves into the shaming consequences of the denial of expression to African Americans and other oppressed groups, the novel brings attention to the oppression of women specifically and the utilization of shame as a tool of patriarchal oppression. The critical nature of speech as symbolic of human existence and freedom and the medium of the soul's creative potentiality are graphically dramatized in the de-tonguing of Louvinie, an enslaved woman on the Saxon plantation. She was the daughter of a family of West African storytellers whose intricate tales would "entrap people who hoped to get away with murder." Though the science of this art was lost, Louvinie was, nevertheless, a great weaver of tales. When young Mister Saxon was scared to death by one of these tales, Louvinie's tongue was "clipped out at the root." It had never been communicated to Louvinie that the boy had a "flimsy heart."[9] Taking no account of Louvinie's innocence, Master Saxon ground her tongue under the heel of his boot.

Mindful of the curse to follow one who lost her tongue, Louvinie was consumed with fear for her soul. "Without one's tongue in one's mouth or in a special spot of one's own choosing, the singer in one's soul was lost forever to grunt and snort through eternity like a pig."[10] Mutely, Louvinie pleaded for her tongue which she buried beneath a "scrawny magnolia" on the Saxon plantation during a solar eclipse. The magnolia outgrew every other tree on the plantation, and as it grew, legends grew up around it: The tree could talk, make music, and was sacred to birds. It was safe harbor for the enslaved, and later when the plantation became Saxon College, it was safe haven for young women. This magical, musical tree was christened "The Sojourner."

The name Sojourner invokes the legendary Sojourner Truth who escaped slavery in the North, in 1826. She had "heard the voice of her God instructing her when to set out on her own as a free woman."[11] An evangelist, abolitionist, and suffragist, Sojourner Truth was an enthralling speaker who could also mesmerize her listeners with song. As her name implies, Sojourner Truth traveled widely and was keen on conveying to her audiences "the *Truth*," "the *whole truth*" about the evils of slavery, the female experience of slavery, the cruelty of enslavers, the rights of women, temperance, and the power of Holy Spirit.[12]

She asserted the truth of her testimonies as there were those who sought not only to discredit her word, but also to deny her identity as a woman. When a congregant at one convention questioned her womanhood, Sojourner showed her breasts to the whole congregation and imparted "that it was not to her shame that she uncovered her breast before them, but to their shame."[13]

Truth's original name was Isabella Bomefree. Her surname, "Bomefree," means tree. Sojourner's father James was given the name because he was "tall and straight," like a tree.[14] This signification enhances the symbolism of the magical, singing tree in Walker's novel. Christened as Sojourner Truth and nourished with Louvinie's organ of articulation at its root, The Sojourner functions in Walker's story as "a World Tree," an *axis-mundi*. It connects heaven and earth and is the instrument through which the lower and higher realms communicate, expressing a spiritual dimension. Connecting the past with the present, it expresses a temporal dimension. As *axis-mundi* or World Navel, The Sojourner also represents the north-south, prime meridian, the selected geographic point on earth which guides the interpretation of the arc of the lives of black women.

As Louvinie's parents wove tales that revealed murderers in their village, The Sojourner tells the stories of murder, rape, slavery, and other criminal acts against African and African American women. As Louvinie's name approximates that of the character Lavinia in William Shakespeare's tragedy *Titus Andronicus*, The Sojourner also weaves into its intricate tale the stories of womankind and the feminine principle in general. Lavinia is the daughter of Titus Andronicus. The sons of Tamora, Queen of the Goths, rape and mutilate Lavinia as part of a plot to avenge their brother's death and to destroy the Andronici family. They both rape her then cut out her tongue and lop off both hands to prevent her any means of communicating.

Lavinia, nonetheless, manages to disclose the rape and name the perpetrators. With grunts and gesticulations, she gets her father Titus to read Ovid's "tragic tale of Philomel." Then steadying a staff with her mouth and guiding it with her stumps, she scrawls: "*Stuprum*—Chiron—Demetrius."[15] Though outraged and distraught by the atrocity, it is Titus who ends Lavinia's life since he construes her shame as his unbearable sorrow.

In the dyad of shame and glory, shame has become the part of the woman. Lavinia experiences the sense of isolation and unworthiness associated with shame. Though Titus displays empathy and grief for Lavinia's state, he experiences her condition as an offense to his sensibilities—"For such a sight will blind a father's eye"—and an offense to his honor and dignity as a father and a Roman general.[16] Even when he kills Lavinia, he does so less as a mercy to her than as consolation for himself and vindication of his pride.

As ideologically rigid forms of patriarchy dictate that females are extensions of males and subject to male authority, the male-female relationship replicates that of master and slave. It is Demetrius and Chiron's prerogative to rape and mutilate Lavinia and Titus' prerogative to kill her, as it is Saxon's prerogative to de-tongue Louvinie. Whether a female has engaged in some behavior considered shameful, whether something shameful is done to her, or whether she has inadvertently committed some act that piques the pride or taints the honor of male vanity, shame is hers alone to face or with which to die.

On many levels, Louvinie's political, social, and metaphysical positionality reflect the overreach of patriarchal authority. Cutting out her tongue was a further assertion of Saxon's self-proclaimed, life-and-death right over her. The de-tonguing was intended to silence her, isolate her, and render her incommunicado. Rather than a physical death, he attempted to impose an existential death wherein her condition of aliveness would leave her just outside the circle of human community. However, as creativity is an essential aspect of self-expression, Louvinie, like Lavinia, found other means through which to communicate. They both found ways to reveal the truth about the societies in which they lived and their identities within those societies.

The truth that Louvinie and Lavinia tell is that patriarchal power knows not its limits and that the masculine principle in its excessive expression is destructive and, therefore, demonic. In Hindu mythology, the male deities found themselves impotent before the *asuras*, the unrelenting demonic, male forces in their social sphere. The Goddess Durgā was sent to them to vanquish the *asuric* forces. During one of Durgā's campaigns "to destroy the most arrogant and truculent man-beasts," the goddess Kālī appeared as "the 'forceful'" aspect of Durgā to take part in the fight.[17]

In this battle, "Kālī manifested herself for the annihilation of demonic male power in order to restore peace and equilibrium." "Kālī" is interpreted as "She who is black." In her expression as Dakṣiṇā-kālī, she is "the south-facing, black Kālī."[18] In *Meridian* the stain-glassed depiction of "B. B., With Sword" in the large, Baptist church Meridian visited conjures the goddess Kālī who wields the sword of enlightenment. The embodiment of the idea of Kālī in the male form of B. B. King suggests the ultimate unity of the masculine and feminine principles and the possibility of balance and peace for which the black congregation longs.

The temperament of Kālī can be traced in the behavior of the students at Saxon College. Once they learn that the president of the college—"a tan, impeccably tailored patriarch with glinting, shifty gray eyes"—will not permit them to use the school's chapel for the funeral services of The Wild Child, something snaps in them. A sorrowful wailing arose from their collective throats. "For five minutes the air rang with shouts and the polite curses of young ladies. . . . They were so ashamed and angry they began to boo and stamp their feet and stick out their tongues through their tears." They flung to the ground their cultured pearls and "gold-plated chastity pins" and "shook loose their straightened hair, and all the while they glared at the locked chapel door with a ferocity that was close to hatred."[19]

The goddess Kālī is renowned for her fierce look, resounding roar, lolling tongue, and "disheveled" hair.[20] "Kālī is free from convention, wild and uncontrolled in nature, and not bound to or limited by a male consort." As an archetypal figure, she is the social subversive who "challenges the socialized ego."[21] As the personification of cosmic power, Kālī's unbound hair symbolizes dissolution of the world, the disruption necessary to annihilate the status quo. At times her fury motivates a rampage that kills everything and everyone in sight. Infused with the spirit of Kālī, the students rioted, but "the only thing they managed to destroy was The Sojourner."[22]

Though they had been indoctrinated to identify with their oppressors, latent in the students was a capacity for resistance they did not quite understand. Though their visceral instinct had been tamped down, the president's treatment of the deceased Wild Child stirred their unconscious anger. The Wild Child, notwithstanding her circumstances, is not a tragic figure. Rather, she is a liminal figure manifesting the spirit of Kālī. The Wild Child did everything of which a woman was socialized to be ashamed. She skulked around the fringes of society, eating from garbage cans, smoking, farting "as if to music, raising a thigh," and she was single and pregnant.[23]

But as archetypal Kālī embraces and embodies the feared and the forbidden, birth and death, and teaches the underlying unity of supposed opposites, The Wild Child reminded the students of that primordial part of themselves they were being taught to reject. She reminded them of the sacredness of all of life. The child she carried inside her was a reminder of the innocence, creativity, and vitality within all beings. The dynamics of her peculiar life offered the students a point of entry into their own unconscious mind and the part of themselves that is beyond shame, and, as certain of Kālī's mudras symbolize, beyond fear.

"MY TONGUE IS IN MY FRIEND'S MOUTH"

Given the iconography associated with Mahākālī, her presence in Walker's novel is indicative of the misuse and overreach of masculine energy. For this prerogative, males like Titus Andronicus, Demetrius, and Chiron claim a "pattern, precedent, and lively warrant."[24] But this age-old misapprehension and misappropriation of the masculine principle disrupts a natural balance. As Albert Camus states, "Man is the only creature who refuses to be what he is."[25] The god-complex to which excessive masculinity lends itself engenders chaos. Suppression of the primal feminine principle effectively inhibits harmony in human society and instigates a false divide between feminine and masculine principles.

"Durga" means "Beyond Reach" and refers to "the woman warrior's fierce, virginal autonomy." Ajit Mookerjee explains that "virginity" is understood in the sense of "belonging-to-no-man" or "one-in-herself." Moreover, it means being beyond "the reach of society's attempt to describe her to herself. The more repressive the images available to women, the more the virgin condition becomes a defence against these." And in extreme situations, "women will reject womanhood itself, if the condition 'unable to move around freely,' both physically and psychically, is seen necessarily to accompany it."[26]

As the saga of Meridian Hill suggests, a black woman's maneuvering beyond society's reach to define her is nothing short of heroic. In rejecting the repressive images of her black and middle-class life, Meridian believed she was the only member of "an unworthy minority." But she discovered her number to be legion. Among them were Louvinie and the confused but defiant Anne-Marion; Fast Mary who tried to stuff pieces of her "illegitimate" baby down a Saxon College commode, then later hanged herself; the imprisoned child who bit then strangled her child; a poor, rural woman who was coquettish with her husband, though she was near death; and 69-year-old virgin Margaret Treasure who finally yielded to sexual desire.

Alice Walker's work gives voice to the legion of women who are tamed, shamed, seduced, raped, de-tongued, and murdered into silence about the truth of their lives. "I am preoccupied with the spiritual survival, the survival whole, of my people," proclaimed Walker. "But beyond that, I am committed to exploring the oppressions, the insanities, the loyalties, and the triumphs of black women."[27] As with her novels, Walker's short story collections In Love and Trouble and You Can't Keep a Good Woman Down bear witness to the oppression of women as they also celebrate the passion, fortitude, and resilience with which women live their lives.

In "Roselily," in In Love and Trouble, the eponymous protagonist hopes that holy wedlock will give her access to freedom and a respectable life. But she weds a man who intends to "redo her into what he truly wants." Roselily feels trapped even as she takes her vows. "Something strains upward behind her eyes. She thinks of the something as a rat trapped, cornered, scurrying to and fro in her head, peering through the windows of her eyes."[28] Like a rat in a maze, the women in these stories are trapped in an internal labyrinth and each woman's particular story is a path initiated in expectation of her freedom.

Myrna, in "Really, Doesn't Crime Pay," believes her talents as a writer will be her escape from a husband who sees her as "a womb without a brain" and denigrates her art as "foolish vulgar stuff."[29] She believes her lover, who is also a writer, will facilitate her path to publication and freedom. But he purloins her work and abandons her to a place in herself "where things have just slipped a good bit off the track."[30] As with Myrna, Mrs. Jerome Franklin Washington, III, in "Her Sweet Jerome," becomes unhinged when she finally realizes that her husband despises her. She, realizes, too, that she despises herself to the extent that she adores her husband. She quenches the rage against her own self-betrayal with self-immolation.

As black women contend with black men who consider themselves superior, they also contend with racist whites who consider blacks inferior. Racial animosity burns in the heart of Hannah in "The Revenge of Hannah Kemhuff." She is humiliated by "that little white moppet" who denies Hannah her allotment of government issued food. In the aftermath of her public shaming, the once proud Hannah lost everything. Her husband deserted her, her children starved to death, and Hannah's self-respect "just up and left all together." She could die easy, she told Tante Rosie the root-worker, if she knew that "something, after all these years, had been done to the little moppet."[31]

The characters in Walker's stories desperately seek to discover or affirm who they are and where they belong. Marriage offers a sense of identity and place for some. Others seek identity and belonging within political and religious institutions where the roles they will play are predetermined. Men like "sweet Jerome" and women like Dee in "Everyday Use" become black cultural nationalists. Roselily's husband looked to the Nation of Islam as did John, in "Entertaining God," who "changed his name and took an X."[32] In spite of white religious hypocrisy, the old woman in "The Welcome Table" dared to integrate a whites-only church service and "The Diary of an African Nun" records the confessions of a young Ugandan woman who suppresses her African heritage and represses her sensuality "to be a wife of Christ, a wife of the Catholic church."[33]

The search for who they are and where they belong often leaves the characters trudging through the backstreets of an even more surreal section of their labyrinthine interior. No matter their effort, they feel "ignorant, *wrong, backward*," and weighed down by a "burden of shame," as they attempt to seek self-affirmation within white and male ideologies and institutions that deny their equality as human beings.[34] But where resignation and suicide typify the responses of characters in *In Love and Trouble*, defiance and self-confidence typify the characters in Walker's second volume of short stories, as the title suggests: *You Can't Keep a Good Woman Down.*

An overall optimism permeates the second collection which begins with "1955," the story of Gracie Mae Stills (Willie Mae "Big Mama" Thornton) and her classic blues song "Hound Dog," which is covered by Traynor (Elvis Presley). Traynor's success with the song transforms his popular appeal and his bank account, but not his life. As he is confused by the song, he is confounded by Gracie Mae who is nonchalant about material possessions and indifferent about popular approval as an artist. Gracie Mae had learned a long time ago in the Hard Shell Baptist Church "that the fellow that sings is the singer."[35]

Like Gracie Mae, the protagonists in *You Can't Keep* are able to nurture and express their creativity. Some are artists, jazz poets, and successful writers, though literary icon Andrea Clement White in "Fame" was never quite convinced that she had arrived. Politically aware and active, the protagonists grapple with the taboos surrounding black female sexuality and American sexual politics. The stories present sexually uninhibited women who take lovers and birth control pills and who sometimes resort to abortion as does Imani in "The Abortion." Though married, Imani is alone in her decision to keep or abort their baby since her husband Clarence insouciantly drops her at the airport for a New York abortion and whispers, "Take care of yourself."[36]

In "Coming Apart," the protagonist engages in the "*necessary fight*" that must be waged in the emancipation of black female sexual identity.[37] She and her husband debate the issue of pornography. He indulges in pornography and feels it is his right to do so. Their discussions bring them to the white patriarchal roots of pornography and the dehumanizing images of women (and men) that derive therefrom. Where white women are objectified, black women are represented as animals. "Where white women are depicted at least as human bodies if not beings, black women are depicted as shit."[38] They each take a "soul-rending look" at the shameful history of rape, lynching, and castration, and the silencing of an entire people through terror and sexual violence. Not to look, would spell complicity in their own dehumanization.

This barbaric and shameful history notwithstanding, the black woman writer in "Advancing Luna—and Ida B. Wells" refuses to submit to the tyranny of history and be silenced about interracial rape. When she initially learned that black activist Freddy Pye had raped her white roommate, she had not wanted to believe her. "Why didn't you scream?" she asked Luna. But they both knew "the power *her word on rape* had over the lives of black men, over *all* black men, whether they were guilty or not, and therefore over [a] whole people."[39] In spite of her misgivings, she wrote the account of Luna's story. As a writer, she was compelled to write what life revealed to her: that some black men do rape white women; that a white woman's word on rape can be true; that "'*rape as a part of rebellion, of "paying whitey back"*'" is "misogynous cruelty" that denies the origins of rebellion.[40]

Like the writer in "Advancing Luna," the feminist-womanist professor Susan Marie in "A Letter of the Times" would not hold her tongue in exposing the racism of her white feminist friend Lucy, whose ideal feminist is Scarlet O'Hara. The black women in *You Can't Keep* are vigilant against the continuation of the master-slave paradigm in any form. They have come to know, as would Anastasia in "Source," that the "*path of obedience*" does not lead to peace, bliss, calm, or freedom; that the construct of race as a sheltering identity is "tenuous" at best; and that identification based on gender is equally fragile.[41]

Light-skinned Anastasia and identifiably black Irene take issue with each other about class and color. Through sober, honest, and brave conversation they reach a place of authenticity within themselves. Anastasia has a clarity about her fragile self which could "shatter and fly away." Irene knows that reducing another person to the function of an "objective correlative" diminishes their humanity and undermines her own.[42] As with several of the stories in *You Can't Keep*, the conversation between Anastasia and Irene exemplifies the kind of respectful dialogue that acknowledges another as equal, the kind of dialogue that can inspire thought that moves toward the meridian.

Even though the name "Meridian Hill" claims a national identity for disenfranchised and historically excluded populations in American society, Alice Walker recognizes that human identity transcends naming and categorization. She shares Jean Toomer's vision of a "new America" as articulated in his long poem, *The Blue Meridian*. In this vision the "new American" defies the dualisms of color, class, and clan, and is freed from the "penalties and proscriptions" attributed to one's sex.[43] In Toomer's poem, the black meridian stone and the white meridian stone symbolize, respectively, the unconscious American and the waking consciousness of the new American. As this consciousness expands, it spiritualizes all form and generates the blue meridian stone which symbolizes the awakened consciousness and the evolved mind of the new American as Universal Human Being.

The new American is neither black nor white but is "blue or purple," the colors of faith and power. The thought of the new American is conscious thought inspired by a strange love that spirals up through "arcs of brightness to the resplendent source."[44] Thought at the meridian lifts rocks. And it lifts branches—like the new one that had begun to grow from The Sojourner.

TEN

Truth Teller, Freedom Writer

TO TELL THE TRUTH, ALWAYS

In her commitment to speak, write, and live the truth of her life, Alice Walker advances the legacy of a people who were denied these freedoms. In doing so, she moves in the current of humanistic social philosophers, writers, and activists from antiquity to modern times. As moving in this current is simultaneously a moving against the status quo, courage, confidence, and faith in humanity and in life, itself, is crucial. Walker's academic training would yield examples of those who held fast to their beliefs about the free nature of human beings and the inalienable rights of individuals in society. In the face of despotism, oppressive government, and certain execution, those of daring spirit and vision maintained their courage to speak. Though his portion was a draught of poison, Socrates was steadfast in his mission to search out the truth in himself and in others. "I cannot hold my tongue," he proclaimed.[1] Cicero, steadfast in his orations and in penning his philippics espousing ideas about freedom and justice and denouncing the evils of tyranny, was beheaded, his hands were cut off, and his tongue was pierced.[2]

As a student of philosophy, a daughter of stalwart sharecroppers, an activist in the Southern Revolution, and as a writer, Alice Walker perceived clearly the truth of her humanity and her inalienable right to freely express her reality. But it was as a little girl, during the time of the injury to her eye, that Walker learned her most poignant lessons about the nature of truth. Coerced by her brothers to lie about what happened to her eye, Alice found herself in a predicament. The lie that confused her parents' response to the situation also left her feeling isolated and disconnected. Her sense of self-betrayal exacerbated the shame she felt around being untruthful and diminished her self-esteem. "It was the first time I abandoned myself, by lying, and it is at the root of my fear of abandonment," said Walker. "It is also at the root of my need to tell the truth, always, because I experienced, very early, the pain of telling a lie."[3]

Paradoxically, Walker's greatest revelations about truth were gained through the telling of a lie. The girl child was intimidated by her older brothers. The woman, however, would stand in her truth and speak up for herself. Walker discerned that the inability to speak on one's own behalf undermines a coherent personal identity. And the inability to authentically communicate with others compromises one's personal integrity, undermining one's sense of self and belonging. Walker, however, was able to transmute her experiences of the physical and existential pain of self-abnegation and separation into a vision of healing and wholeness for herself and for a people. Thus, her preoccupation with "the spiritual survival, the survival *whole*, of my people" and her commitment to exploring the truths of black women's lives.[4] In emphasizing the term "whole," Walker underscores the significance of coherence and unity both within the individual and in society. Aware of the power of falsehood to disrupt the whole, she stands vigilant and rebellious against it.

"WHAT WOULD HAPPEN IF ONE WOMAN TOLD THE TRUTH ABOUT HER LIFE? . . ."[5]

One woman who told the truth about her life was Celie Harris Johnson. Through a network of letters and shared confidences, Celie communicates both the oppressive and brutal conditions of her reality as well as the excitement and delight she discovers in life, once she finds her strength to rebel against the absurdity of existing in life as a tree. In forming the character of Celie in her novel *The Color Purple*, Alice Walker brought to light the obscured reality of poor black women in the rural South. By virtue of being born into this American "underclass," Walker had firsthand knowledge of their experiences. Observations she made during her seven-year tenure in Mississippi enhanced her knowledge and shaped her understanding of what she saw and heard in her own household and surrounding community. *The Color Purple* distills these experiences and observations.

The first statements made in *The Color Purple* are declarations of domination and terror: "*You better not never tell nobody but God. It'd kill your mammy.*"[6] Alphonso Harris, as a seemingly disembodied voice, restricts Celie's freedom of speech. He tells her to whom she may speak, and about what. Since she can speak only to God, and no other human being, she is effectively silenced and burdened with a knowledge of something about which she can tell no one— ever. She is therefore isolated and cut off. A barely literate fourteen-year-old, she is vulnerable and feels herself helpless. The second declaration promises violence and establishes a threat of harm against a loved one—the mother whose constitution is already weakened by a series of births. The prison of silence in which she is locked and the fear of killing her own mother immobilizes Celie—and turns her into a tree.

Celie's unspeakable burden is that Alphonso, whom she yet believes is her father, has raped her: "You gonna do what your mammy wouldn't," he said.[7] Children are conceived from two of the rapes, and Alphonso gives them away. Walker's woeful tale disclosing incidents of incest and domestic violence within black families is also a reworking of the story of incest as presented in Ovid's *Metamorphoses*. In Book X, the poet Orpheus sings a dreadful tale of the "unlawful lust and passion" Myrrha felt for her father, King Cinyras.[8]

Ruled by her "obscene love," Myrrha steals into Cinyras's bed and seduces him.[9] When he learns that the young woman he deflowered was his own daughter, he tries to kill her. Myrrha escapes, pregnant with her father's child and grandchild. Full of guilt, shame, and self-loathing, Myrrha does not want to live, nor does she want to offend the dead by killing herself. So as she spoke her wish, her toes grew roots into the ground and her body morphed into a tree.

Alphonso's words paralleled Orpheus's warning against a tale of dread. Whereas Orpheus's rhetorical device was meant to inform the listener, Alphonso's words were intended to deceive and to present himself as honest and Celie as someone untrustworthy. Years after Alphonso made his declarations, Celie tells her story. In the arms of Shug Avery, she recounts the horror of violation at the hands of one she respected as "Pa." "Seem like it all come back to me, laying there in Shug arms," writes Celie. "How it hurt and how much I was surprise. How it stung while I finish trimming his hair. How the blood drip down my leg and mess up my stocking."[10]

With her tears flowed the long-dammed up story of the rape, the pregnancies conceived in incest, the shame of lying to a mother who also mistreated her, a loveless marriage, and the loss of her sister Nettie, the only one in the world who ever loved her. As Walker's development of the relationship between Celie and Alphonso draws on Ovid's story of Myrrha and King Cinyras, her development of the relationship between Celie and Nettie draws on and revises the relationship between Philomela and Procne in Ovid's myth of Philomela.

In the development of the character Louvinie in *Meridian*, Walker indirectly alludes to Ovid's Philomela whose tongue was also cut out. In *The Color Purple*, Walker's allusion is more apparent as the love between two sisters is emphasized in both *The Color Purple* and in the myth of Philomela. Philomela and her sister Procne, like Nettie and Celie, have an inseparable bond. But Procne's husband King Tereus disregards the sisters' relationship and lusts after Philomela, just as Albert lusts after Nettie. When neither Tereus nor Albert succeeds by flattery, both resort to force. Tereus rapes Philomela in a hut in the woods. Defiant, Philomela intends to expose the villainy. She vows she will cast aside her shame and she will tell her tale until it reaches the gods.

Where Tereus acted on his "foul passion," Albert was foiled. In Nettie's very first letter to Celie, she informs her sister that Albert "ain't no good." She tells Celie how Albert tried to kiss her and drag her into the woods. But that she fought him and thwarted his intentions. "But he was some mad," writes Nettie. "He said because of what I'd done I'd never hear from you again, and you would never hear from me."[11]

In a more gruesome fashion, Tereus sought to silence Philomela. Holding her tongue "with a pincer," he cuts out her tongue, then continues to indulge his lust. Afterwards, he imprisons Philomela in the hut and spins "a cunning story of her death" to tell his wife.[12] Even so, Philomela is determined to tell her story. On a loom she hangs white threads into which she weaves "purple signs" denouncing the "savage crime." Philomela has a servant take the cloth to Procne who reads in the warp and woof its threads that her sister lives, her husband lies, and "revenge is what she needs."[13]

Where letters are used as Celie's medium of revelation in the novel *The Color Purple*, quilting is Celie's mode of revelation in "Watch for Me in the Sunset or The Color Purple," Walker's screenplay of the novel. In the screenplay, Celie sews together pieces of cloth that symbolize her story. Among the *"precise shapes"* are pieces from the dress she wore when "Pa" raped her and a piece representing the star embroidered on the hat of her second child. *"As she works, totally absorbed, cutting, placing, contemplating, sewing,"* directs Walker, *"we should have the feeling that in putting these poor scraps of her life together CELIE is in fact praying—and telling her story to God."*[14] Finally reunited, Nettie tells Celie, "I wrote to you because when I didn't I felt like I was choking on my own heart." Nettie asks Celie whether she had ever written to her. Celie replies that she wrote to Nettie all the while. "Here your letter," she says, giving Nettie the quilt.[15]

As Philomela communicates her harrowing experiences to Procne with embroidered cloth, the screenplay of "The Color Purple" ends with the display of the quilt and Nettie's reading of Celie's life. In the novel as in the screenplay, communication is a key element in the development of and transformation of the characters. This is so in general, but particularly so in relation to the female characters. As they are collectively silenced in a patriarchal social structure, the only succor is within each other's listening. The novel *The Color Purple* pays homage to this sisterhood among black women. It is a paean to women who refuse to be silenced and those who struggle for self-expression. It dramatizes the importance of relationships between sisters and sisterly relations, as it highlights the women's collective efforts in literally and figuratively creating comfort for one another.

The suffering that occurs in the wake of forced separations, imposed silences, and disrupted communications in the lives of the characters, results in tragic situations. The poignancy of such situations speaks to the importance of communion for the characters. Communion signifies authentic relationship between and among individuals and respectful and dignified interaction that recognizes a society of equals whose intrinsic value can never be greater or lesser than another. As the novel highlights the various forms in which communion is expressed among women, it calls into question the "patterns and precedents" of patriarchy which interrupt and disrupt the communion which is the nexus of the women's identity and belonging. It brings attention to the destructive and nihilistic ideologies, structures, and discourses which support patriarchy in its malevolent form, as a social system rooted in the falsehood of male superiority.

Nettie's letters illustrate that the idea of male superiority is atemporal, cross-cultural, and intercontinental. As a missionary in Africa, among the Olinka people, Nettie observes the sexist attitudes toward females. They are not allowed to be educated and they are perceived more as a useful support in the livelihood of males rather than as free and autonomous human beings. Tashi's mother is socialized to believe that if a woman is unmarried and childless, she is nothing. That women hold such views is even more significant as it suggests to what extent an individual's own mind can be enslaved and made subject to external authority, even to the detriment of the individual. Among the Olinka, men have the power of life and death over women, the power of a god.

The reality of the doctrine of absolute power is also evident in the repercussions of colonial rule which Nettie and her family witness in Africa. Like Marlow aboard the *Nellie* in Joseph Conrad's *Heart of Darkness*, Nettie takes Celie and the reader through the nefarious history of European imperialism which lies at the heart of Africa's troubles. Her letters describe the devastation and terror suffered among the Olinka and surrounding villages consequent to the installation of rubber plantations. Her letters raise the specter of King Leopold II and reveal the devastation that occurs when a man is not satisfied with the cultivation of his own fields, when his appetite exceeds what he produces, and even when he intimidates and terrorizes others to produce on his behalf, he finds his appetite unquenched.

As the speaker in Muriel Rukeyser's poem "Käthe Kollwitz" describes herself as being between and among wars, so the women in *The Color Purple* find themselves between and among oppressions. The sexism, racism, classism, and imperialism are all wars, each with its own declaration of inequalities, each with its own bill of denied rights, and each with its own flavor of the master-slave, subject-object paradigm. The sexism and violence Sofia faced at home with Harpo rendered her vulnerable to the hostilities of the larger society wherein the rule of white superiority and class privilege prevailed. This sense of privilege had the mayor's wife presume that Sofia would love to be her maid, as the sense of omnipotence inherent in white patriarchy authorized the mayor to bend Sofia to his will.

Because neither the mayor nor his wife recognizes Sofia as a human being, a speaking subject, they cannot concede her right to speak, even on her own behalf. As Sofia's "Hell no" is translated as "[s]assing the mayor's wife," her knocking the mayor down in reaction to his slapping her is perceived as a capital crime, as the mayor's attending officers nearly kill her.[16] "When I see

Sofia," writes Celie, "I don't know why she still alive. They crack her skull, they crack her ribs. They tear her nose loose on one side. They blind her in one eye. She swole from head to foot. Her tongue the size of my arm, it stick out tween her teef like a piece of rubber. She can't talk. And she just about the color of a eggplant."[17]

As Sofia is blind in one eye, Harpo and Albert are blind in both eyes for a major portion of the novel as they don't see the correlation between their domination of the women in their lives and the domination that these women experience in the racially and economically stratified hierarchy of male supremacy. They cannot connect oppressions. But the women see it. As the sap begins to rise in Celie, her perception becomes clear and her words bear true witness. "If you hadn't tried to rule over Sofia," she tells Harpo, "the white folks never would have caught her." "That's a lie, say Harpo." "A little truth in it, say Sofia."[18]

Celie realizes that the men in her life are all variations of the white, male personification of god in her head. She discovers that this god is not only blind and "deef," but asleep as well, unavailable to poor colored women. When Mary Agnes hesitates to disclose that her uncle Bubber, the warden, raped her when she approached him on Sofia's behalf, Shug asks her with irony, "[I]f you can't tell us, who you gon tell, God?"[19] Although the women have their differences, ill-treat and fight each other, they still recognize their common plight and their common humanity and will sacrifice for one another. As there is no greater expression of love than "that a man lay down his life for his friends," so the women literally lay themselves down for one another.[20] Mary Agnes lays down for Sofia as Celie lays down for Nettie. Nettie's second letter to Celie acknowledges this great expression of love: "I miss you, Celie. I think about the time you laid yourself down for me. I love you with all my heart."[21]

Once she awakens to a sleeping god and a living sister, Celie addresses her letters to Nettie. The letters that make up *The Color Purple* expose the trauma of poor and black women in the American rural South, as well as the condition of females in patriarchal societies in Africa. Together the letters constitute a dialogue in the fashion of Plato—seeking truth, contemplating justice, and ultimately, envisioning unity. As a dialogue implies at least two speaking subjects, the letters imply the need for black women to claim their subjectivity as human beings, assume their rightful status as equals, and to speak their truth both in the home and in the larger society.

In both private and public spheres, just to speak at all can be a dire business, as the situations with Celie, Sofia, and Albert's first wife Annie Julia suggest. Yet as the housewife in "Coming Apart" dramatizes and as the historical legacy of Fannie Lou Hamer demonstrates, "it is a necessary fight." And because "power concedes nothing without a demand," as Frederick Douglass stated, the individual women in *The Color Purple* are encouraged in their necessary fight for freedom and justice by a supportive community of women.[22]

Support and courage notwithstanding, the individual must find her own will to resist, to demand the respect due her as an equal human being. "You've got to fight and get away from Albert," Nettie advises Celie. Her sister-in-law Kate helps Celie all she can before Albert sends her packing. She tells Celie before leaving that she has to stand up for herself. "I can't do it for you. You got to fight them for yourself." But Celie is immobilized by Albert's aggression. "I make myself wood. I say to myself, Celie, you a tree." Kate sympathizes with Celie as she sympathized with Annie Julia. Albert married her, dropped her at the house, and "kept right on running after Shug Avery."[23] Annie Julia sought comfort in the arms of another man who murdered her. In his recurring nightmares, Harpo replayed the event: "He grab hold of her shoulder, say, You can't quit me now. You mine. She say, No I ain't. My place is with my children. He say, Whore, you ain't got no place. He shoot her in the stomach. She fall down."[24]

The Color Purple unveils the ruthlessness of a malevolent patriarchy. The novel reveals that, whether it is robed as European imperialism or black male sexism in Africa or America, unconscious masculinity knows not its limits and is destructive. As the ideology of patriarchy assumes domination over women and children and dominion over the earth, it also sanctions the emasculation of even those males who subscribe to it. The white men in town think nothing of lynching black men like Celie's father whose success and independence is considered an affront to them. And even though the white sheriff might agree with Albert—that as men they "know how womens is, anyhow"—Albert must anyhow remember that he is "colored."[25]

But there is no safe haven from the assault Albert faces as a man even in the sphere of home. Albert resents being dominated by his father who keeps him in a position of dependency. He has not the wherewithal to stand up to his father or stand up for himself—let alone stand up for Shug whom his father forbade him to marry. Albert's miserable life without Shug does not prevent him from contributing to Harpo's domestic misery in relation to both Sophia and Mary Agnes.

As the women find their voices and find their feet, the men are left to come to terms with a rebalancing of power and a reexamination of who they are and what their place is in the home, in society, and in life in general. In his solitude, Albert examines his life and contemplates whether it is worth living at all. He shares his philosophical investigations in conversation with Celie when she returns from Memphis. "Anyhow, he say, you know how it is. You ast yourself one question, it lead to fifteen. I start to wonder why us need love. Why us suffer. Why us black. Why us men and women. Where do children really come from. It didn't take long to realize I didn't hardly know nothing."[26]

In recognizing that he is not omniscient, Albert admits he is not a god. He expresses the wisdom of Socrates, and in his hard-won humility, he expresses the wisdom of being what he is—a natural man whose value is neither greater nor lesser than any other human being. "And if you ast yourself why you black or a man or a woman or a bush it don't mean nothing if you don't ast why you here, period." Albert's inquiry takes him to an enlightened view of the mystery that is life: "I think us here to wonder, myself. To wonder. To ast. And that in wondering bout the big things and asting bout the big things, you learn about the little ones, almost by accident. . . . The more I wonder, he say, the more I love."[27] And he is surprised and delighted when the love is returned.

As Walker undresses male superiority, Celie undresses Albert. When she rebuffs his overture of being together again as "man and wife," "He say, Celie, tell me the truth. You don't like me cause I'm a man?" But Celie has never looked at men. "Take off they pants, I say, and men look like frogs to me. No matter how you kiss 'em, as far as I'm concern, frogs is what they stay.'" In a gesture of kindness and understanding, Albert carves Celie "a little purple frog" that she places on the mantel in her house.[28] Frogs symbolize transformation and metamorphosis. The color purple symbolizes wisdom, knowledge, spiritual protection, and higher consciousness.

". . . THE WORLD WOULD SPLIT OPEN"[29]

Splitting the world open is the work of the novelist. The writer rejects the world before her and creates one that reflects the ever-elusive unity and coherence to which she aspires. No longer dubious about the efficacy of her art, Alice Walker came to embrace Albert Camus's perspective that art is rebellion in its purest form. And given that the novel "is born at the same time as the spirit of rebellion," the novel is its consummate literary form of expression. The writer rebels against an absurd existence and is compelled by her passion for a better world to create alternative realities. "The world of the novel," states Camus, is "a rectification of the world we live in."[30]

In *The Color Purple* Walker rebels against the suffering endured by black women and the mutilated spirits of those black men dominated by the dogma of patriarchy. She resists totalitarianism and the catastrophic consequences of excess. She bears witness against the silencing of women, extirpation of whole societies, historical erasures, and the lunacy of self-made gods. But as Camus's treatise on rebellion and art makes clear, the writer's response to the world cannot be a total negation. The writer may denounce total injustice and demand total justice but "cannot affirm the total hideousness of the world." To create a better world, the writer "must simultaneously reject reality and exalt certain of its aspects." In the realm of "the literature of rebellion," "better does not mean different, it means unified."[31]

Unity, in *The Color Purple* is fostered, first and foremost, by authentic communication between equals and is symbolized in the letters between Celie and Nettie. It is expressed in the spoken and written word and in behaviors and actions that inspire personal integrity within individual characters and those that promote community among characters. *The Color Purple* is a world wherein there is freedom to speak and live one's truth. It is a world where reason triumphs, uplifts, and transforms. It is a magical place wherein men have fingers with eyes and a kiss can turn a tree into a woman. It is a mystical realm where God is "[e]verything that is or ever was or ever will be."[32] It is a dimension in which laughter bubbles up and giggles forgive, and where existence is a call to wonder, to inquire, and to love.

The Color Purple is a vision of a better world wherein the unitive power of unconditional love prevails. A transcendent Miss Celie is the personification of this ideal. Celie's love for Shug Avery precedes Shug's actual presence in her life, and it only changes to become more expansive and truly unconditional. Celie's love transforms Shug Avery from a destructive woman who was merciless in her disregard for Albert's wives to a conscientious and reflective woman who would come to love and protect Celie. The loving relationship between Celie and Shug and Celie and Nettie become the foundation of *The Color Purple*'s beloved community.

SECTION III
Air

Ubiquitous. Life-breath. *The gaseous form of cosmic creative forces vibrates as air. Nitrogen mingled with oxygen mingled with Goddess spirit mingled with God spirit, air is everywhere, surrounds everything, permeates all that exists. As atmosphere, it envelops Earth in blue gauze.[1] Infused with prana, it inspirits and sustains rivers, plants, animals, humans. Element of the east, air is as essential as the rising sun. Air is a cooling luminous green.[2]*

Air is life. "Air allows flow and movement" and so it encourages flexibility and inspires adventure.[3] Invisible, air is known by its effects—a felt sense of pressure, a whistling, a breeze. And so air impresses and teaches subtlety. Charged with the intelligence of currents, air gusts, spins tornadoes, sees through the eye of hurricanes. Air purifies, cleanses, purges. Air expresses as the winds of change, teaching curiosity, engendering vitality, encouraging movement.[4] Empowered with wisdom and grace, air is transformative: Hate relents to love. Greed acknowledges generosity. Egoism acquiesces to peace. Balanced with earth and water, air is regenerative. Omnipresent, air connects all, facilitating equanimity, communication, and healing, carrying wave and sound.[5]

As air animates the body, it is required for rebirth. As it sustains the body, it connects the body to the mind and "allows the mind to move in new directions, to see things from different perspectives, and this allows the accumulation of knowledge and understanding."[6] It is the example of freedom. Associated with the illumination of dawn, air expands the mind, shifts consciousness; its molecules blossom as enlightenment. Life is a dance we do with air—like a butterfly.

"The Clitoris Knows When and How"
by Phyllis McEwen

Satin baby,
That nipple of skin folded softly and safely away.
This is a smart and feeling
Woman sea—bead sex thing
Knowing when to be all things
And then, demurely, nothing but a hint
Of her turgid self, after all.

They are so like sacred beads
Hidden, their names unsaid
People fearing them
Feeling their orblet selves
Even in the soft mouth crack split
Liquid torrid tightness
Centers of her name.
When they are set into motion
They weave then, spinning off
Waves of threaded gold.

It is this finger tip that
Begins the world
Sets it to bowing Out
Back
Dancing in Her own lips
Teaching a woman to sing.

ELEVEN

Apologia: Honoring the Difficult

The Color Purple won the 1983 Pulitzer Prize and the National Book Award for fiction, making Alice Walker the first black woman to win the Pulitzer in the category of fiction. Though "stunned" to learn she had received the award, Walker was tempered in her response to the rising media frenzy that touted her success. Having perceived herself as the medium of her characters, Walker was more inclined to see the honor as theirs. "I feel really happy for the people in *The Color Purple*. They'll really like this," she told reporters.[1]

Walker was suspicious of prizes and vigilant against the vaingloriousness she critiqued in the philosophers and writers she admired. Writing with the goal of winning distinguished awards had not been an aspiration. Walker declined the celebratory presentation of the Pulitzer in New York and received the $1,000 cash prize in the mail. Though a recipient of two major literary awards, Alice Walker's attitude echoed the sentiment of her character in *You Can't Keep a Good Woman Down* who believed that, unlike prizes, her life "*was* a reward she could count on." Moreover, Walker added, "I love being a black Southern woman. All three add incredible enlargements to being a writer."[2]

Mindful of the unique perspective that she brought to literature, Walker also valued the publications and potential contributions of other writers. She therefore collaborated with poet June Jordan to found The Sisterhood, an organization that provided black women with mutual support. Toni Morrison, Ntozake Shange, Verta Mae Grovesnor, and Audrey Edwards were among the regular participants.[3]

In her role as *Ms.* magazine's poetry and fiction editor, Walker introduced to the magazine and its readers the voices of African writers Bessie Head, Buchi Emecheta, and Ama Ata Aidoo. And her reviews recommended works that were unconventional in subject matter and fresh and bold in style. To write, Walker believed, was to connect with others who cared to move forward "the discussion of survival, with grace and justice and dignity." A variety of voices, perspectives, experiences, and creative expressions were critical to the advancement of human society and appreciation of the planet. "We will need to know many different kinds of things to survive as a species worth surviving."[4]

Walker's ideas align with those of writer-activist Doris Lessing whom Walker read and held in high esteem. Lessing believed that "writers everywhere are aspects of each other, aspects of a function that has been evolved by society." If you see writers in this light, comments Lessing, "as a stratum, a layer, a strand, in every country, all so varied, but as together making up a whole—it tends to do away with the frantic competiveness that is fostered by prizes and so forth."

That function, says Lessing, can be seen in the novelist. "I think novelists perform many useful tasks for their fellow citizens, but one of the most valuable is this: to enable us to see ourselves as others see us."[5] Even as Alice Walker perceived *The Color Purple* as a mirror, she understood the complexity and risk in performing the task of providing that mirror: "I belong to a people, heart and mind, who do not trust mirrors. Not those, in any case, in which we ourselves appear."[6] Nonetheless, Walker had based *The Color Purple* on family history and lore. "The characters are 'composites' of people I love from my childhood."[7] The novel explored relationships between black women and men, and between and among black women. As it candidly questioned sexual mores and presented graphic scenes of sex and lesbianism, it also raised the issues of sexism, domestic violence, incest in black families, and sexism in African societies. In comparative fashion the novel addressed American racism and European imperialism.

Given the taboo status of some topics addressed or the unconventional treatment of those topics, the novel generated intense discussion. Once it was selected for the Pulitzer, *The Color Purple* became a *New York Times* best-seller, and remained on the list for over a year. When Walker agreed to have the novel adapted to film, the discussion intensified: "from the moment word went out there would be a movie, it was attacked by people who loathed the idea." "The attacks," said Walker, "many of them personal and painful, continued for many years, right alongside the praise, the prizes, the Oscar award nominations."[8] The novel and the film were at the center of heated debates across the country.

The author, herself, had to contend with fierce public opposition. "Still there is no denying the pain of being not simply challenged publicly, but condemned," Walker recollected. The list of allegations against her were severe: "It was said that I hated men, black men in particular; that my work was injurious to black male and female relationships; that my ideas of equality and tolerance were harmful, even destructive to the black community. That my success, and that of other black women writers in publishing our work, was at the expense of black male writers who were not being published sufficiently."

She was "accused" of being a lesbian.[9] She was believed to be in conspiracy with white feminists to vilify black men. And she was called obscene names. "Of all the accusations," Walker confessed, "it was hardest to tolerate the charge that I hated black men." She contemplated "the fiercely sweet spirits of black men" that had inspired her life and her work. "But even more important," she reflected, "I felt close to, and always affirmed by, the black male spirit within myself."[10]

Calvin Hernton's essay "Who's Afraid of Alice Walker?" discusses "The Color Purple" phenomenon. The essay analyzes the novel and film and offers an even-handed summary of the debate surrounding both, delineating the arguments that ensued and the issues that were raised. At the bottom of the controversy, wrote Hernton, were the issues of historical shame and the attending fear of punishment consequent to exposure: "Walker should not have aired 'dirty laundry' before the eyes of white people who will use The Color Purple to justify their genocide against the black race." Besides, the consensus was adamant: "Nobody knows any black people like those portrayed in the film, beyond imagination, not believable, false depiction, unrealistic."[11]

Some blacks took issue with what was revealed in the novel while others found nothing in the film with which to identify. "The empty mirror," writes Walker, "the one that reflects noses and hair unlike our own, and a prosperity and harmony we may never have known, gives us peace. Our shame is deep. For shame is the result of soul injury." Nevertheless, mirrors are sacred, says Walker. They allow us to witness the physical form we inhabit which reveals "the condition of the eternal that rests behind the body, the soul. As an ancient Japanese proverb states: when the mirror is dim, the soul is not pure."[12]

Walker surmised early on that her path as a black Southern woman writer who was committed to authentic expression would be marked by adversity. In researching the work and life of literary foremothers, Walker was daunted by the conditions under which they wrote, the intimidation to which they were subjected, and the unsympathetic and biased assessments of their work. Walker said her investigations into the critical reception of Zora Neale Hurston, a writer whose work she had come to love, was a decided "mistake."

"After reading the misleading, deliberately belittling, inaccurate, and generally irresponsible attacks on her work and her life by almost everyone, I became for a time paralyzed with confusion and fear." Riddled with self-doubt, Walker, a novice writer, pondered her potential fate. "Would I also be attacked if I wrote and spoke my mind? And if I dared open my mouth to speak, must I always be 'correct'? And by whose standards?" Rather than be cowed, Walker was encouraged to fight back, to rescue Hurston and her work from "a sneering oblivion," and to resist the politics of intimidation and the silencing of women's voices.[13]

Though poised for the necessary fight, Walker was deeply affected by the raging controversy over her work and by the notion that her critique of black male oppression of black females was construed as her desire for "racial divorce."[14] The idea that a work she considered a gift to her people and to the world was seen as an act of race betrayal was devastating to the author who "felt isolated, deliberately misunderstood and alone." But, she understood, "This too is the writer's territory."[15]

Nevertheless, Walker was steadfast in the authenticity of her depiction of black rural Southern life—its beauty and its violence. "Ever since I was a child, I had been aware of the high rate of domestic violence in our town, among our people; wives shot or stabbed to death, children sometimes abused and beaten." She was unapologetic about scenes portraying "women-loving women" who were "lesbian, heterosexual, bi-sexual, 'two-spirited.'" "We needed to see how we looked," concluded Walker, "behaving as if still under the spell of a religion that made it nearly impossible to love the female body that was our source."[16]

Walker wanted readers and viewers to see "womanist women" who were independent-spirited and sexually autonomous. She wanted them to see men who could love as full human beings. Thus, in the novel Odessa's husband Jack is portrayed as a man who had a sensibility that allowed him to see by touch. And in her screenplay, the biographical sketch of Albert emphasized Albert's awakening, his process of becoming present to his full humanity. It highlights his love for Shug Avery as the alchemical component in his personal transformation.

In modeling her male characters, Walker's novel and screenplay reflect the idealism of Rainer Rilke's philosophical perspective on sex, masculine energy, and the masculine principle. "Sex is difficult," Rilke counsels "My Dear Mr. Kappus," who expressed concerns about a relationship. "But those tasks that have been entrusted to us *are* difficult; almost everything serious is difficult; and everything is serious." Rilke urges Kappus to trust in what is difficult; for difficulty "is a certainty that will never abandon us." Solitude, too, is difficult, Rilke continues. However, the difficulty of something "must be one more reason for us to do it."[17] In dealing with issues of sexuality with her characters, as well as within her own life, Walker followed Rilke's advice to honor "the difficult and the good."[18]

In honoring the difficult, Walker was able to find meaning in all that transpired in the wake of the publication of *The Color Purple*, and specifically in the decade that followed the film adaptation. In retrospect, she could see she had been on a journey. She came to realize that she, herself, had answered a call. Jean Shinoda Bolen states that we all have. In *Crossing to Avalon*, Bolen writes that we are invited to an adventure by some exceptional circumstance or simply by a knock at the door. For Alice Walker it was the latter.

While in the midst of going about her day-to-day life, Walker writes that there came "an unexpected knock at the door."[19] Steven Spielberg and Quincy Jones had come to invite her on an adventure—collaboration on making a film based on her book. She had set out on a journey fraught with all the elements of the heroic path, a path which she depicts in the epigraph of *The Same River Twice*.

Walker describes her initiation as an entry into the labyrinth, a journey that commenced with a delightful going off with two strangers to engage in a strange, magical, and bewildering creative project of filmmaking. Spielberg would direct the making of the film. Quincy Jones would write the musical score, as well as coproduce the film with Spielberg and Kathleen Kennedy. Walker would write the screenplay—which she did. "It was however not the script that Steven loved."[20] Menno Meyjes would write the screenplay that would guide the film's production.

Though Walker would play the role of consultant to Meyjes and to the cast and crew in general, her overall ability to be fully present—in body as well as spirit—to the vicissitudes of production was severely compromised. Having been struck with a condition that only later she had learned was Lyme disease, she was left, in the meantime, to manage its chronic symptoms. "I sat under a tree and offered speech lessons and tarot readings, painfully conscious of my fuzzy thinking and blotchy skin, my soul-deep exhaustion and an almost ever-present nausea." Her inability to intercede at critical junctures where the integrity of a character or the spirit of the novel came into question, tried Walker's own sense of personal responsibility and integrity. "I was unequal to the task of pointing out to Steven every 'error' I saw about to be made, as my critics later assumed I should have, or even of praising the exquisite things he constantly thought up. . . . This pained me; I felt it an unexplainable and quite personal failing."[21]

Moreover, because of her ambition to share with the larger world the re-created world of her parents, grandparents, and ancestors, Walker was particularly anxious about their representation on the silver screen. An initial viewing of *The Color Purple* film left her feeling "terrible." "It looks slick, sanitized and apolitical to me." In a December 6, 1985, journal entry she confided her disappointment that the film "turned out as well as it could have done." Yet, she "*saw* how hard everyone worked. How earnestly they tried to do it right." In spite of having given her best, she feared she had failed the ancestors, and she simply wanted to weep. "I do so hope it's true that there are no mistakes, only lessons. This one could be big."[22]

While negotiating the public outcry against the film and decrying her own inability to have done more to influence the final version of the film, Walker was emotionally stymied by the fear of losing her mother, Mrs. Minnie Tallulah (Grant) Walker. Mrs. Walker had suffered a major stroke in 1981, with smaller strokes before and after, which left her largely incapacitated for over 10 years. Alice Walker had endeavored through those years to provide for the care and comfort of her mother, a woman she knew only as strong, active, and resilient, and a woman to whom she felt a sacred connection. "There was a strong green cord connecting me to this great, simple seeming, but complicated woman, who was herself rooted in the earth. I felt this cord weakening, becoming a thread."[23]

At the same time that she was contemplating the "irremediable loss" of her mother, Walker was blindsided by the sexual infidelity of her partner Robert Allen. Monogamously partnered for over thirteen years, Walker and Allen had a relationship in which Walker felt happy and secure. Yet Allen informed Walker of his sense of insecurity and neglect: "[B]ecause I had been 'distracted by my work and sexually inattentive' he'd had an affair a year or so earlier with an old girlfriend from the past."[24]

Walker and Allen elected to remain in their relationship, "hopeful of honoring both the difficult and the good, and especially that place where they meet."[25] Walker also remained in the relationship because she felt too vulnerable to leave. "I was too weakened and confused by my illness, and by my mother's illness, to make such a painful break." Walker bemoaned the ironic "humiliation of being in this position with a black man, at a time when I was being publicly and venomously accused of 'attacking' black men." She dismissed the accusations as "crass" and "simpleminded." But as the situation was "especially enervating," the accusations "found their target just the same."[26] At the time, Walker kept a public silence about what she experienced as a shameful situation. She felt "trapped to still be trying to stay with him and not be ashamed. This is the feeling of being deep in the messy stuff of women's secret lives, that place from which unscathed survivors are so rare."

The labyrinthine pathways Walker trod were physically, emotionally, and psychologically harrowing and, at turns, life-threatening. "It felt exactly as if I were being attacked from the inside at the same time I was being attacked from the outside. Would I survive it? I thought not."[27] But if the traveler does not give up, does not turn back, the center of the labyrinth will be found. And there in the center, one would ascertain the Holy Grail—"the rose, the Goddess, the Grail, a symbol of the sacred feminine."[28]

"At the heart of the most mysterious labyrinth lives the greatest mystery," writes Walker. And because she followed love and curiosity through the winding labyrinth and had managed to keep going despite the boulders that rose up in the river, she found the sacred feminine: "all the women in *The Color Purple*." And because of the accessibility of film, they could be "beamed across a world desperate for its return."[29] She found there also, at the heart of the labyrinth, the sacred masculine, resonating in the persons of Spielberg and Jones, and especially in the spirit of her grandfather Henry Clay Walker, the prototype for the "much maligned character of Mister." Walker regretted that few could "really see him" as she intended to reveal him in his full humanity.[30] In the film, Albert is astride his horse, separate from the others, outside the circle of kin. But in both her screenplay and in the novel, he is an integral part of the family that has finally united as one.

Loving her grandfather was difficult, Walker conceded, not knowing how to reconcile her adoration of a man who was "extremely misogynistic." But in taking him apart and putting him back together, in the novel and screenplay, as the complex human being she understood him to be, she could then come to terms with a granddaughter's love. Her treatment of Henry Clay Walker aligns with Rainer Rilke's prompting to embrace love as one of those difficult mysteries that is to be honored. "It is also good to love," says Rilke, "because love is difficult. For one human being to love another human being: that is perhaps the most difficult task that has been entrusted to us, the ultimate task, the final test and proof, the work for which all other work is merely preparation."[31]

The Same River Twice symbolizes Alice Walker's exit, her having found her way out of the labyrinth. The way back is not obvious and the adventurer has no way of knowing as she emerges how or when she will take the experience back into the world until she does. *The Same River Twice*, a compilation of reflective commentary, journal entries, letters, articles, and *The Color Purple* screenplay, all document Walker's experiences, newly gained insights, and wisdom as they are also emblematic of her having reached the center—her center.

Walker's journey confirmed her childhood beliefs: "The world *is* magical; there *are* good people in it. *Inherent in life is fun.*"[32] It revealed knowledge that is critical for the growth and advancement of the individual and society: the ability to be self-critical; the courage to live one's unique self-expression; awareness that violence to others is soul abuse; oppression of others destroys the beauty of the self.[33] And it offered healing balm, a trust that all will be as it is—whether in terms of people, nature, creative collaborations, or difficult situations. Come what may, Walker breathed deeply, "Love is the way to feel."[34]

Coming out of the labyrinth and publishing *The Same River Twice*, Alice Walker performs the ritual ceremony of shedding the old skin—which is symbolic of rebirth—and growing into a new one. In shedding the old, Walker writes that she was letting go of that which was no longer needed, releasing herself from years of pain and suffering. Growing a new skin, Walker embraces a deeper self-love. One that is detached from the images others have of her. One that is unconditional in her own self-acceptance:

> For that great gift, that I am me: with this spirit, this hair, this skin, this fluid, whole sexuality, this vision and this heart, I dare not apologize. I am too grateful.[35]

The Same River Twice was published a year after the transition of Walker's mother. Among the writings in the compilation is a journal entry that captured a difficult conversation between them:

> One of the last things my mother said coherently to me before she died, while looking at me as if seeing me for the first time (also a possibility), was "You('re) a little mess, ain't you." Meaning someone selfish enough to fully express her being. We looked deep into each other's eyes. I said "Yes." It was a long moment and the only moment in which I felt my mother understood who she'd brought into the world and that she and I were well matched. That I wished to share that being with her, and that this Being that I am loves her completely, I hope that is the message she fully understood.[36]

The Same River Twice is the answer to questions Walker had posed; answers that Rilke had promised would come, but not in the moment of asking—thus one must love the questions, he had exhorted. The work documents the essentially philosophical response she received. The title of the work comes up in Walker's discussion of commentary about her writing of the screenplay for the film adaptation. According to conventional wisdom, Walker's writing of the screenplay would be like "giving birth to the same baby."

Pointing out the differences between the novel and her screenplay, Walker rebutted the idea, stating moreover, that "you really cannot step into the same river twice. Each time it is different, and so are you." Walker describes this pearl of wisdom as an "old idea."[37] But it is a little more than that. It is a foundational tenet in the philosophical ideas of Heraclitus, one of the first Greek philosophers, and it represents Heraclitus's belief that change is the nature of the universe: "Just as the river where I step / is not the same, and is, / so I am as I am not."[38] And it represents his belief that the universe invites our participation.

Ever the artist-activist, Walker maintained her faith that inherent in art is the ability to transform the individual and change society. Walker repeats Albert Camus's conclusion that to create "is to create dangerously." Yet the artist is compelled "to find out how . . . the strange liberty of creation is possible."[39] Being one of those who cannot live without art, Walker is heartened by Camus's clear-sightedness, Rilke's strength and integrity, and Heraclitus's eternal truths. She is emboldened to create mirrors "in which we can see our true collective face." She knows her sacred calling and that her work is "a prayer to and about the world."[40]

TWELVE

Helped Are Those Who *Know*

DREAMS

Journal Entry
  December 3, 1986

> . . . My new novel is coming along. Good people, interesting sinners. . . .
> I'm enjoying a new freedom in the writing of this book. I let myself go with the
> voices of the people even when they take me to foreign countries and don't speak
> much English. . . . I think I will call the novel something that came to me in a
> dream: *The Temple of My Familiar*. . . .[1]

Alice Walker writes in *The Same River Twice* that during the time of her illness
with Lyme disease and the emotional trials of familial and personal affairs, she
felt alone. In time, however, she had come to understand that she "had never
been truly alone. Always with me," she realized, "was the inner twin: my true
nature, my true self, . . . the self that came in dreams, to be pursued in the
essays I was writing at that time." And, Walker continued, "I frequently had
dreams, visions, and spiritual revelations of extraordinary power."[2]

In *The Temple of My Familiar*, dreams are revelatory and empowering. Dreams
are, says Carl Jung, messages from the unconscious, "a normal psychic phenomenon that transmits unconscious reactions or spontaneous impulses to consciousness." They are "the almost invisible roots of our conscious thoughts," the
evidentiary emissaries of the existence of the unconscious stratum of the human
psyche or soul.[3] He emphasizes that the conscious mind is but one aspect of

the human psyche. And if humankind is to truly know itself and appreciate its earthly origins, it must understand the conscious mind as an integral part of the other, unconscious aspect.

The sharp and weighted divide between the intellect and intuition or the conscious and unconscious mind has resulted in a dangerous psychic fragmentation, states Jung. In the space of this divide, modern humanity experiences a crisis of personal identity, social isolation, and disconnection from other life forms. *The Same River Twice* and *The Temple of My Familiar*, suggest that this divide is superficial. As Walker has addressed the issues of social, cultural, and political identity in previous works, she addresses in *Temple* the issue of psychic identity. The novel demonstrates the consequences of a fragmented psyche and illustrates the means by which the psyche can be integrated and unified. In its narratological structure of concentric stories, *Temple* is a labyrinth which takes the reader to the Holy Grail of a totality of self and the possibility of a progressive humanity that is harmonized within nature.

The unconscious mind is "the really complex and unfamiliar part of the mind, from which symbols are produced." And these symbols or archetypes are critical to human identity. Yet because it is characteristically denied, dismissed, or disparaged, the unconscious mind "is still virtually unexplored."[4] Walker explores this "unfamiliar" aspect of the human psyche in *The Temple of My Familiar*. Functioning in the manner of the collective unconscious, *Temple* contains the experiences and memories of humanity extending back to time immemorial, transmitting messages to the conscious mind of the reader through stories, dreams, dream-memories, journal accounts, taped recordings, conversations, letters, and notes.

Dreams are a kind of lifeline in *Temple*. They signal psycho-emotional health and psychic integration when characters express a desire to know and begin to remember their dreams for the first time or for the first time in a long time. In a kind of psychoanalytic dialectic, Walker's characters reveal their thoughts and resurrect their memories in the listening of one another, through story. And some of them, like Celie's granddaughter Fanny Nzingha, undergo psychoanalytic therapy. Fanny struggles to understand her recurring racist fantasies that floated up from repressed memories of racial trauma experienced during her childhood. Walker's novel embraces Sigmund Freud's approach to reaching the subconscious mind through psychoanalytic therapy. But it is Jung's more expanded perception of the unconscious that captivates Walker's imagination and inspires her narrative.

NIGHTMARES

Where the subconscious or individual unconscious mind holds the repressed memories of one individual, the collective unconscious contains millennia of repressed, forgotten, and willfully jettisoned human history. The resulting disconnection of the present from its past yields within modern humanity a fragmented psyche that adjusts itself to the violence of misogyny, imperialism and colonialism, and the destruction of Earth.

Temple concerns itself with both the "forgotten or repressed" contents of the personal unconscious, as well as the inherited, universal contents of the collective unconscious—the instincts which govern passion and intuition and the archetypes which are codifications of knowledge, wisdom, and prophecy. This psychic dyad is embodied in the character M'Sukta, a woman who remembers forever. A liminal character who functions as an archetype, M'Sukta is imprisoned in the British Museum of Natural History. She is the living, human component of an African village exhibition and is literally "on view" as a relic of the conquered and vanishing "barbarous" states of the human species. She is the sole survivor of the Balawyua people whose village was demolished: "Intertribal warfare, slave raiding, that sort of thing."[5]

Lady Eleandra Burnham Peacock learns about M'Sukta while sampling London's prurient nightlife in the company of her cousin T. "For, as T. says so well, how am I to be a great painter if I never *see* anything?"[6] Once she actually *sees* M'Sukta, Eleandra sees a civilized human being for whom nothing in her background or her books has prepared her. What she sees is what had been erased from historical memory. "The history I knew was not hers, . . . the literature I read talked about savages and blackamoors, and that was when it was being polite. The languages I knew failed me entirely when I stood before her."[7]

Eleandra experienced M'Sukta's circumstances as a familiar memory triggered by the smell of fear that permeated the room. "And then it seemed to me perhaps I had smelled it in a dream, for the whole room now had an aspect of dream."[8] As nothing from her personal nor academic background could inform Eleandra's perception of M'Sukta as a civilized person, Eleandra's identification with her is apparently informed by knowledge transmitted from the realm of the collective unconscious, triggered by her olfactory senses—the sense most strongly linked to memory.

Eleandra's identification with M'Sukta inspired frequent visits to her replicated compound. Over the years, they develop a pidgin and Eleandra penned their conversation in her journals, capturing M'Sukta's "primitive philosophy." The Balawyua believed "that all that has ever happened is stored as memories within the human mind. . . . The life of my people," conveyed M'Sukta, "is to remember forever; each head granary is full. The life of your people is to forget; your thing granaries ('museums'), and not yourselves, are full."[9]

What the English, Europeans, and Americans chose to forget filled their museums. The willful choice to "forget" generates both psychic and social schisms. Denial of the subjectivity of and identification with others allowed for the objectification of "others" under Western imperialism and colonialism. Western imperialism figures as a prominent theme in *Temple*. Walker addressed the topic of imperialism in earlier works, focusing specifically on the impact of colonialism in Africa. Her treatment of the subject is embedded in a love for Africa inspired by eldest sister Mamie who taught her songs and history about a continent she never knew, "But learned to love."[10] During her years at Spelman, Walker conducted research on this continent she "never knew" and wrote papers for her history classes that explored the effects of colonialism and the pan Africanist response to European expansionism.

Much of the material derived from Walker's research would serve as a basis for the political insights and historical knowledge presented through Nettie's character in *The Color Purple*. *The Temple of My Familiar*, like a dream, continues the resurrection of the suppressed chronicles of Africa from the catacombs of world history. The novel conjures those stories that continue to be denied in modern human consciousness: African intertribal warfare and collaboration with European traffickers and colonialists; African resistance and detention in barracoons and slave pens; the horrors of the middle passage; and the uniquely female experience in all spheres of the destruction and defamation of Africa. Fanny Nzinhga, who later spends time with her father Ola, in Olinka, harbors fears for an Africa she has never known. Her fears are manifested in nightmares featuring a ghoulish image of "Prince Charles grinning at her, but with Africa's teeth."[11]

Temple also weaves into its remembering the tales of other civilizations ground beneath the wheels of Western imperialism. Through the story of Carlotta, in which is interwoven the stories of her mother Zedé and her grandmother Zedé, the elder, Walker foregrounds the myth, lore, and history of indigenous populations in South and Central America. Carlotta and Zedé live in California. Carlotta, having been rescued from her Latin American home when yet a child, feels bereft of family and cultural history and suffers from a diminished sense of self. She wants to know who she is and whence she came. She longs to feel whole. Her mother Zedé holds Carlotta's history, but her mother is a broken woman.

Zedé survived the conquistadors and the relocation of her people, but dehumanizing experiences shamed her into silence. She cannot speak directly to her daughter. But she can talk to Arveyda, the renowned musician who is Carlotta's husband and who becomes Zedé's lover. A comforting familiarity allows Zedé an ease of expression with Arveyda. In the dream-memory that unfolds in his listening, Zedé returns to a sacred time of mythic dimension and relives the communal and ceremonial life where stones have protective powers and the delicate artistry of the capes her mother designed inspired the village priests. She relived, too, the destruction and carnage that marched in company with the Spanish conquistadors who killed Carlotta's father, the "rough-haired priest" who had become guardian of the sacred stones. Softened by the melody of guitar strings, Arveyda sings this story to Carlotta.

Temple makes it clear that the story of the West can never be a singular, solo voice above and disconnected from the chorus of the silenced voices of those whose lives and lands were decimated, then pillaged, for the benefit of the West. No matter how meticulously and murderously constructed is this history, it is insufficient to deracinate humanity's common origin or to expunge from the collective unconscious our common identity. Thus Lady Eleandra Burnham Peacock glimpses herself in the "savage" ballet that shocked her parents. And Fanny, Olivia, and Ola, recognize and discuss the Choctaw roots of Elvis Presley and the Cherokee heritage of Johnny Cash—extant despite the Trail of Tears.

DERACINATION AND THE POLITICS OF FORGETTING

In suppressing the unconscious aspect of the psyche, modern, Western humanity cuts itself off from instinct—"the age-old forgotten wisdom stored up in us"—and it cuts itself off from intuition—the numinous quality of nature.[12] Carl Jung postulates that this disconnect is foreboding. "For it is the body, the feeling, the instincts, which connect us with the soil. If you give up the past you naturally detach from the past; you lose your roots in the soil, your connection with the totem ancestors that dwell in your soil. You turn outward and drift away, and try to conquer other lands because you are exiled from your own soil."[13]

Loss of roots whether for traditional peoples or moderns is equally disastrous. "Age-old convictions and customs are always deeply rooted in the instincts," says Jung. "If they get lost, the conscious mind becomes severed from the instincts and loses its roots, while the instincts, unable to express themselves, fall back into the unconscious and reinforce its energy, causing this in turn to overflow into the existing contents of consciousness." This rootless condition of consciousness "results in a hybris of the conscious mind which manifests in the form of exaggerated self-esteem or an inferiority complex." The loss of balance that occurs creates conditions for an individual's psychic injury, as well as societal disaster.[14]

King Leopold of Belgium epitomizes exaggerated self-esteem and the inferiority complex that belies it. Through Nettie's letters in *The Color Purple* Alice Walker draws a portrait of Leopold that recounted his cruelties as King of the Belgium Congo. In *Temple*, she recalls these atrocities while also alluding to Leopold's misogynistic disposition. In *King Leopold's Ghost*, Adam Hochschild writes that the "refined cruelty" Leopold perfected in the Congo expressed itself also in his misogynistic treatment of his sister Carlota, the erstwhile Empress of Mexico. He was also tyrannical with his daughters.

Hochschild relates that in his attempt to obliterate evidence of his activities in the Congo, Leopold ordered the state archives in Belgium to be burned and records and witnesses in the Congo to be destroyed. The "politics of forgetting" that are evident in the destruction of historical records are also present in the means by which the patriarchal mind attempts to banish women to the realm of the unconscious. Leopold, who firmly believed that "thrones and royal property were for men only," attempted to rewrite Belgian law in order to deny his three daughters an inheritance.[15] As he had his sister locked away in a chateau in Austria, he also had eldest daughter Louise committed to an insane asylum.

Through signifying parallelisms, Walker subtly but emphatically calls attention to the commonalities of the conditions of women's lives across time, culture, and class. Carlotta, in *Temple*, shares a name and a history with Carlota, the Empress of Mexico. Lady Eleandra Peacock was threatened with being remanded to a nunnery because she refused to marry, just as Louise, the daughter of Leopold, was committed to an asylum for refusing to remain in a forced marriage. And the life of Ola's wife—we know her only by her code name "Harriet, as in Tubman,"—bears comparison to Leopold's sister Carlota in that both women represented their nation and both were later labeled insane and were abandoned to oblivion.[16]

Excessive masculinity was an integral aspect of European imperialism that expressed itself, as well, in the destruction of natural environments. As Jung's work explained it, the destruction of nature inherently meant the undermining of the feminine principle—and by extension, the human spirit. The wave of environmental destruction that crossed the African continent rippled across the Atlantic. Woven into Zedé's reminiscences were stories of both the desecration of the land and the ongoing effort of men to dominate women. Zedé recollected how the Spanish conquistadors forced the people of her village to clear the forests: "The men used machetes and pickaxes and saws to fell and uproot trees and vines, and the women used hoes and rakes to complete the slaughter of the earth." The guards forced the women to mate with them, and before long each guard had chosen his favorite slave "wife."[17]

This will to subjugate women was true also of the men of her village long before the coming of the conquistadors. But this had not always been so. According to Zedé's mother and grandmothers, "in the beginning, at about the same time the toucan was created, there was also woman."[18] She was one with nature and had the power to create human life. Finding her powerful, beautiful, and mysterious, man feared and revered her and in doing so, made her the priest. Over time, the story goes, man forgot that he bestowed this sacred function on woman and resented worshiping her. "In short," says Zedé, "it was during this period of rebellion that the man decided they would be priests. That they could be the ones through whom life passed!"[19]

REMEMBERING

In his forgetting, Ola, who had become a playwright, had risen in the new government to become its minister of culture. Ola exemplified the behavior of men benighted with complexes of inferiority. He could never admit of anything that would deny the superior profile he had fashioned for himself. He lived his life as though his wife "Harriet" did not exist. "Harriet" was an Olinka guerrilla soldier who had joined the Mbele in the struggle against colonialism and white supremacy. She had saved the lives of many Olinka including Ola. A sanguine matriot, she helped institute a postcolonial government run by the Olinka people.

But that government, "once in power, conveniently forgot she existed. This was true of all the women: they were forgotten."[20] Once his wife died, however, Ola began to remember his true nature and the sacred nature of Harriet. From this place of remembering, he began to write plays that honored the heritage of his people and that critiqued the "government of men" who were absorbed in "beer drinking, women, and soccer."[21] He dedicated the first of such plays to the wife very few knew he had.

Ola's play brought to the conscious level of mind the sexist attitudes among the Olinka who behaved "as if they'd never before thought of women or the possibility that women were human beings in their own right at all."[22] "My father's insights into the oppression of women, black women by black men, who should have had more understanding—having criticized the white man's ignorance in dealing with black people for so long—made many of the people uncomfortable," Nzingha Ann shared with her sister Fanny. Yet Ola's work had stirred the people who were "stimulated to change."[23] And it was the first of his plays to be banned by the government of men.

In the socially constructed, twin hierarchies of race and sex, there is a corresponding assignation of value. The effect of this in the mind is to relegate undervalued or devalued ideas, concepts, and perspectives to a subliminal sphere. "The lower the value of a conscious content falls," says Jung, "the more easily it disappears below the threshold" of consciousness into the unconscious mind which then functions as "a receptacle for all lost memories"—those without the energy of value to become conscious, as well as intentionally repressed memories that are painful or perplexing.[24] Through a process of associative activity in the unconscious, these memories surface in dreams and can emerge through artistic creations like the drama created by Ola or the "Tombstone and Fruit" still life painting by Lady Eleandra.

In the minds of all but a few of the male characters in *The Temple of My Familiar*, the idea of woman was devalued. That women could be human beings "in their own right" was a concept that had fallen below their conscious level of awareness. Fanny's husband Suwelo viewed women objectively and believed them to be possessions, which were his right to own. He was obsessed with making some woman "his woman," preferably one "without the kind of painful past that would threaten his sense of himself as a man or inhibit his enjoyment of her as simply a woman."[25] Suwelo counted himself among the "generation of men [who] had failed women." "For all their activism and political development during the sixties, for all their understanding of the pervasiveness of oppression, for most men, the preferred place for women had remained the home; the preferred position for women, wherever they were, supine."[26] Suwelo's awareness of this did not prevent his affair with Carlotta.

As Hochschild writes in *Leopold's Ghost*, the politics of forgetting also entail the active deed of turning things upside down. "It is not a moment of erasure, but the strange reversal of the victimizer mentally converting himself to victim."[27] Thus Suwelo sees himself as victimized by Fanny's decision to live as though she had a right to her own life. His attitude accorded with the strange reversal of woman's identity from a free, sacred, and powerful being to an appendage. During Fanny's stay in Olinka, Suwelo indulges in pornography and prostitutes and, as if to insure that his male prerogative of ownership is accommodated, he also enjoys viewing "naked women in quarter-to-peek glass cages," and in "bondage films."[28]

With few exceptions, the men in Temple are insecure and possessive. They deny women their autonomy and insert themselves between women and their children and between women and their familiars. According to Miss Lissie Lyles, the central, archetypal character of the novel, from time immemorial "women alone had familiars."[29] Like M'Sukta, Lissie Lyles was "a long-memoried woman." In Temple Lissie's name means "the one who remembers everything."[30] Miss Lissie had lived many lifetimes and remembered a period of time when women and their children constituted their own tribe apart from the tribe of men.

In a taped recording she left for Suwelo, Miss Lissie reminisced about Husa, the lion who was the familiar of her mother. During another lifetime when Lissie assumed the form of an albino male, the winged serpent with feet called Ba, was the familiar of Lissie's mate. Almost every female had a familiar that they'd known since childhood. In an incarnation as a lion, Lissie was, herself, the familiar of a woman and her children. "I can still sometimes feel the sun on my fur, the ticks in my mane, the warm swollen fullness of my tongue," recalled Lissie.[31]

But the life Lissie lived with her companions was unceremoniously upended when the tribe of men merged with that of the women, a merger in which each group lost its freedom to the other. Men assumed authority and proceeded to impose their order on things. In doing so, "they lost the freedom of their long, undisturbed, contemplative days in the men's camps." The women, subject to the laws decreed by men, "became emotionally dependent on the individual man by whom man's law decreed they must have all their children." Women thereby "lost their wildness, that quality of homey ease on the earth that they shared with the rest of the animals."[32]

THE INNER TWIN AND TOTALITY OF THE PSYCHE

Walker's treatment of the concept of a familiar corresponds with Jung's concept of a "bush soul." Jung writes that the bush soul is incarnate in a wild animal or a tree or other form "with which the human individual has some kind of psychic identity." The bush soul or familiar shares its qualities with and is protective of its human counterpart. The relationship between familiars is hallowed and apparently symbiotic, writes Jung; for "an injury to the bush soul is interpreted as an injury to the man."[33]

In a dream, she shares with Suwelo, Lissie is a tall and stately woman. She is at odds with her familiar, a bird-fish-reptilian creature that is arrayed in spectacular color and vibrant with life. She has covered her familiar with glass and ceramic bowls and, later, a metal washtub so she can have an uninterrupted conversation with a Suwelo-like white man who is interested in her temple.

The familiar breaks through the barrier each time. It finally dawns on Lissie that her familiar is compelled by its will to freedom and that Lissie's behavior was destroying their relationship. The familiar took flight and Lissie found herself alone "on the steps of a cold stone building . . . in a different world from my own, in a century that I would never understand. Except by remembering the beautiful little familiar, who was so cheerful and loyal to me, and whom I so thoughtlessly, out of pride and distraction, betrayed."[34]

Disconnection from one's familiar, like an injury to one's bush soul, is essentially one's perceived separation from nature and a turning away from the natural self. The Lissie of the recounted dreamtime, found herself in a cold, hard, friendless place. To remember the familiar would be to restore her sense of self and belonging. In her dream, the familiar symbolizes the indivisible interrelationship of nature and humans, the intuition and the intellect.

Remembering is key. To remember is to reconnect, to facilitate articulation and communication. To restore an erstwhile disrupted flow. To regenerate. To forget is to disrupt the flow of memories, to fragment the psyche, to disconnect from nature, from other humans, and from one's full humanity. *Temple* illuminates all the ways in which a disconnected, hostile, and paranoid humanity persists in disruption and dismemberment. *Temple* also illustrates how nature, in its form as the collective unconscious, persists in assisting human beings to be what they are.

THIRTEEN

A Woman of One's Own: Womanist Philosophy and Revitalization of the Sovereign Feminine

lice Walker appraised herself as "unsuited for marriage" and filed for divorce in 1979. She had agreed to joint custody of daughter Rebecca then left New York for San Francisco. There she would deepen her relationship with newly divorced Robert Allen. Having vowed never to utter marriage vows again, she preferred to partner with Allen rather than to marry. "I am more committed to learning to speak Spanish," quipped Walker, "than I am to the institution of marriage."[1] To secure her personal freedom, the couple kept separate apartments, sharing weekends in the country.[2] Alice Walker was clear about her status as "one-in-herself." As Walker reclaimed herself in matters personal, she asserted herself in matters professional. She continued to teach, to write, and to work as consulting editor to Ms.

Walker had gained national and international recognition and acclaim with The Color Purple. Her 1983 publication In Search of Our Mothers' Gardens, like The Same River Twice, testified to the kind of industry, dedication, mental tenacity, and emotional resilience that underscored Walker's hard-won achievement. A collection of womanist prose, In Search maps the course of Walker's path as an activist-writer. In the first essay of the collection, "Saving the Life That Is Your Own: The Importance of Models in the Artist's Life," Walker pays homage to artists and ancestral folk whose lives and work prepared the ground over which she walked.

Referencing a letter written by artist Vincent Van Gogh just months before his suicide, Walker states that society makes the existence of artists "wretchedly difficult at times." And the more original the art, the more wretched the difficulty. Van Gogh's major difficulty was that he suffered "under an absolute lack of models," a condition, says Walker, that was exacerbated by narrow and ridiculing criticism of his work. "The absence of models, in literature as in life," she writes, "is an occupational hazard for the artist, simply because models in art, in behavior, in growth of spirit and intellect—even if rejected— enrich and enlarge one's view of existence."[3]

Only incidentally did she begin a search for models that would lead her to the discovery and recovery of writer and social scientist Zora Neale Hurston. "I sat down at my desk one day," Walker recollected, "in a room of my own, with key and lock, and began preparations for a story about voodoo."[4] The story, "The Revenge of Hanna Kemhuff," was based on a story Walker heard her mother tell many times. Walker's version of the story was informed and authenticated by folklore materials collected by Hurston, whom she had discovered "in a *footnote.*"[5]

During her matriculation at prestigious black and white women's colleges, Walker "had heard not one word about early black women writers."[6] Though she experienced the literature of early white women writers as influential in her thought and development as a writer, she also found it necessary to reject those aspects of their work that negated her. The majority of Southern writers, female and male, were benighted with a racial blindness that prevented them from writing about whites and blacks as they saw and *knew* them. And it was the exceptional black male writer who could, like Jean Toomer, express an authentic and empathic black female sensibility.

There was a dearth of available historical and literary material that valued the black female experience in America. Thus, like Toni Morrison, Walker would write the stories she wanted to read. She would also write those works she "*should have been able to read.*" For even as she searched for models, Walker was ever the writer in search of a tradition. She found guiding inspiration for her search in those "belatedly discovered models," who understood that the value of their experiences and of those around them were "in danger of being misrepresented, distorted, or lost."[7] Those models who inspired her search included Zora Neale Hurston, Jean Toomer, Sidonie-Gabrielle Colette, Anaïs Nin, Tillie Olsen, and Virginia Woolf.

Of Virginia Woolf, Alice Walker writes that she "has saved so many of us."[8] "Saving the Life That Is Your Own" and "*One* Child of One's Own: A Meaningful Digression Within the Work (s)" are essay titles that allude to and play on the title of Woolf's classic work *A Room of One's Own.* These essays frame Walker's collection of womanist prose and are suggestive of the impact of Virginia Woolf's work on Alice Walker.

Woolf's *A Room of One's Own,* is an elaboration on two lectures she delivered at Newnham and Girton women's colleges in 1928 in Cambridge, England. The work contemplates the quality of a woman's existence in a patriarchal society and the possibilities of her creative expression as a writer under patriarchal authority. Woolf rummages through libraries and ambles through graveyards for answers to a cluster of questions related to her lecture topic, "Women and Fiction": "Why did men drink wine and women water? Why was one sex so prosperous and the other so poor? What effect has poverty on fiction? What conditions are necessary for the creation of works of art?"[9]

Woolf deduced from her research that the patriarchal perception of women as inferior creatures, together with the force of law and custom that articulated and reinforced male supremacist ideology, explained much about a woman's impoverishment, her repressed creativity, and her consequent inability to generate literary works of genius. To remedy the situation, she concluded that a woman writer requires a room of her own with a lock and a minimum of 500 pounds a year. The former to assure her a private sphere. The latter to support her material independence and encourage her intellectual freedom.

Having examined woman's image and personality across several millennia, Woolf gathered that one would have to infer that woman was "certainly an odd monster":

> Imaginatively she is of the highest importance; practically she is completely insignificant. She pervades poetry from cover to cover; she is all but absent from history. She dominates the lives of kings and conquerors in fiction; in fact she was the slave of any boy whose parents forced a ring upon her finger. Some of the most inspired words, some of the most profound thoughts in literature fall from her lips; in real life she could hardly read, could scarcely spell, and was the property of her husband.[10]

If she refused to marry, she was "liable to be locked up, beaten and flung about the room, without any shock being inflicted on public opinion."[11]

Woolf's investigation into her topic led her to "an avalanche of opinion hot as lava, discoloured as dish-water." She mused that "nothing is known about women before the eighteenth century. I have no model in my mind to turn about this way and that." Narrowing the scope of her research to the middle-class Elizabethan Englishwoman, Woolf found so little information about her, that her existence could be doubted. The woman for whom Woolf searched never wrote her own life, scarcely kept a diary, and left few letters. Of the flood of literary works created during the age of Elizabeth, "no woman wrote a word."[12] To interpret this silence, Woolf imagined a blood, flesh, and bone Judith Shakespeare—a female version of William Shakespeare.

Woolf hypothesizes that given the absurdly hostile world of Elizabethan England, Judith's life as an artist who was her brother's equal, would have been impossible. Her talk of writing plays would have been discouraged, for the intellectual inferiority of woman was a matter of official record. Reputable university professors had conducted scientific examinations that proved that "the best woman was intellectually the inferior of the worst man." Moreover, they deduced that woman's essential purpose was the propagation of the species: "when children cease to be altogether desirable, women cease to be altogether necessary."[13] Woolf visualized Judith's likely path: denial of access to theatrical facilities, humiliation, seduction or rape or both, pregnancy, and suicide. Judith's ambition would issue forth stillborn.

From time to time in her essay, Woolf pauses to address her reader, as one imagines Woolf might have paused to directly address her audience in the actual delivery of her lectures: "What one wants, I thought—and why does not some brilliant student at Newnham or Girton supply it?—is a mass of information; at what age did she marry; how many children had she as a rule; what was her house like; had she a room to herself; did she do the cooking; would she be likely to have a servant?"[14] Woolf might well have added Spelman and Sarah Lawrence to the list of prestigious women's colleges attended by "some brilliant student."

The fluidity of time and space and the intercourse between the conscious and unconscious mind allows one to imagine Alice Walker present in the audience of Virginia Woolf, enrapt with a portrait of the artist as Judith Shakespeare, as Woolf was painting her. One imagines Walker touched by the artist's deplorable condition. Moved by her anonymity. Inspired by Woolf's call to accumulate the details of her unrecorded life. The information "must be scattered about somewhere, could one collect it and make a book of it," Woolf hinted. "It would be ambitious beyond my daring," Woolf thought—aware of the books that were not to be found on the shelves—"to suggest to the students of those famous colleges that they should re-write history."[15]

In Search of Our Mothers' Gardens is such a rewriting. It adds to the store of knowledge of woman in general and it brings to light the unrecorded, obscured, lost and neglected experiences of African American womanhood. On many levels, *In Search* is an answer to Virginia Woolf's call to young women to take an adventure of discovery, to investigate the misconstrued history of woman, to write the missing ethnographies and biographies and studies, and to trace their literary lines of descent. *In Search* answers the call to young women to examine woman's interior life, to feel the emotional lives of their female ancestors in relation to the likely discouragement, disappointment, and customary and customized abuse they each faced. "Among your grandmothers and great-grandmothers," Woolf impressed upon them, "there were many that wept their eyes out."[16]

Charged with her mission, Alice Walker pursued the past and the meaning it held for black women. In the title essay "In Search of Our Mothers' Gardens," Walker initiates a dialogue with history that guides her efforts in tracking down a tradition: "What did it mean for a black woman to be an artist in our grandmothers' time? In our great-grandmothers' day? It is a question with an answer cruel enough to stop the blood."[17] As Walker's questions echo those of Virginia Woolf, Walker's enthusiasm for the rewriting of a history that "often seems a little queer," resonated with that of Woolf.[18] By way of illuminating the circumstances of early black women writers, Walker quotes from Woolf's narrative of the spectral Judith Shakespeare.

Interpolating the quoted passage with aspects of race, class, and time, Walker inflects Woolf's narrative of a fictive Judith Shakespeare with details from the actual life of Phillis Wheatley:

> What then are we to make of Phillis Wheatley, a slave, who owned not even herself? This sickly, frail black girl who required a servant of her own at times . . . and who, had she been white, would have been easily considered the intellectual superior of all the women and most of the men in the society of her day.
>
> Virginia Woolf wrote further, speaking of course not of our Phillis, that any woman born with a great gift in the sixteenth century [insert "eighteenth century," insert "black woman," insert "born or made a slave"] would certainly have gone crazed, shot herself, or ended her days in some lonely cottage outside the village, half witch, half wizard [insert "Saint"], feared and mocked at. For it needs little skill and psychology to be sure that a highly gifted girl who had tried to use her gift for poetry would have been so thwarted and hindered by contrary instincts [add "chains, guns, the lash, the ownership of one's body by someone else, submission to an alien religion"], that she must have lost her health and sanity to a certainty.[19]

As Virginia Woolf focused on the middle-class English woman, Alice Walker focused on the enslaved African woman and her descendants, particularly the working poor of the rural South. In "But Yet and Still the Cotton Gin Kept on Working . . .," for example, Walker extols the fortitude and foresight of Mrs. Winson Hudson of Harmony, Mississippi, who defended her life and property from the Klan and documented her experiences. "She wanted other people to know what it meant to fight alone against intimidation and murder, so she began to write it all down."[20]

Walker had met Mrs. Hudson during her stint of teaching black history to women in rural Mississippi. In helping the women to see the events of their lives in context of the web of history, she encouraged them to write their autobiographies. Walker's research and her own experiences corroborated Woolf's supposition that creative intelligence was no respecter of class structure even as circumstances too predictably hindered creative expression. To Woolf's understanding about the prejudices against British women, Walker would add her understanding of the enslaved black woman and the black female working poor:

> Yet genius of a sort must have existed among women as it must have existed among the working class. [Change this to "slaves" and "the wives and daughters of sharecroppers."] Now and again an Emily Brontë or a Robert Burns [change this to "a Zora Hurston or a Richard Wright"] blazes out and proves its presence. But certainly it never got itself on to paper. When, however, one reads of a witch being ducked, or a woman possessed by devils [or "Sainthood"], of a wise woman selling herbs [our root workers], or even a very remarkable man who had a mother, then I think we are on the track of a lost novelist, a suppressed poet, of some mute and inglorious Jane Austen. . . . Indeed, I would venture to guess that Anon, who wrote so many poems without signing them, was often a woman.[21]

For as much as Walker can be imagined in the audience of Virginia Woolf, drinking in her talk, one can imagine Virginia Woolf striding across the campus of Spelman College, just barely overhearing a white, middle-aged, male Northerner chiding a daughter of a sharecropper against her foolish aspiration of becoming a poet. Perhaps Woolf's steps slowed when she heard him caution the student that "'a farmer's daughter' might not be the stuff of which poets are made. . . . A shack with only a dozen or so books is an unlikely place to discover a young Keats."[22] The sharecropper's daughter would later learn from Woolf that even the genius of the belatedly celebrated Keats was treated with such scorn that he left instruction on his deathbed to omit his name from his headstone and engrave instead, "Here lies one whose name was writ in water."[23] Both Woolf and Walker would come to know from their own struggles that even if a shack is an unlikely place to discover a Keats, it does not follow that Keats was not living there.

That the creative spark of literary forerunners survived at all to blaze and get itself onto paper was a miracle worthy of note. Woolf encouraged her enthralled audience to honor their forerunners by excavating the circumstances of their lives and by reading their works in context of the traditions to which they belong and to which they have contributed. "For books continue each other," Woolf told them, and were not anomalies. As a book and its author stand in conversation with other books and their authors, so a masterpiece expresses the mystery and genius of an entire people and crowns a given moment in the movement of a people's literary tradition. "For masterpieces are not single and solitary births; they are," Woolf informed her audience, "the outcome of many years of thinking in common, of thinking by the body of the people, so that the experience of the mass is behind the single voice."[24]

Thus Woolf impressed upon her young apprentices the importance of recognizing their inheritance; the importance of dignifying the existence of their forebears as flesh and blood and bone women endowed with creative intelligence; and the importance of commemorating the lives of their forebears. "Jane Austen should have laid a wreath upon the grave of Fanny Burney, and George Eliot done homage to the robust shade of Eliza Carter." "All women together," she said, "ought to let flowers fall upon the tomb of Aphra Behn."[25]

In similar spirit, Alice Walker bade her readers to recognize Phillis Wheatley in context of the nascent African American literary tradition that her writing was instrumental in generating. Walker enjoined them to take "the larger perspective," in their critical analysis, one that desisted from the kind of sneering ridicule that condemned rather than connected and to look for "the common thread, the unifying theme . . . that enlarges the private and the public world."[26] In gathering the pieces of Wheatley's life story, Walker strove to understand the "contrary instincts" at work in the breast of Phillis Wheatley and that lay just beneath the surface of her verse.

Snatched from her African homeland at seven years of age, thrust into the absurd reality that was American slavery, Wheatley came of age. With the "incorrectness" of a Sammy Lou and the audacity of a revolutionary petunia,

Wheatley dared to bloom as a poet. Though lauded in America and England, her writings were also mocked and her humanity denigrated. In his assessment of her poetry, President Thomas Jefferson dismissed Wheatley and all blacks as incapable of creating poetry. "Among the blacks is misery enough," he scoffed, "but no poetry." He considered blacks too obtuse to obtain to the station of a poet. "Religion indeed has produced a Phyllis Whately; but it could not produce a poet." He concluded, "The compositions published under her name are below the dignity of criticism."[27]

In "In Search of Our Mothers' Gardens," Walker sounds the depth of Wheatley's contribution to a tradition: "It is not so much what you sang, as that you kept alive, in so many of our ancestors *the notion of song*." In noting the magical transitioning from the oral to a written tradition, Walker's essay conjures up the mothers and grandmothers, who, by virtue of expressing their own innate creative intelligence, were midwives to a literary tradition. "Perhaps Phillis Wheatley's mother was also an artist"—a painter, singer, weaver, storyteller, ponders Walker. "Perhaps in more than Phillis Wheatley's biological life is her mother's signature made clear."[28]

Walker's essay "A Talk: Convocation 1972," is derived from a lecture delivered to the brilliant minds at Sarah Lawrence College. In a reflective, stream-of-consciousness style that honors Woolf as it resurrects Wheatley, Walker invites readers to let flowers fall upon Wheatley and a host of other early, unknown, and otherwise obscured women writers—among them Lucy Terry, Frances Harper, Nella Larsen. And as though following the promptings of Virginia Woolf, Alice Walker recounts her search for Zora Neale Hurston's gravesite in "Looking for Zora." The essay retraces Walker's pilgrimage to Fort Pierce, Florida, to Hurston's grave, to lay a wreath. But finding bramble bushes where the grave was understood to be, Walker marks the spot and erects a headstone. "A Genius of the South" was engraved on the light gray granite. Taken from a line in Jean Toomer's poem "Georgia Dusk," the inscription at once pays tribute to Toomer as it recognizes the rural Southern ethos that sourced and was expressed through the genius of Zora Neale Hurston, the same cultural ethos in which Walker herself was enveloped.

The young women at Newnham and Girton (and Spelman and Sarah Lawrence) were encouraged to understand themselves as originators, as well as inheritors, of tradition. In her peroration, Virginia Woolf impressed upon her listeners that their originality was intrinsically bound up with their ability to stand in reality and to know that "it is much more important to be oneself than anything else."[29] Standing in one's reality, vigorously living one's truth is at the heart of Walker's self-description as a womanist. Walker originated the term "womanist," which encapsulates her sense of inheritance and reflects her originality.

In the front matter of *In Search of Our Mothers' Gardens*, she defines "womanist." The first entry traces the word's etymology. Accordingly, "womanist" is of African American origin and is derived from the black folk expression used by black mothers in relating to their daughter or other female children.

It is typically used to admonish female children who display bold, outrageous, or *willful* behavior. (It is sometimes used by adult women in tacit admiration of the same *willful* behavior.) The second entry describes a womanist as a woman who loves other women—sexually or nonsexually; appreciates women's emotionality and strength; and prefers women's culture. She sometimes loves men—sexually or nonsexually. And she is committed to survival and wholeness of entire people—male and female.[30]

The womanist is inclusive in her embrace of all humanity. Characteristically she is a universalist, but will seek restorative solitude. An inheritor of a history of black women achieving the impossible, she is confident. Entry three of Walker's definition denotes the behavioral aspects of a womanist and the activities with which she is likely to be involved—song, dance, spirituality, struggle. Entry four defines "womanist" in a political sense, its meaning implied by its comparison with "feminist." Its meaning is also implied in the symbolism of colors and their comparative relationship: "Womanist is to feminist as purple to lavender."[31]

In her essay "Gifts of Power: The Writings of Rebecca Jackson," Walker expounds the concept of womanism as it relates to the politics of identity. *Gifts of Power: The Writings of Rebecca Jackson, Black Visionary, Shaker Eldress* is a volume edited by Jean McMahon Humez. Walker's essay is both an assessment of Jackson's writings and a review of Humez's work as editor. Rebecca Cox Jackson was an early-nineteenth-century spiritual mystic who was led by her "true" inner voice to become a minister. The male leadership of the Bethel African Methodist Episcopal church branded her a heretic; for she was "a woman aleading the men."[32] Jackson's inner voice had dictated that she be celibate. Jackson's husband contested. Directed by the voice within, she left husband, church, family, and friends. She found a spiritual community among other black women and formulated a bond with Rebecca Perot, with whom she lived, worked, and traveled for over 30 years. Both women joined the Shakers, a religious sect that practiced celibacy, and later founded a black Shaker community which consisted only of women and their children.

Humez read the relationship between "the two Rebeccas" as sexual and labeled them "closeted lesbians."[33] Walker questioned the attempt of a non-black scholar "to label something lesbian that the black woman in question has not." Jackson and Perot were self-described celibates, explained Walker, "the name they *did* accept, and *embrace*, which caused them so much suffering and abuse." "My guess," she continued, "is that, like Virginia Woolf, whom many claim as a lesbian but who described herself as a 'eunuch,' the two Rebeccas . . . cared little for sex, which Jackson repeatedly states."[34] Walker held that the term "lesbian," derived from the Greek "Lesbos," evoked a reality that was at variance with the cultural tradition and values of the black community of which Jackson and Perot were a part.

"I simply feel that naming our own experience after our own fashion (as well as rejecting whatever does not seem to suit) is the least we can do—and in this society may well be our only tangible sign of personal freedom," writes

Walker. The importance of this, Walker suspects, is what compelled Jackson to leave a record of her spiritual path. "This, that makes her an original," proclaims Walker. "This that makes us thankful to receive her as a gift of power in herself."[35]

In her commitment to free and authentic expression, Walker, like Virginia Woolf, established her own publishing enterprise in 1984. She called it Wild Trees Press. Among the works she published were J. California Cooper's *A Piece of Mine* (1984) and Cynthia Stokes Brown's *Ready from Within: Septima Clark and the Civil Rights Movement* (1986).

Walker intuited black women's self-affirmation and rebellious creativity as she observed the exquisite reality of her mother's everyday life. As some black women inscribed their sovereign selves in the written word, Mrs. Walker expressed hers in the stories she told, the clothes she sewed, the quilts she pieced, the foods she canned, and the garden she maintained. Moreover, what Walker bore witness to in her mother was the "creative spark." Working in her garden, her mother was radiant. "Her face, as she prepares the Art that is her gift, is a legacy of respect she leaves to me, for all that illuminates and cherishes life."[36]

Symbolic of the black-Southern-rural everywoman, Walker's mother expressed the archetypal Divine Feminine. This was Walker's inheritance. Along with a suitcase, a typewriter, and a sewing machine, Alice Walker left home at the age of 17 with a treasury of stories secreted in childhood memories, a legacy of respect for beauty, a respect for the strength to grasp the possibilities of one's life, and a realization that spirit was "the basis for Art."[37]

Walker found that the possibilities of her life were expanded by the birth of her daughter Rebecca. "*One* Child of One's Own" traces Walker's fears and concerns about becoming a mother who is also an artist. She feared that the quality of her writing would be "considerably diminished." After all, she observed, "Most women who wrote in the past were childless . . . and *white.*" And consensus had declared, "Women have not created as fully as men because once she has a child a woman cannot give herself to her work the way a man can. . . ."[38] Through the fog of opinion concerning children, Walker found her own wisdom: *One* Child of One's Own.

Rather than a threat, Walker experienced Rebecca's birth as "the one genuine miracle in life." The experience expanded Walker's consciousness and shifted her perspectives. "Her birth was the incomparable gift of seeing the world at quite a different angle than before, and judging it by standards that would apply far beyond my natural life."[39] And it was her daughter, at two years of age who marveled at the world in her mother's eye, reminding her that she was "beautiful, whole and free."[40]

In *In Search of Our Mothers' Gardens*, Alice Walker vindicates the life of women and the life of the child. It demystifies the shadows that fall on the path of the black woman artist and writer. This collection of womanist prose restores woman to her true sovereignty, as one-in-herself whose spirit resonates with life in all its forms. Inherent in the theory and ideology of womanism is a philosophy about existence, about value, about how to live. In examining the lives of her mother, grandmothers, and great-grandmothers, Alice Walker discovered the source of their existence and their creativity: "their spirituality."[41]

Alice Walker's novel, *The Color Purple*, embodies the philosophy of womanism and presents Sofia, whose name means wisdom, as "one of the first womanists."[42] The novel recognizes spirit as the source of existence and creativity. In Walker's portrayal of Celie, black women's lives are reclaimed. In telling Celie's story, Walker synthesizes fact and fiction and creates a voice resonant with the nuances of the lives of women who constitute Walker's own ancestral line. Based on the life of Walker's step-grandmother Rachel, Celie's character articulates a history of resistance to everything that would vanquish the life of a black woman, everything that would violate her creative intelligence.

As kidnapped children tried to walk back to their African motherland, "right into the sea," so they regularly risked their lives "to walk back to, or to find, the woman who brought them into the world and loved them, to whom their return was the essence of 'holding up the light for her to see by' through the long dark nights of slavery [as she spun thread or pieced a quilt]."[43] Through *In Search of Our Mothers' Gardens*, Alice Walker walks back to her mother and grandmothers to save her own life and to hold up the light for the rest of us to see by.

FOURTEEN

The Sacred Masculine

They'd *left* us! Hell, these bitches were so tough, they'd left *God*! This was when they were just discovering the Goddess, and it was all the time Goddess this and Goddess that. I once asked a black woman on the street where the new bus stop was—the city was repairing the old bus stop part of the street we were on—and she just looked at me, shrugged, and said an easy "Goddess knows." It blew me away.[1]

In this passage Suwelo shares his uncanny experience with Miss Lissie and Mr. Hal in *Temple of My Familiar*. They are elders whom Suwelo has come to regard as parents. His relationship with them is warm and comfortable, allowing Suwelo to relax into and express his deeper thoughts and feelings. Characteristically the listener in their circle of ritual talk, he feels encouraged, little by little, to share with them "small stories" from his life. Suwelo was confounded by his inability to persuade his wife Fanny to remain married to him. He found the role of man and wife to be to his liking, and he relished the privileges that came with it, particularly delicious meals and the availability of sex—without too much fuss.

Their ritual talk encourages him into something of a confession. He exposes his vulnerability and discloses his fear that Fanny could leave him for a woman. He had begun to closely observe women: "Beautiful, beautiful women, though some often didn't look too hot, . . . on their outings together . . ., climbing the hills, sunning in the parks, eating noisily at the largest tables in restaurants . . ., made you want to cry." They had become his competition. "The only

men who don't have this fear are living in caves and jungles somewhere with
their women still tethered to the floor at night by their nose rings."[2]

With Fanny in Africa for several months, he feels deprived. "My woman had
left me, you see, taken my rightful stuff off to another continent, totally out of
reach of my dick, and left me high and dry. Well, I knew how to get off without
her." Plenty of other women in the world was his attitude.[3] He was pleased
with his selection of the "superfeminine" Carlotta who Suwelo said "had no
substance." He assessed her as all image: make up, tight-fitting sweaters, short
skirts, stilettos.[4]

Suwelo described Carlotta as "a space cadet"—the same descriptive he had
also used for his wife Fanny. Though enchanted by Fanny's paganism and her
mystical relationship with various spirits, he was annoyed by it. He was resentful of her "dubious gift" of second sight, and jealous of her "seriously magical"
ability to conjure what she wanted.[5] Fanny resonated with the words of the
Egyptian Goddess Nut, "Whatever I embrace, becomes."[6] "To her, 'marriage'
was a bonding of souls that was eternal, *anyway*." What need of preachers, the
state, and a wedding band—"a remnant of a chain." "I wasn't so sure," Suwelo
said, "being a man within a patriarchal system. I could see some privileges."[7]

Beneath Suwelo's objectification of women lay a misogyny hidden deep in
his unconscious mind, but it surfaced one night in a dream. He was shopping
"in the Great Supermarket of Life" for enough food to last a lifetime when he
realized he was without a means to get his items home.[8] He sat on the floor
like a confused child, bewildered by a loss of what to do. Suwelo awoke to
his own whimpering. Lying in bed, shopping carts rolled through his every
thought.

The dream triggered the memory of his conflict with Fanny over shopping
carts. He refused to use one. "The cart," he said, "reminds me of little old
ladies with funny-colored hair, net scarves, and dowager's humps . . . of young
women who are suddenly too stout in their jeans . . . of bright young race-
horses of women who willingly put themselves in harness." His mother and his
grandmother had pushed and pulled shopping carts, and so did his then wife,
Fanny, who inferred that it was "of women," in general, that carts reminded
Suwelo. He had refused to utilize their cart to pick up items necessary for a
meal she was preparing. Fanny halted her preparation of dinner. A "little murder" had happened.[9]

With the logic he could muster—"I was raised to be a certain way"—Suwelo
continued to kill softly and justifiably the feminine principle within himself.[10]
Though he presumed his prerogative to enjoy, use, and possess them, Suwelo
rejected any fundamental identification with women. His inability to relate
to their complexity, fullness, and mystery reflected his inability to touch his
own feminine essence. The name Suwelo is derived from the rune alphabet
"Σ" ("Sowilo"), "the rune for wholeness."[11] However, Suwelo's personality
and behavior contradicted this meaning. Carlotta, far from being "simply a
woman" who lacked substance, was aware of the meaning of Suwelo's name
and was equally aware that Suwelo was a man "in fragments."[12] Yet as the rune

character had other layers of meaning, so the character Suwelo would have opportunities to explore his own complexities and heal his fragmented self.

A major factor in Suwelo's path to wholeness was his willingness to finally allow the memory of his mother to rise. Both his parents were killed in a car wreck, with his alcoholic father behind the wheel. With all the major characters in the novel, remembering the past is essential to a full life in the present. And remembering or otherwise learning more about both parents was central to restoring the past, to healing the fragmented psyche.

With Suwelo, as with Carlotta's mom Zedé, disconnection from the past undermined his sense of groundedness. It was important that he come to understand that knowledge of parents or ancestors was integral to a balanced sense of self. There is an insistence in the novel on balance. Imbalances in a character result in an exaggerated sense of self which requires the character to seek balance, restoration, or harmony. In *The Temple of My Familiar*, the emphasis on reconnecting with both parents reflects Walker's engagement with Carl Jung's theory pertaining to the syzygy of the anima and the animus. Accordingly, the anima personifies the feminine nature of the male unconscious, and the animus personifies the masculine nature of the female unconscious. These archetypes, says Jung, perform a compensatory and complementary relationship between the female and male principles within the psyche: "the anima gives relationship and relatedness to a man's consciousness, the animus gives to woman's consciousness a capacity for reflection, deliberation, and self-knowledge."[13]

As Suwelo must first allow the memories of his mother to rise before he can be restored to balance, Carlotta must ascertain the knowledge she seeks about her father in order to gain stability and self-confidence. And even Fanny does not feel quite whole until she experiences the African homeland of her conception and meets her father Ola for the first time. Implicit in Walker's writing is the idea that integration of the feminine and masculine principles within the human psyche is essential to an individual's psychic identity and full human expression.

In the character sketches she composed for *The Color Purple* screenplay, Walker correlated characters' attitudes about gender with the degree to which they were capable of maturing into their full humanity. In her sketch of Mister (Albert) for instance, Walker comments on the passionate love Albert has for Shug Avery that "saves him from total failure as a human being" and from "the blind alley of misogynism" that balked his father's maturation.[14] Jungian psychologist Jean Shinoda Bolen, whose work Walker also respects, discusses the tendency among men to "sacrifice their *anima*, suppressing the feminine aspect of their psyche for power. The feminine aspect is not allowed to develop and contribute to the creativity, sensitivity, and perspective of the male personality."[15]

The character of Celie makes it clear that women, too, resist maturation and the fullness of their personality. Fear keeps Celie from heeding the advice of virtually every woman around her who tells her to stand up for herself. "All I know how to do is stay alive," is Celie's ready defense.[16] But as Alice Walker stated, her preoccupation was not only with the survival of her people, but with the survival *whole* of her people:

> It is a mistake to assume that Celie's "meekness" makes her a saint and Mister's brutality makes him a devil. The point is, neither of these people is healthy. They are, in fact, dreadfully ill, and they manifest their dis-ease according to their culturally derived sex roles and the bad experiences early impressed on their personalities. They proceed to grow, to change, to become whole, i.e., well, by becoming more like each other, but stopping short of taking on each other's illness. Celie becomes more self-interested and aggressive; Albert becomes more thoughtful and considerate of others.[17]

As characters integrate contrasexual aspects of the unconscious into the conscious mind, they become balanced and whole.

In Jungian theory, the male animus that manifests in the female and the female anima that manifests in the male express the bisexual aspect of the human psyche. "This psychological bisexuality," says Jung, "is a reflection of the biological fact that it is the larger number of male (or female) genes which is the decisive factory in the determination of sex. The smaller number of contrasexual genes seems to produce a corresponding contrasexual character, which usually remains unconscious."[18]

Although she could "work like a man," Celie had not the spirit, confidence, or independence typically associated with men. As the animus within Celie becomes more present, Celie becomes more self-aware and interested in the fact of her existence and the life surrounding her. She is no longer stuck in survival mode. Albert, who can "clean like a woman," likewise becomes emotionally open and generous as he embraces the anima, the feminine principle which is integral to his humanity.

This movement of contrasexual energy from the unconscious to the conscious realm is evident in Celie's and Albert's actions and attitudes. It is apparent in their dialogue as they discuss their favorite subject—Shug Avery:

> He say he love her style. He say to tell the truth, Shug act more manly than most men. I mean she upright, honest. Speak her mind and the devil take the hindmost, he say. You know Shug will fight, he say. Just like Sofia. She bound to live her life and be herself no matter what.
> Mr. _____ think all this is stuff men do. But Harpo not like this, I tell him. You not like this. What Shug got is womanly it seem like to me. Specially since she and Sofia the ones got it.
> Sofia and Shug not like men, he say, but they not like women either.
> You mean they not like you or me.
> They hold they own, he say. And it's different.[19]

Walker coined the term "womanist" to describe and define this quality that Albert discerns: Different. Unique. Singular. Authentically individual. Free. Albert and Celie's discourse suggests that they have moved beyond the stereotypes and the projections that are consequent to a narrow and limited perspective. They have become conscious of the complexities of human sexuality and the way it expresses differently in each human being.

As archetypes, the syzygy of the anima and animus is primordial and inherited and, therefore, a part of the collective unconscious. As such, both are born anew in every human birth. In accordance with Jung, the *anima* and *animus*—along with the *shadow*, the repressed part of the personality—"have the most frequent and the most disturbing influence on the ego." Typically, these psychic phenomena remain hidden and are "always unconsciously projected upon the person of the beloved, and is one of the chief reasons for passionate attraction or aversion."[20] Bringing these elements to a conscious level seems to be an important part of Walker's efforts in her writing.

Walker's perspectives also reflect those of Virginia Woolf, whom Walker described as "a beloved mentor, muse, sister, a crazed Aquarian."[21] Woolf had explored the fluidity of the sexes in the character of Orlando in her eponymous novel *Orlando*, a book to which Walker alludes in *Temple of My Familiar*. In *A Room of One's Own*, Virginia Woolf theorizes about the bisexuality of the human brain and emphasizes the importance of an androgynous mind versus a "single-sexed mind" for the writer. "It is fatal to be a man or woman pure and simple; one must be woman-manly or man-womanly," Woolf writes. "Some collaboration has to take place in the mind between the woman and the man before the act of creation can be accomplished. Some marriage of opposites has to be consummated."[22]

To maintain that one sex is completely distinct from another, says Woolf, takes great effort and "interferes with the unity of the mind."[23] Upon observing a woman and a man meeting and entering a cab together, Woolf pondered "whether there are two sexes in the mind corresponding to the two sexes in the body, and whether they also require to be united in order to get complete satisfaction and happiness."[24] Woolf envisioned a complementary "plan of the soul" that compares with Jung's theory of the anima and animus:

> that in each of us two powers preside, one male, one female; and in the man's brain, the man predominates over the woman, and in the woman's brain, the woman predominates over the man. The normal and comfortable state of being is that when the two live in harmony together, spiritually co-operating. If one is a man, still the woman part of the brain must have effect; and a woman also must have intercourse with the man in her.[25]

However, Woolf writes, patriarchal ideology would have the sexes separate and demand the superiority of the male over the female. She notes that such a position exacerbates the already complex problem of human existence. "Life for both sexes . . . is arduous, difficult, a perpetual struggle. It calls for gigantic courage and strength. More than anything, perhaps, creatures of illusions as we are, it calls for confidence in oneself. Without self-confidence we are as babes in the cradle." Rather than devote one's energy to the cultivation of this valuable and "imponderable quality," Woolf observes, many prefer to acquire their confidence at the expense of others: "By thinking that other people are inferior to oneself. By feeling that one has some innate superiority . . . over other people. Hence the enormous importance to a patriarch who has to conquer, who has to rule, of feeling that great numbers of people, half the human race indeed, are by nature inferior to himself. It must indeed be one of the chief sources of his power."[26]

Rather than an authentic *self*-confidence, the confidence of the patriarch is fraudulent and fragile, as it is externally derived; and therefore it requires a great deal of force to hold intact. Rather than integrate the anima, the feminine principle within himself, the patriarch projects it outward onto woman as the inferior other who becomes for him, not another human being of equal value, but a being whose value is in her ability to reflect back to him the self-image he has contrived. She becomes "a looking-glass." In *The Color Purple* Mister uses Celie in this manner. When he dresses for the evening to attend Shug Avery's opening, he looks in an actual mirror to check his appearance, but he is confident in the image he fashions only once Celie approves:

> He dress all up in front the glass, look at himself, then undress and dress all over again. He slick back his hair with pomade, then wash it out again. He been spitting on his shoes and hitting it with a quick rag.
> He tell me, Wash this. Iron that. Look for this. Look for that. Find this. Find that. He groan over the holes in his sock.
> . . . . Anything happening? I ast.
> What you mean? he say, like he mad. Just trying to git some of the hick farmer off myself. Any other woman be glad.
> I'm is glad, I say.
> What you mean? he ast.
> You looks nice, I say. Any woman be proud.
> You think so? he say.[27]

Woolf says that the woman writer must be courageous to tell the truth. "Women have served all these centuries as looking-glasses possessing the magic and delicious power of reflecting the figure of man at twice its natural size." That figure, however, is augmented in proportion to the diminishment of the figure of women; "for if they were not inferior, they would cease to enlarge."[28] Woman, as looking-glass, is essential to the patriarch's confidence and power. Should she register a flaw or cease to render the appropriate reflection, she is subjected to indignant anger and chastisement.

Mister is indignant when Shug announces that Celie is going to Memphis with her. "I thought you was finally happy, he say. What wrong now?" Mister performs a "strange reversal," as he is convinced that he is a long-suffering, benign patriarch. But Celie sees him as "a lowdown dog," and, having mustered some courage, she tells him so.[29] Celie dresses him down, and when he attempts to shut her up with a slap, she stabs a knife into his hand.

Mister's self-image is challenged; thus his self-confidence is threatened. He tries to stabilize his wavering identity by deflating Celie's growing sense of self-worth: "Look at you," he scowls. "You black, you pore, you ugly, you a woman. Goddam, he say, you nothing at all." But Celie, who has done the work of getting man off her eyeball, has gradually integrated her masculine attributes, her animus, becoming increasingly confident and has come to see and value her own existence: "I'm pore, I'm black, I may be ugly and can't cook. . . . But I'm here."[30] She defends her life, her burgeoning self-knowledge and sense of freedom, and leaves for Memphis. In her absence, Mister struggles with the despair born of a hollow existence. In her absence, he has to see his true reflection. Then, he is able to see how he looked to Celie.

Revealing what is hidden from one's view is a service one sex can provide for the other, says Woolf. "For there is a spot the size of a shilling at the back of the head which one can never see for oneself." Men have long pointed out this spot to women, she writes. As women have been used as a looking-glass, for centuries, they may very well reflect back what they, too, actually see. "A true picture of man as a whole can never be painted until a woman has described that spot the size of a shilling." Woolf urges the woman writer to "go behind the other sex and tell us what she found there."[31]

Having detected a seething anger in the writings of the patriarch-professors whom she read, Woof emphasized the need for a woman writer to be both honest and brave: "For if she begins to tell the truth, the figure in the looking-glass shrinks; his fitness for life is diminished. How is he to go on giving judgment, civilizing natives, making laws, writing books, dressing up and speechifying at banquets, unless he can see himself at breakfast and at dinner at least twice the size he really is?" Though the looking-glass vision of himself may flatter the patriarchal ego, a true picture, says Woolf, has the potential to contribute to his fuller expression as a whole human being. In Walker's portrayal of Mister, one sees that "dark place at the back of the head!"[32] The vanity, insecurity, mean-spiritedness, brutality, and fear. One also sees that Mister has the wherewithal to do the necessary work of cultivating a healthy ego personality, one that includes the feminine principle, his anima, and one that is interdependent and reflective of his authentic self as a whole, "man-womanly" human being.

In Living by the Word, Walker describes Mister as a character she deeply loves—"not, obviously, for his meanness, oppression of women, and general early boorishness, but because he went deeply enough into himself to find the courage to change. To grow."[33] In The Same River Twice, she writes that the character of Mister is based on her own grandfather, Henry Clay Walker. In attending to the growth and transformation of the fictionalized version of Henry Clay Walker, Alice Walker reveals her efforts to understand and redeem the person and spirit of her grandfather. For she felt infuriated that she could love and adore someone who was so "extremely misogynistic." In reconciling herself to all that her grandfather was, Walker was honoring the difficult. This, Walker sees as part of her responsibility and joy as a writer; for she came to understand "that the creation of art is truly a prayer for the souls of those we love, the 'good word' before the throne of God."[34]

In the reclamation of this ancestor and in the exploration of the mystery that was her grandfather, Walker discovered in him the sacred masculine, or what Jung described as the archetypal "Wise Old Man." In reconciling herself to Henry Clay Walker, it may be that Alice Walker embraced a certain aspect of her own animus, and thus was receptive to what her grandfather's life, as the personification of the sacred masculine, could teach. In the novel, *The Color Purple*, the denouement of Mister's life speaks to lessons of compassion, forgiveness, and acceptance. In Walker's own life, it speaks to unconditional love: "My grandfather taught me one of the best things I know: you don't have to be perfect to be loved. . . . If I love you, Grandfather, surely that means the Universe does too."[35]

In Jungian psychology, the sacred feminine (or anima) and the sacred masculine (or animus) symbolize "the Self, the innermost nucleus of the psyche." In the dreams of a woman, this principle is personified in the figure of "a priestess, sorceress, earth mother, or goddess of nature or love." In the dreams of a man, "it manifests itself as a masculine initiator and guardian . . ., a wise old man, a spirit of nature."[36] In *Temple of My Familiar*, Suwelo has a recurrent dream. "He was sitting at the bedside of a very old man, and, though neither of them seemed to be talking, much information was being exchanged. No, not exchanged, for even in the dream Suwelo had had little to say. He was there simply to listen to the older voice of experience, for the sake of his own present pitiful life."[37]

This dream materializes when Suwelo goes to visit Mr. Hal in the Mary McLeod Bethune Memorial Nursing Home. Mr. Hal, life companion and familiar of Miss Lissie, became despondent at her death and perplexed over the images she had painted during her last days. He was particularly put off by a painting which Suwelo thought of as "the tree of life": "That big tree with all the black people and funny-looking critters, and snakes and everything . . . and even a white fellow in it. Then all those lions."[38]

Mr. Hal knew of the many metamorphoses Miss Lissie had experienced. But he could not embrace them all. He particularly rejected those parts of her, of which he was afraid—white men and cats. So he turned a blind eye to her paintings. And he lost sight of his world. "Was it Freud who said we can't see what we don't want to see?" Suwelo ponders. They, "the middle-aged man and the very old man," sat together on Mr. Hal's bed talking about the paintings Mr. Hal brought with him to the nursing home.[39] Miss Lissie's paintings were something of a looking-glass for Mr. Hal. They showed him blind spots he would not otherwise see.

Yet Mr. Hal loved Miss Lissie more than he was committed to his prejudices and phobias. His friendship with old Pete, a white resident at the nursing home facilitated his freedom from the former. Though he knew old Pete "was a jerk all his life," Mr. Hal felt only compassion for him. "The heart just goes out to the man." "Only the lord and his ledger keeper know how much misery he's caused. But he's here now, and he's scared. And he's deaf, and he's old." Regarding the latter, Mr. Hal still retained a fear of cats, but having listened to the tapes Miss Lissie left, and encouraged by his talk with Suwelo, he was "willing to work on it."[40]

Personifications of archetypes may express light or dark aspects. As the Wise Old Man, Mr. Hal's blindness points to the darkness and disconnection that comes as a consequence of hate and fear. It points to the separation and sense of isolation one experiences when one is unable to accept a part of someone or something and unwilling to see the whole. Though he is a very old man, Mr. Hal continues to learn. "And to think," Mr. Hal choked. "And here I am, out here at the home, and being out here I've had to learn so much."[41]

Because he is no longer so afraid, when Suwelo holds up a painting of a maned lion wearing a red shoe on its back left paw, Mr. Hal can make out a "'reddish spot,' which marks the return of Mr. Hal's lost vision."[42] In stillness and quiet, Suwelo witnesses the miracle, absorbing both the lessons garnered from the wise old man he sits next to, and from Miss Lissie, the archetypal feminine principle, whose voice and paintings continue to teach messages of connection, communion, relationship, forgiveness, acceptance, and a fearlessness about being everything that one is.

FIFTEEN

The Gnostic Gospel of
My Father's Smile

BARDIC ROMANCE

It opens with poetry and song and closes with song and poetry. It tells the tale of a beautiful maiden, the dragon who would possess her, and the knight who saves her and with whom she gallops across the mountains on the back of a steed. It follows their movements through and between worlds of peaks and valleys, mythic and mystical love, life and afterlife.

In "Angels," the opening chapter of *By the Light of My Father's Smile*, the reader's eye is brought into alignment with the gaze of Mr. Robinson who hovers around daughter Susannah. He seems voyeuristic, watching her every movement, even when she is in the throes of sexual passion. But his interest has less to do with Susannah's relationships and sex life than it has to do with the guilt he feels over his reaction to the blossoming sexuality of older daughter Magdalena, nearly thirty years ago.

Though sexually active, Susannah was sexually repressed, so much so that even as a writer, she found it difficult to include sex scenes in her novels. Mr. Robinson felt responsible for her rather sterile imagination. He wanted to give her permission to feel good about something he himself had made sinister. Where she hesitated, he silently shouted encouragement: "It is not so big a deal! I want her to know. As I see her, crippled in a place that should be free, and still, after all these years, perplexed by the memory of her sister's stubborn face and the sound of the whistling silver belt."[1]

Robinson and wife Langley had children only after Langley felt they could provide a safe and protected environment for a child. They had agreed to use "reason and consistency" as their discipline. But Robinson was present to none of their agreements when he beat Magdalena "to the point of actually drawing blood."[2] She was sixteen. She had walked out of her house at high noon toward a distant hill where her lover Manuelito waited. He reached down to pull her up behind him, astride Vado. Her arms encircled his waist, and they strode to their "home," a cave in the mountainside. There, they made love. Magdalena called it worship.

This was not the first time they met, but on this last occasion, Robinson punished her. It seemed a particularly pernicious punishment, as he used the silver belt, that Manuelito had made and given to Magdalena, to execute the punishment. Bewildered by the vehemence with which her father struck her, Magdalena was rendered mute—they both were: "he thrashed me in silence. I withstood it, in silence."[3]

Through the keyhole of the door behind which her father and sister played out an ancient pantomime, Susannah witnessed the beating that broke her sister's spirit and transformed her father "into Godzilla," into someone she could not recognize and against whom she closed a door within herself. Years later, in his afterlife, nose pressed against her life, her father wondered what Susannah had seen in his face; "what did she read there, what message about consequences of a searing passion, ecstatic sex?"[4]

Robinson regretted beating Magdalena. In the cool estrangement that infused their home, he contemplated his baffling behavior. "I could find no justification for it," he admitted. He knew well Magdalena's boldness of spirit: "She was born that way." What baffled Robinson was that he had committed an act with which he consciously knew he did not agree. "I prayed over it. Spare the rod, spoil the child. One says that and swallows down one's immediate protest. Stifles the voice that hates the rod. Would never, on its own, have even thought about the rod."[5]

Yet Magdalena embarrassed him. He tried to hide her wild spirit under long dresses and below high necklines and he refused to call her by the name the Mundo people felt matched and expressed her spirit—"Mad Dog." "She is the daughter of a minister!" he bellowed.[6] But in truth, this was a lie. Robinson and Langley were anthropologists. They wanted to live among and study the Mundo people of Mexico, an African-Amerindian maroon society whose numbers were diminishing. But they had no funding for their project. Their church agreed to support them in exchange for their agreement to carry out the church's mission among the Mundo.

Once they accepted the church's money, Robinson felt he had died to himself. Langley, too, saw the deception as their downfall; "it was the one big lie that, as the Mundo would say, definitely unraveled our world."[7] They masqueraded as pastor and pastor's wife for 10 years. "I was an atheist," Robinson stated. "More accurately, an agnostic. How was I to pretend to know whether God existed, and in what form?" Robinson's philosophical perspective spoke to what he didn't know and didn't believe, but he knew not what he did believe. He realized that there was something in him that was submissive and "this 'something' was like an internalized voice, a voice that drowned out my own," Robinson reflected. "And when I allowed myself to think about that submission I thought of myself as having been spiritually neutered." Dressed in "the long black coat and black hat and trousers," Robinson experienced himself as having no substance: "I was a shadow."[8]

In the absence of a strong sense of self, Robinson's personality became a vehicle for ideas and edicts that reflected a perspective he had not consciously chosen. When he betrayed Langley's trust and physically disciplined their daughter, his emptiness was revealed anew. He was a man split in two. In the moment of his raising the silver belt to strike Magdalena, Robinson did so as pastor, as priest, and in "the name of God." He had taught "rectitude and chastity" to the Mundo girls and would not have his willful daughter defy his teachings. But in the moment of his bringing the belt down upon her body, he did so in the name of patriarchy. "It seemed to be necessary to tame her," he confessed.[9]

Robinson had imbibed the ideology of patriarchs who believed that sexual expression was a male right and a male rite. And the rod of chastisement against transgressors of this code was in his hand. A minister of the church was to literally and figuratively "be a father figure to the congregation. He must be a man whose wife and children are 'submissive [to him] in every way'; this power proves his ability to keep 'God's church.'"[10] He had worn the garb of the clergy for a decade and, as Manuelito observed, Señor Robinson had been "sucked into the black cloth."[11]

DISAPPEARANCE OF THE FEMININE

In the chapter titled "God the Father / God the Mother" in *The Gnostic Gospels*, Elaine Pagels writes that the question concerning the sexual identity of the Divine Source is an important one, as the answer would eventually be institutionalized in political and social structures. Her investigation into the history of early Christianity "('the field called "patristics"—that is, the study of "the fathers of the church"')" showed clearly that orthodox Christians conceived the nature of god as monistic and masculine. "[T]he God of Israel shared his power with no female divinity, nor was he the divine Husband or Lover of any. He can scarcely be characterized in any but masculine epithets: king, lord, master, judge, and father."[12]

Whereas Catholics recognized Mary as the Divine Mother of Jesus, Pagels observes that "she is not 'God the Mother' on an equal footing with God the Father!" And even as orthodox Christianity reformulated the description of god as a Holy Trinity, only the masculine aspect was expressed: "Yet of the three divine 'Persons,' two—the Father and the Son—are described in masculine terms, and the third—the Spirit—suggests the sexlessness of the Greek neuter term for spirit, *pneuma*."[13] Robinson's plaint in his existential angst was that he felt spiritually neutered. The part of himself that was feminine had been forcibly suppressed over millennia, just as he intended to forcibly suppress "his girls."

Religious traditions that perceived the feminine as divine were demonized and suppressed by the orthodox faction of the Christian movement. Among those suppressed were Gnostic Christians who characterized the Divine Mother in three distinct ways: as part of an original couple; as Holy Spirit (the maternal, and therefore gendered, element of the Trinity, "both Mother and Virgin, the counterpart—and consort—of the Heavenly Father"); and as *sophia* or Wisdom who brings forth all creatures and endows human beings with insight or *gnosis*.[14] Such ideas were anathema to orthodox church fathers and teaching them was deemed heresy.

By the year 200, writes Elaine Pagels, "virtually all the feminine imagery for God had disappeared from orthodox Christian tradition."[15] Jungian psychology would intimate that Gnostic ideals had not disappeared altogether, but had been suppressed, hidden within the collective human unconscious just as actual Gnostic scriptures had been hidden in a jar and buried in the earth. Carl Jung was a devoted student of Gnosticism. In his search for a connection between Gnosticism and modern analytical psychology, he discovered Alchemy to be its historical link.

Jung realized, too, that Christian Gnosticism represented but one strand of Gnostic religious beliefs and spiritual practices. Alchemical Gnostics numbered among and blended with the various strands. An essential aspect among Alchemical Gnostics was "the primordial image of the spirit as another, higher god who gave to mankind the *krater* (mixing vessel), the vessel of spiritual transformation." "The *krater*," imparts Jung, "is a feminine principle which could find no place in Freud's patriarchal world."[16] Like Gnosticism, Alchemy was vigorously suppressed.

Alice Walker was influenced by both Jung and Pagels. The philosophy of Gnosticism, particularly in its mystical and alchemical aspects, is the underground river that courses through the narrative of *By the Light*, only here and there revealing itself. Encoded in the names of her characters and in the archetypal imagery that pervades the novel is the tension between Gnosticism and orthodox Christianity and its suppression of the divine feminine in tandem with its suppression of the voice, figure, and sexuality of woman.

MAKING THE UNKNOWN KNOWN

Mr. Robinson is a character without a first name. A first name describes a person's primary identity "on a day-to-day basis," and is a powerful expression of one's personality traits and destiny.[17] The lack of a first name speaks to Robinson's lack of a distinct identity, and consequently, his inability to be self-directed. His condition is what Gnosticism describes as "'roadlessness,' not knowing where to go."[18] He is also without "the spark" that, according to Gnosticism, is necessary for his personal transformation and unification with the divine whole.

Other than "father," Robinson is only ever referred to as Señor Robinson. "Señor" is Spanish for "sir" or "senior," and translates into "lord" and "master." Señor functions as Robinson's given name. Thus, on a day-to-day basis, Señor Robinson identified as someone of superior ranking and as lord and master. His surname, a variation of Robert, inherently means "Bright in Counsel" and carries the spiritual connotation of "Abiding in God."[19]

Robinson's elder daughter Magdalena recalls the biblical Mary Magdalene. "Magdalene" identifies Mary as being "from the town of Magdala."[20] She figures in the canonical gospels of the New Testament as a staunch follower and supporter of Jesus, the Christ, and one who bears witness to his crucifixion and resurrection. The aspersions cast on the character of Mary Magdalene as whore and prostitute are configured into the characterization of Magdalena in By the Light. In her father's eyes, Magdalena is a whore. But in Manuelito's arms, she is sacred.

Awakened to the divine within her, Magdalena christened herself June, after the Roman Goddess Juno. Associated with love, marriage, and the moon, Juno, "the Three-in-One deity cognate with 'yoni' and Uni-verse," was embodied in every woman, "her own soul a juno."[21] Magdalena embraced her sacred self and her sexual passion. She ignored her father's judgment of her when she deliberately set out to meet Manuelito in broad daylight, as if to signal her intent to no longer be cast, in his dark drama, as a shadowy woman of the night.

Just who Mary Magdalene was in relation to Jesus and her role in the new dispensation was contested in her time as in modern times. Where the New Testament gospels portray her as a faithful follower of Christ, the Gnostic gospels of Mary portray her as "the model disciple."[22] The Gnostic gospels narrate the events depicted in the New Testament, providing additional detail. In The Gospel of Mary the disciples dispute Mary Magdalene's relationship to Christ and resist her authority to convey his teachings. Where Andrew questioned the validity of her teachings, Peter rejected Mary Magdalene altogether: "Did he, then, speak with a woman in private without our knowing about it?" contended Peter. "Are we to turn around and listen to her? Did he choose her over us?" Levi defended Mary Magdalene and reasoned with Peter: "For if the Savior made her worthy, who are you then for your part to reject her? Assuredly the Savior's knowledge of her is completely reliable. That is why he loved her more than us."[23]

In By the Light, the idea that Mary Magdalene was not only a model disciple but an intimate companion or wife of Christ is suggested in the literal and symbolic partnering of Magdalena with Manuelito. "Manuelito," is the Spanish derivation of "the Hebrew name Emanuel."[24] The book of Matthew indicates that Emmanuel is one of the names of the Christ: "Behold, a virgin shall be with child, and shall bring forth a son, and they shall call his name Em-man'-u-el, which being interpreted is, God with us."[25]

Like his biblical counterpart, Manuelito is respectful of women and their power. He has self-knowledge, is one with nature, and he understands the spirit realm. As Jesus, in The Gospel of Mary, taught Mary Magdalene about the nature of the material world and the ascent of the soul, so Manuelito taught Magdalena. He also enlightened Señor Robinson about the sacred nature of his daughter and the feminine principle in nature, while also assisting Robinson with his soul's ascent through the afterlife.

Walker also uses the literary technique of twinning in sounding the mythic and historical dimensions of her characters. Susannah was the psychic twin to her sister Magdalena. As they are joined as sisters in the novel, Susannah and Magdalena are joined as Christian sisters in the New Testament. Among the women who ministered to Christ along with Mary Magdalene was "Su-san'-na, and many others."[26] Susannah's character may also be informed by Susanna in the apocryphal chapter of the Old Testament book of Daniel where Susanna was subjected to the voyeuristic surveillance of two elders who failed in their attempts to seduce her.[27]

In the novel, Susannah is married to Petros. Their relationship is seen against the backdrop of ancient Greek culture and Western civilization. In the Greek village of Skidiza where Petros was born, Susannah meets Irene, the village pariah. Irene represents those aspects of Petros's history and culture of which he feels ashamed. Many women had been stoned "before they got their vaunted 'democracy' in these parts," Irene told Susannah. She informed Susannah about the stoning pillars at the top of the cliff beyond the church. Her own mother had been stoned there. "They say," she told Susannah, "that even a hundred years ago, the base of it was still pink from blood."[28]

Petros angrily denied this bloody history and complained that his wife should think of such things. He complained about women in general. "Whatever a woman was, was never enough, or right enough, for him."[29] Petros's attitude toward women resonated with that of Peter in the gospels. "Petros" is the Greek word for rock. And in the New Testament, Peter is spoken of as the rock upon which Jesus would build his church. The narrative in *By the Light* engages the statement and asks just how this was to come about. Would it come at the silencing of women? And because women, like Susannah, like Irene, like Magdalena would not be silenced, would it come at their demise?

Susannah is also paired with Pauline, her nomenological twin. Susannah's name is derived from Hebrew *Shoshana*, which means lily. Lily is Pauline's actual first name. Irene points out that Lily is a variation of Lilith, the forgotten, willful first wife of Adam. Lily, is the flower of the Goddess Lilith and indicative of her parthenogenetic capacity, "the self-fertilizing power of the yoni (vulva)." The meaning inherent in Lilith's name underscores the sexual nature of the conflict between Adam and Lilith, as "Adam tried to force Lilith to lie beneath him in the 'missionary position' favored by male-dominant societies." But Lilith refused and absconded to her home by the sea.[30] Lily Pauline's character expresses the psychological and sexual autonomy of Lilith. Lily Pauline left a marriage that she was tricked into, went to night school, and absconded to the navy.

Pauline's name is the feminine and adjectival form of Paul. As Irene explained him to Susannah, the apostle Paul was established as the authoritative voice of the orthodox church. It was in accordance with Paul's writings, or those purported to be his writings, that orthodox Christian patriarchs established the official attitude toward women, their treatment and place within the church, and by extension, in society. Pauline's character interrogates the symbolism of the biblical Paul and is the means through which the issue of church-sanctioned sexism is addressed.

THE WORK

Where Pauline had felt enslaved, Susannah felt "roadless"—until she encountered her angel, Irene. "Angel," from the Greek *angelos*, means "messenger."[31] Through conversation and Tarot readings, Irene conveyed messages that assisted Susannah on her path. Like Pauline's, Irene's character serves several functions. "Irene" is derived from the Greek "*eirene*, meaning 'peace.'"[32] As "Peace," Irene is one "of Aphrodite's three Horae" who danced the ritual of time (*hora*). She is the goddess whose temple crowned the acropolis at Constantinople, and in her Christian adaptation she is Saint Irene.[33] In *By the Light*, in her role as caretaker of the church and the church cemetery, she is a pagan priestess.

The pronunciation of Irene's name—"E-ree-ne"—articulates her connection with Saint Irenaeus. She serves as a foil to this church father who was instrumental in establishing the "universal," catholic, Christian church and determining the New Testament canon. Irenaeus aligned himself with church patriarchs on the "precepts of ecclesiastical discipline concerning women": "It is not permitted for a woman to speak in the church, nor is it permitted for her to teach, nor to baptize, nor to offer [the eucharist], nor to claim for herself a share in any *masculine* function—not to mention any priestly office."[34]

In the figure of a dwarf, Irene's character heightens the mythic and numinous quality of Walker's novel. In ancient Egypt and Greece, dwarfs were revered as gods or messengers of gods, and they functioned as psychopomps that served as protectors, helpers, angels, messengers, and guides to souls migrating to the realm of the afterlife or living souls moving through transitional stages in life. The distinguished place of dwarfs in ancient society, however, was the domain of male dwarfs.[35] Yet in her configuration of Irene, Walker invokes the divine and empowered heritages of dwarf, goddess, dancer, saint, and woman. And it is through Irene that Robinson hopes to recover his daughter.

Where Magdalena's spirit was broken, Susannah's was fractured. Under Irene's guidance, Susannah, like the mythic Psyche, had come to see her need of a lamp and a knife. She needed the light of awareness to interpret the image of the swords in the spread of Tarot cards, indicating that it was "time to cut the illusions." Susannah had suffered under the illusion that she had not suffered. She was also unaware that her spirit had "left her body long ago" when she closed the door against her father. "But now," Irene read, "it is as if you are calling to yourself, Susannah, Susannah, come back; come home."[36] To return to herself, Susannah, as with Pysche, had four tasks to achieve: understand that her father was neither God nor Godzilla; cut the marital contract that bound her to Petros; have compassion for her own suffering; and end her codependency with Magdalena whose sacred "Mad Dog spirit" had been transmuted into the viciousness of a Cerberus.

Throughout her ventures, Susannah, like Psyche, was accompanied by the spirit of Eros, "Bisexual Greek deity of erotic love." Plato had praised Eros as "the oldest of deities . . ., the one who gave souls strength to ascend heaven after death." He was perceived as "a kind of Savior, before cults of asceticism began to replace the older worship of sexuality as a primary life-force."[37] Susannah had experienced the power of erotic love with Pauline. "Without our relationship," she tells Pauline, "I would never have known how far away I was from what could be. What heights of spirit one might reach through such a physical act. No wonder the church has demonized it."

Though she experienced the bliss of sex, Susannah was always peering through the mist of her orgasm, "seeking what is essentially beyond it."[38] As Psyche was required to cut through the illusion that she could live ignorantly blissful with Eros, Susannah needed to extricate herself from "the muddled territory of the blissfully deluded."[39] Irene had been the only living soul to see the spirit fracture Susannah had suffered. She was there to "properly set" the fracture, but Susannah was responsible for saving her own soul. "What does it mean, being saved?" Susannah asked. "I think it means becoming aware," Irene says. "And what this card says is that you are gaining that possibility."[40]

THE PHILOSOPHICAL EGG

The characters in Walker's By the Light of My Father's Smile embody the pathos and pleasures inherent in the human condition. Whether alive or in the afterlife, there is the work to be done. Susannah's journey suggests that the willingness to become aware, to know, is the beginning of spiritual maturity. In her "marriage" to experimentation and transformation, Susannah's journey reflects the processes of alchemical Gnosticism. Gnosticism and alchemy account not only for the metamorphosis of Walker's characters, but also for the graphic sexual imagery and attention to death that pervades the novel.

While engaged in the Gnostic enterprise of revelation—making the unknown known—Alice Walker does so, paradoxically, by utilizing the stylistics of secrecy. Where both Gnostics and alchemists mythologized their doctrines and drew on the literary device of allegory, the writings of alchemists were more systematically and heavily encrypted. In the outset of their science, alchemists employed the coded language of Decknamen to openly hide their experimentations. "Decknamen" means "cover names." Lawrence Principe writes in The Secrets of Alchemy that decknamens allowed "for discreet communication among those having the knowledge or intelligence to decipher the system. They simultaneously conceal and reveal."[41]

During the Middle Ages, the figurative descriptions that marked the writings of both scientific and philosophical alchemists became highly complex, and the sexual imagery in these works became "shocking or outlandish." Sexuality, sexual intercourse, and reproduction "are among the most universal and common experiences of human beings," writes Principe, and so would have been a natural source for a scientific practice whose "aim is to give rise to new substances or new properties by combining existing ones." The same was true in relation to death. "Thus death, with all the attendant Christian doctrines of the departure of the soul and of final resurrection, appears in alchemical imagery as prominently as sex."[42]

Sex and sexuality in *By the Light* signify more than alchemical and philosophical truths and theorems. They symbolize the very fire that is essential to alchemical transmutation and transformation. Principe's discussion of the *Opus Magnum* highlights the critical role of the alchemist in regulating the heat, a part of the process "sometimes called 'women's work and children's play.' But this duty," Principe made clear, "like 'women's work' . . . actually constitutes an enormous burden of labor. . . . The early modern chymist had only carefully sized pieces of charcoal added at regular and frequent intervals day and night, and the manipulation of the air vents on brick or iron furnaces, to maintain and control the heat."[43]

By the Light looks at the ways in which women, across time, have stoked the embers and rekindled the flames that ignite personal growth and societal transformation. It looks into the fire of sex as a uniquely feminine force that corresponds with the primacy of the feminine principle in nature. And it advances a womanist-alchemical perspective, encoded in the description of pottery making among the Mundo women. The women used three colors: "the red of earth, which was the pot itself and came from the local clay; the black of charcoal; and the white of lime, used as decoration, which after baking in the fire was not white but gray."[44]

The colors described are the "primary colors" of alchemy. In his discussion of these basic colors, Principe notes their symbolism and standard order: Black or *nigredo* represents decomposition, putrefaction, and death—"the beginning of the work" of combining materials. White or *albedo* represents the state of purification attained after material substances have mutated through a variety of colors called "the peacock's tail." This phase yields the White Elixir or the White Philosophers' Stone. And red or *rubedo* signifies success—attainment of the Red Elixir or the Red Philosophers' Stone which transforms base metals to gold or, for the philosophical alchemist, signifies attainment of spiritual salvation or enlightenment.[45]

Significantly, Walker changed the order of these colors. The Mundo women do not begin their work with death, but with life. They work with the living, fertile red clay of Earth. They knead the red clay to form the pots that store the food and drink of their people. Potters, are among the first alchemists, and theirs is a "life-sustaining craft."[46] In rearranging the primary colors, Walker restores women to a primary position in human culture and society. She simultaneously pays homage to Maria Judaea or Mary the Jewess, "the first great alchemist," and to other women alchemists who were persecuted as witches.[47]

Langley and Susannah both studied pottery making. Where Susannah was awed and fascinated, Langley had contemplated the process from an anthropological stance: "There was in building a pot a distinct feeling of prayer. . . . [F]rom watching their mothers make pots, primitive man would assume God made men from clay. Though why, seeing their mothers' work they'd think God male, she could not grasp."[48] Langley's insights, like her instincts, were keen, but she did not adhere to them. She was a woman who lived in the shadow of her husband. Langley's name means "from the long meadow." And like a meadow at the foot of a towering mountain, she lay in the shadow cast by Señor Robinson. Innately peaceful, Langley became subdued, like a fire whose flame had been dowsed.[49]

Through Susannah, the sovereignty of woman is reasserted and the fire rekindled. It is at his funeral that Susannah began to come out from her father's shadow. "That night. Eating a pomegranate seed by seed beside the fire, she did not miss me," Robinson noted. "She felt rather as if something heavy and dark, something she could never explain, had rolled away, off her soul."[50] Yet Susannah's soul had left her. Retrieving it was her path home. Where Psyche was challenged with the task of sorting a pile of seeds in order to regain her lost love, Susannah had the task of eating the seeds of a pomegranate, one by one, to regain her soul.

"The pomegranate with its red juice and many seeds was a prime symbol of uterine fertility. Therefore pomegranates were eaten by souls in the underworld, to bring about rebirth."[51] Symbols of the primal feminine were essential aspects of religious iconography. "The Bible says the pillars of Solomon's temple were ornamented with the female-genital symbols of lilies and pomegranates."[52] That Susannah eats a pomegranate not only suggests that living in someone's shadow is tantamount to being in the underworld, but it also speaks to the nature of the work she must engage in, if she is to reignite her divine spark. The fire, beside which she eats the fruit, reflects her emerging flame.

Having experienced a kind of apprenticeship among the Mundo women, Susannah would correlate the alchemist's fire that stimulates mutation and transformation with the fire generated through sexual passion. Susannah's mother knew something of "the fire of life" inherent in the body, but it smoldered beneath the dark clothing she wore in her role as pastor's wife. Susannah's father was very much aware of the power of sex as a primal life-force. However, he perceived sex as a male prerogative and more as a force to control within himself and others rather than a force that reveals, transforms, and unifies.

Robinson's path to a more cosmic understanding of sexuality began with his desire for Susannah to live a life that included sexual ecstasy. He is initiated into a liberating *gnosis* once he enters the cave, the womb of the mother, and fathoms that making love is making life. Like the prisoners in Plato's allegorical cave who were deceived by the flames behind them, Robinson learned to discern reality from illusion. His growing understanding of the feminine principle in nature, as in all life, waxed like the moon into its fullness. And in this light, the long-cast shadow of the orthodox church withdrew. In this light, Robinson reclaimed the name "Father" and could embrace a now-transcendent Magdalena as the daughter he loved.[53]

THE DANCE OF LIFE

The title of Walker's novel implies her embrace of the Egyptian origins of the term "alchemy." "In Arabic, alchemy meant 'matter of Egypt,' Al-Khemeia, from Khemennu, 'Land of the Moon,' an old name for Egypt."[54] *By the Light of My Father's Smile* (Por la luz de la sonrisa de mi padre), the novel's title, is the refrain of the initiation song of the Mundo people, whose name means the earth or the world. The song refers to the moon, the symbol of feminine, regenerative energy. In its crescent phase, the moon smiles an invitation to the masculine principle to enter into sacred and harmonious participation in the rhythm of life.

Like substances combined in a *krater*—the glass vessel or "the philosophical egg" of alchemy—the African-Amerindian Mundo people, evolved a cohesive, syncretic culture and a society that radiated love and valued wisdom. Their way of life is portrayed as a response to the questions that initially compelled Robinson to live among them: "How to organize life in a better way than the white man has. How to live in a way that permitted others to live as well."[55]

As the Mundo can be seen to offer a life-affirming mode of social organization, Susannah's journey can be seen as a woman's successful escape from "the general pressing down of life that passes for the male notion of civilization."[56] Susannah's quest for spiritual and sexual freedom was first quickened in Kalimasa, the town she visited in the outset of the novel. The town reverberated with the primordial energy of Kālī Ma. And the "winged mermaids, their bronze scales dusted with gold" evoked the presence of Aphrodite. There, in the village of Wodra, Susannah gifted herself with a ring. "Black onyx, an oval shape. Its sides splashed with gold."[57] Afterwards, she ventured beyond the town, as far as the Elephant Walk.

What she began to remember and to dream thereafter had opened her up to "the dance of life."[58] Susannah died dreaming of Anand, Petros's dancing brother, who was also her lover. To die while dreaming of Anand, whose name is akin to "Ananda," meaning bliss or joy, implies Susannah's transcendent state. She had rekindled the divine spark that was reflected in the ceremonial fire that engulfed her body. Her soul, mingled with the smoke of the fire, rose up into the aether.

SECTION IV

Water

*C*osmic moisture. Swirling mists of hydrogen and oxygen, Water is the alpha and omega of divinity and creation. Spreading everywhere, it births infinity and is the language of eternity. Defying separation, water unifies. The vapors of heaven merge with the waters of ocean at the "altar of God."[1] Water meanders West. Nurturing, sensual, introspective. It is identity, itself. An element of initiation, water activates and inspires all. And it shimmers blue, luminously.[2]

Water is sacred. Within its mysteries abide life, death, birth. Water purifies and cleanses and invigorates. It quenches thirst and dissolves density. Troubled, water is fierce and formidable, as implacable in destruction as it is inexorable in creation. Water, resolute, carves canyons through mountains. Compassionate, water soothes, lolls, and buoys. It is the "Great wetness." Its numinous fluidity encircles egg, sperm, and seed. Water empowers creation to taste life.[3]

"All water is one—one whole, one awareness. All water is continuously aware of all the other water in the world."[4] Thus, water claims humanity as its own. Pouring over rock, eddying at the knees of trees, trickling from fissures, water teaches acceptance, ease, destiny.[5] Its ebb and flow demonstrates reciprocity, giving and receiving, renewing and returning. Mutable, water appreciates tears. Relentless, it is the wisdom of sweat. Mingling with blood, it knows balance and restraint. Water evaporates, teaching temporality and uselessness of a grudge. In its capacity to float whatever is cast upon it, water invites surrender. The face of water is mirror. Its reflection transcending duality, it is the mother of philosophy, teaching humans to swim.

"My Body Is a Farm"
(For My Son)
by Phyllis McEwen

I never noticed when the breasts grew in;
There was always the backward memory of bras
That cut my shoulders like knives
promising to slice me and feed someone
before I was present to it.
And not needing any milk myself, gave freely
letting it run when they sang "Precious Lord!"
In church my baby nestled
snug asleep.
Who was calling for this milk I asked a Jesus thought
and realized I am
not ready to be this food.

It is not an easy thing to be made into hay,
to be somebody's lunch and quiet time
purchased with the change in a free man's
pocket.

Demons sense the nipples first, then
moving to the aureole sun-thing
that colors the world worse
than any eyes ever have,
what they see is jugs of milk
dangling from a proud chest that chose Female
not really knowing all the consequences but
hurrying to taste the prizes,
Knowing
there were prizes.

I can never deny the happy thumping of my heart:
It was my heat breaking.
When they laid him on my chest
I saw my true love,
A squirming, uncomfortable, angry man,
small but unencumbered.
He would draw in rage like a tuber,
Gather strength from the space around my knees,
Breathe life into life.

I worship you in secret;
Tell no one of my devotion.
Send you small but constant prayers.
Brag about your beautiful cleansing;
The way you swallowed a name, found it inside my promise,
Labeled me Mama, and proceeded with the process.
In the hospitals of light, forgiveness and sin
You folded your other-self away
because the body
had finally taken control.

SIXTEEN

Mbele Aché

In *Possessing the Secret of Joy*, the suppression of the feminine principle is symbolized in the demonization of the vulva—and the woman who has one. This demonization is dramatized in the life experience of Tashi Evelyn Johnson Soul. Interwoven monologues of other characters add dimensions and perspectives that connect her one life to the cosmic whole. Her perspective, like that of Mr. Robinson in *By the Light of My Father's Smile*, is told from the realm of the afterlife.

Early chapters convey that Tashi Evelyn has been executed by a firing squad. She had been found guilty of depriving the people of a "national monument," their "Grandmother of the race!"[1] Anticipating her execution, Tashi Evelyn was as collected as Meursault, in Camus's *The Stranger*, who had been found guilty of murder and awaited the guillotine. But Tashi was not indifferent. And where Meursault felt washed clean of hope, Tashi was a symbol of hope.

She was more like Kaliayev, in Camus's *Just Assassins*, who was held in a tower at Butiriki Prison, condemned to death for the assassination of the Grand Duke Serge. Finished with life and having squared his accounts with death, Kaliayev "walked quite calmly to the scaffold."[2] In similar attitude, Tashi Evelyn Johnson faced death. "There is nothing more of this life I need to see," she said.[3] Refusing the blindfold so that she could spy the distant blue hill of eternity, Tashi awaited the roar that would split open the world.

IN THE BEGINNING. . . .

Tashi was taboo. Among the Olinka, it was customary that females undergo the initiation ceremony of circumcision shortly after birth or by the onset of puberty. Contrary to custom, Tashi was uncircumcised. It meant that she still possessed her external female genitalia—her vulva. For this she was ridiculed. To Tashi's age-mates, her uncircumcised vulva was a monstrosity. "After all, none of them had vaginal lips; none of them had a clitoris." Only a few other girls were uncircumcised. "The girls who had been would sometimes actually run from us, as if we were demons."[4]

Tashi was caught in the cultural clash between Africa and Europe, between Western religions and the traditions of the Olinka. Along with the loss the Olinka suffered as Europeans colonized one village then the next, Tashi was also losing her sense of self. To save what was left of her, she felt compelled to save what was left of the Olinka, which meant joining the rebel Mbele. Doing so would prove that her relationship with the African American missionaries Adam and Olivia had not made her a potential traitor. To become an Olinka warrior meant keeping all of the old ways, including the initiation rites. Facial scarification and circumcision seemed all that was left to Tashi in claiming her identity as an Olinkan, as a woman, as a human being.

Tashi's dream of running and leaping to the attack of the enemy, however, was halted by the wound tradition had given her. At the Mbele encampment, Tashi lay on a grass mat, "her head and shoulders propped against a boulder." She was suffering the wounds of her facial scars and the trauma of a pharaonic circumcision. Her legs, ashen and wasted, were bound.[5] Adam had crawled to where she lay and gathered in his arms all the parts of her he could reach.

Tashi had renounced her friendship with Adam and Olivia though they had been childhood friends and Adam had been her lover. In her patriotic zeal, she had come to see them as "the white people's wedge."[6] But in her suffering, it was Adam who came for her. Though Tashi and Adam would marry and begin life anew in America, their lives would be subject to the effects of the circumcision and the long-cast shadow of the circumciser, the tsunga M'Lissa.

The character of Tashi appears first in *The Color Purple*. Young, nubile, and spirited, hers is a minor role. In *Possessing the Secret of Joy*, Tashi's story takes center stage. Her youthful spirit has been subdued as her motherland had been pacified. The ostracism she endures and the consequences of the circumcision factors into a lifetime of anxiety for which Tashi would undergo psychoanalytic treatment. In monologues from the beyond and in dialogues with her therapists, Tashi expresses her anguish and rage as she struggled to define herself.

She had been a wife and a mother and in both roles she suffered traumatizing emotional and physical pain consequent to the circumcision. Tashi required fifteen minutes to urinate. Ten days to complete her menses. M'Lissa had fastened the raw sides of Tashi's vagina "with a couple of thorns and insert[ed] a straw so that in healing, the traumatized flesh might not grow together, shutting the opening completely." The small opening slowed the menstrual flow, causing severe cramps and stagnation and stench.[7]

Pleasure during sex was impossible anymore. "After three months of trying," Tashi's spirit said to anyone listening, "he had failed to penetrate me. Each time he touched me I bled. Each time he moved against me I winced. There was nothing he could do to me that did not hurt."[8] Thus her pregnancy was perceived as an "immaculate conception," but the miracle of Benny was cause for alarm rather than celebration. After an excruciating delivery, Tashi had to reshape Benny's head while worrying about the trauma to his brain. And her obstetrician was challenged to figure out what to do about "the hole." "My doctor sewed me up again, much as I'd been fastened originally," Tashi said into the aether, "because otherwise there would have been a yawning unhealable wound."[9]

NIGREDO: THE DARK TOWER

Tashi's physical pain correlated with her emotional and psychological pain. She was anxious, depressed, neurotic, and psychotic. Her first therapist excelled more in imitating "the father of psychoanalysis," Sigmund Freud, than in curing Tashi's neurosis.[10] He nevertheless compelled Tashi's attention with the declaration that "Negro women . . . can never be analyzed effectively because they can never bring themselves to blame their mothers . . . for anything."[11] Beyond this provocative statement, the sessions yielded little as the therapist could not ascertain the *prima materia*, the material essential to psychoanalytic treatment—Tashi's dreams. "I tell him I do not dream," Tashi lied. "I do not dare tell him about the dream I have every night that terrifies me."[12]

What little he knew about her dreams was derived from his interview with Adam:

> There is a tower, she says. I think it is a tower. It is tall, but I am inside. I don't really ever know what it looks like from outside. It is cool at first, and as you descend lower and lower to where I'm kept, it becomes dank and cold, as well. It's dark. There is an endless repetitive sound that is like the faint scratch of a baby's fingernails on paper. And there are millions of things moving about me in the dark. I can not see them. And they've broken my wings! I see them lying crossed in a corner like discarded oars. Oh, and they're forcing something in one end of me, and from the other they are busy pulling something out. I am long and fat and the color of tobacco spit. Gross! And I can not move![13]

The obstetrician addressed Tashi's gaping physical wound, but the gap in her mind, between actuality and fantasy widened. The physical wound that the doctor feared might become unhealable manifested in Tashi as the archetypal psychic "wound that does not heal." Carl Jung named this condition "the Amfortas wound," based on the Arthurian legend of "a 'fisher king' whose wound would not heal."[14] Such wounding symbolized a schism, a split in the psyche or a repression of some aspect of the self that undermines the whole.

Carl Jung is fictionalized in *Possessing the Secret of Joy* as Mzee, The Old Man who embodies Walker's conception of the ideal therapist. His philosophy and psychology informs the narrative. And Jung's Bollingen Tower hermitage in Switzerland, with its rising turrets, becomes the womb of Tashi's psychic rebirth.

PEACOCK-BLUE SKY GODDESS NUT: *MAGNUM OPUS*

At the end of his career, Mzee honors the request of his niece Lisette, who is Adam's lover, to take Tashi as his client. Mzee invites Adam and Tashi to his hermitage. In the care of the "pinkfaced witchdoctor" at Bollingen, Tashi confronts her shadow.[15] Viewing a film from one of Mzee's African expeditions, she is terrified by the image of a large fighting cock. The image triggers a flood of memories that leave Tashi in a faint upon the floor. Unable to verbally communicate, she paints her distress onto the walls of her guest bedroom in the turret. From the bowels of her unconscious, she draws "The Beast," the cock that loomed in her mind.

With "The Beast," she painted a foot and a fold of cloth designed in a "crazy road" pattern.[16] In the protective environs of the Tower at Bollingen, Tashi was empowered to look the beast in its menacing eye:

> It no longer frightened me. Indeed, I felt as if I were seeing the cause of my anxiety itself for the first time, exactly as it was. The cock was undeniably overweening, egotistical, puffed up, and it was his diet of submission that had made him so.[17]

Tashi stared into "the wicked gaze" of the creature she penned in glaring strokes onto the walls, but she shuttered before the synecdoche of foot and cloth that summoned the spectral M'Lissa and the cache of forbidden memory over which M'Lissa presided.

As she painted, Tashi remembered the day she had hidden in the elephant grass, near the hut where her sister Dura and her age-mates were undergoing the initiation of circumcision. She heard the "howls of pain and terror" that came from the hut. As Dura was not among the "dazed row of little girls" that Tashi could see in her mind's eye, the screams emanating from the hut could only have been those of her sister. But Tashi could not have heard the "howls of pain and terror," because taboo dictated that Tashi was not there. Just as taboo required her to expunge from her vision M'Lissa's lame foot flinging the excised, "unclean," part of her sister to the witless fowl that "in one quick movement of beak and neck, gobbled it down."[18]

Dura had not simply, passively, died. "I took a deep breath and exhaled it against the boulder blocking my throat. . . . I remembered my sister Dura's *murder*," said Tashi, "exploding the boulder."[19] This was the beginning of the avalanche to come. In anticipation of his death, Mzee had arranged for Tashi to continue her therapy with Raye. An African American woman who knew little about circumcision, Raye studiously learned about it and empathized deeply with Tashi, which allowed Tashi to continue The Work. But even as the boulders dislodged, the energy of ambivalence, of desire and prohibition, intensified and discharged itself as suicidal and homicidal thoughts. Small acts of violence. Eventually, the killing of the *tsunga*.

Tashi had watched M'Lissa from the blind of the elephant grass. But the elephant grass, too, was witness and portent. Grass symbolizes renewed growth, fuller mental or spiritual development, and protection. And elephants are known for their exceptional memory and they never forget someone who has injured them. "They have been known to seek revenge if the opportunity presented itself."[20] As if assisted by the elephant hair bracelets she fingered on her wrist while talking with Raye, Tashi's repressed memories of everyone and everything involved in Dura's death gave themselves up. Even the boulder that covered up Tashi's responsibility in her own wounding rolled away.

But Tashi's conscious memories could not unravel the mystery of her nightmare. "A psychology of consciousness can, to be sure, content itself with material drawn from personal life, but as soon as we wish to explain a neurosis we require an anamnesis which reaches deeper than the knowledge of consciousness."[21] Everyone committed to Tashi's well-being formed a collective of support that assisted Tashi with the anamnesis—the recollection of experiences that were pristine and that reached beyond her conscious memory.

Pierre was a keystone figure in the collective's communal structure. He was the son of Adam and Lisette. Since childhood and throughout his academic studies and his career as an anthropologist, Pierre had gathered information and conducted research toward the end of interpreting and understanding the primordial image of the dark tower that haunted Tashi's life. During their exploration of the countryside beyond the prison where Tashi was held, Pierre, Adam, and Benny discovered the natural symbol that correlated with the figurative tower of Tashi's nightmares. They captured on film the small and towering termite structures that resembled huts in an African village.

Tashi immediately made the connection. Excerpts Pierre had read to Tashi from *Conversations with Ogotemmêli* floated up to her conscious mind. Ogotemmêli, a Dogon priest, had said that the God Amma created the earth from clay and that the vertical line of the earth was female and the anthill was its sexual organ and the termite hill was its clitoris. "At God's approach the termite hill rose up, barring the passage and displaying its masculinity. It was as strong as the organ of the stranger, and intercourse could not take place. But God is all-powerful. He cut down the termite hill, and had intercourse with the excised earth. But the original incident was destined to affect the course of things forever. . . ."[22]

The Olinka had apparently been influenced by the neighboring Dogon whose knowledge of their insect kin was integral to their cosmology. "This, Madame Johnson," says Pierre, observing the projected image, "is your dark tower." *She* was the queen who loses her wings and lies in the dark surrounded by millions of worker termites who stuff her with food at one end while continuously removing her eggs, "millions of them," at the other end. It was she who had been reduced to "a tube through which generations of visionless offspring pass," only to die at the end of it, "and be devoured by those to whom you've given birth."[23]

Seeing the termite tower was like seeing "The Beast." This time, though, Tashi does not faint. In a trance-like vision, she is transported to a scene from her early life, a child amidst the male elders of her village. Insignificant and therefore invisible to them, Tashi serves them water and food while they chant their esoteric knowledge about the prerogative of God and man, the role of woman as "Queen" and as *tsunga*—the helpmeet of God. "They were discussing her, determining her life. And at the time she did not, could not, know. And yet, there in her unconscious had remained the termite hill, and herself trapped deep inside it, heavy, wingless and inert, the Queen of the dark tower."[24]

Tashi's time at Bollingen Tower had prepared her for the meaning of the dark tower. In pairing the Tower at Bollingen with the tower of terror in Tashi's nightmare, Alice Walker illustrated the Jungian principle of *coniunctio*—the combining of opposites, which was "the major concern of 'philosophical' alchemy."[25] In the combining of opposites, one achieved a third, transcendent element.

SUNRISE: *MBATI* MEANS "THE HOPE OF WHOLENESS"

In the Arthurian Grail legend, The Fisher King, Amfortas, was wounded in the thigh or genital area, symbolizing suppression of the masculine principle. Amfortas's wound corresponds with Tashi's circumcision and symbolizes suppression of the feminine principle. The Amfortas wound is a metaphor for the psychic split inherent in all humanity. This psychic wound in the Fisher King could be healed only when an innocent lad—Parsifal—posed the appropriate question: "Whom does the grail serve?"[26] But like Tashi, Parsifal was forbidden by his mother to ask any questions. It was taboo. As long as he blindly submitted to the taboo, he was doomed to wonder and blunder through his labyrinthine life, fighting one war and slaying one dragon after another. But once he found his tongue and asked the question, the wound of the king healed and the erstwhile wasteland that was his kingdom, flourished.

Likewise, Tashi was doomed to wander the dark towers of her nightmares until she dislodged the stones that held her tongue and reclaimed her innocence. Tashi's psychic wound, could not be healed until she posed the primary question of the novel: "*Why is the child crying?*"—which begged the question, Whom did female circumcision serve?[27] Tashi's questions opened an internal space of healing that generated outward, creating the possibility of wholeness for her spiritual daughter Mbati and generations to come. Her questions broke taboo and ended the reign of blind submission, of unconscious existence.

Pierre is made in the image of Parsifal, a mythological "helper," who assists Tashi on her journey. Pierre's character is polyvalent. Professionally, he contrasts Mr. Robinson in *By the Light of My Father's Smile*. They are both anthropologists. Where Mr. Robinson's work as an anthropologist was compromised by his entanglement in the cloth, Pierre represents the apotheosis of his discipline. Psychologist Ludwig Feuerbach stated that " 'theology is really anthropology' (the term derives, of course, from *anthropos*, and means 'study of humanity')."[28] Gnostic Christians believed that "when God revealed himself, He revealed himself in the form of *Anthropos*." "*Anthropos*" was understood as "the underlying nature of that collective entity, the archetype, or spiritual essence, of human being." Where Robinson became a man of the cloth, Pierre manifested as "Son of *Anthropos*."[29]

THE LANTERN: NYNANDA

"Pierre," like "Petros" in *By the Light*, means stone. In alchemy stones are sacred and mystical; they hold celestial secrets. They are conveyers of knowledge and light and are emblems of eternity. In *Possessing*, stones constitute a singular motif. They function as a kind of mineral totem that connects Tashi and Pierre, as they also connect Tashi—through Pierre-to Lisette (who enacts the role of a second wife). At Pierre's birth, Tashi began to collect stones. At the first sight of Pierre, she pelted him with stones she had stockpiled by the steps of her home. For his part, Pierre knew Tashi's condition and did not judge the violence she directed toward him. He continued his ardent pursuit of information that would help her to remove the boulders that blocked her memory.

Pierre is also the spiritual reflection of the biblical Peter and he is presented in *Possessing* as the rock upon which a re-envisioned society—a society that remembers its divine heritage as *Anthropos*—can be built. As he is the son that Tashi would have rejected, Pierre is also the cornerstone in the life Tashi was refashioning in her own image, as from the bag of clay given her by Mzee. Pierre's role as cornerstone evokes the cornerstone that stands slightly to the left of the path that leads to the actual Towers of Bollingen. And Pierre's characterization resonates with the image and inscription Jung carved into this stone.

Jung recounted in his memoir that the cornerstone for the foundation of his retreat home had been improperly cut. Yet he kept the stone rather than return it. On the front face of the stone, Jung carved a circle and in the center or "eye" of the stone, he "made a tiny homunculus. This corresponds to the 'little doll' (*pupilla*)—yourself—which you see in the pupil of another's eye."[30] On her visit to Bollingen, Alice Walker was photographed touching this cornerstone. The photograph became the basis of a painting of the cornerstone whose image graced the book cover of *Possessing*.

Carl Jung perceived his cornerstone in light of "the alchemist's stone, the *lapis*, which is despised and rejected." The homunculus at its center symbolized the inner *Anthropos*, the soul. Around this figure Jung chiseled a quotation from alchemy:

> Time is a child—playing like a child—playing a board game—the kingdom of the child. This is Telesphoros, who roams through the dark regions of this cosmos and glows like a star out of the depths. He points the way to the gates of the sun and to the land of dreams.[31]

Telesphorus, which means "accomplisher," was the dwarf son of Asclepius and the Greek god of health and convalescence. He was invoked to "restore to full health the person who is ready to receive him."[32]

Pierre and his great uncle Mzee share a relationship analogous to Telesphorus and Asclepius. And Pierre, in stature and temperament, embodies the attributes of Telesphorus. Much is made of Pierre's small stature. His mother called him "petite Pierre." His father assessed him as "petit (for a man)." Tashi described him as "absurdly small for a man," "skinny and short, as if still a child."[33] Pierre is diminutive like Jung's homunculus. Pierre is versed in the healing arts as is Telesphorus. He personifies the spirit of philosophical alchemy and expresses that spirit when he combines his efforts with those of others in helping Tashi step out from the shadow of the unconscious—guised as tradition—into the light of her authentic Self.

The light of knowledge Pierre brings, like the lantern Telesphorus carries against the darkness, is the light of awareness. Tashi's work with the imitative Freud, Mzee, Raye, and Pierre performs a "transcendent function," allowing Tashi to see. Though the success of the first therapist was minimal, it was nonetheless significant. His statement, that black mothers might be blamed in relation to the wounded bodies and lives of their daughters, exposed a boulder over which Tashi had blindly stumbled. The statement had set off "a kind of explosion in the soft, dense cotton wool of [her] mind." The quiet explosion shifted a boulder, enabling her to pose an equally explosive question: "Blame them for what?"[34]

In *The Same River Twice*, Alice Walker notes a revelatory moment with her own mother. It became clear to Walker that homophobia factored into her mother's refusal to have *The Color Purple* read to her. "One of the most painful things for me to accept," wrote Walker, "has been my mother's fundamentalist Christian prejudice against many of the people and things I love. . . . This is the shadow side of her I can face even now only by calling on the most loving but determined spiritual force."[35] With *The Color Purple*, Walker had given people she loved an opportunity to see into the relationships of "women-loving women" and to see *her*. Having assessed her daughter as "a little mess," Mrs. Walker rejected this opportunity.

With a growing awareness of her condition, Tashi proved to be "a little mess," too, as she put the pillow over M'Lissa's face and lay across it for an hour. Neurotic and psychotic, Tashi was "unquestionably mad." However, just before she killed M'Lissa, Tashi was quite lucid. She took on the demeanor of the just assassin who kills, consciously. Tashi had awakened to the tyranny of custom and tradition and saw it personified in M'Lissa. Though Tashi felt her own life had been taken long ago and that M'Lissa was guilty in the theft, Tashi knew she could not keep the life she had begun to feel stirring inside her.

Tashi and M'Lissa were well matched; for the first time, they, too, saw each other clearly. Their incisive and blunt talk emboldened Tashi to ask every question required to unlock the meaning of her life, to break taboo and feel the full force of her woundedness, and tell the truth about all of it. In her unwillingness to submit to a life of lies or defend herself against the unjust act of killing M'Lissa or to do anything beyond beholding "the beauty of one blue hill in the distance," Tashi was alive and fully inhabited her body for the first time.[36]

Tashi's interrogation of M'Lissa had uncovered the absurd reality of Tashi's existence. It revealed the culpability of her mother Nafa (Catherine) and the trusted women elders of her village in Dura's death. Tashi and Lisette had both discovered their mothers to be collaborators in a ceremony that unceremoniously killed, maimed, and wounded the daughters of a people. "I recognized the connection between mutilation and enslavement that is at the root of the domination of women in the world," said Lisette. And she saw that women are mesmerized by "our unconscious knowledge of what men, with the collaboration of our mothers, do to us."[37]

Resistance was not a new idea for Tashi. She had resisted domination and tyranny all her life. Resistance was even the essence of her animal totem, her familiar—the leopard. Tashi's first drawings with Mzee were of the leopard that charged her pregnant mother, hastening her birth. "For this, after all, represented my birth. My entrance into reality," Tashi proclaimed.[38] Leopard signifies the reclamation of one's true power and its cycle of power rises with the new moon, which is to say, in darkness.[39] What Tashi discovered, as she reclaimed her power and dispelled the darkness, was the discernment of who and what to resist. Such wisdom charted the path to one's integrated Self—one's *elixir vitae*.

FIRE: DYEING TO LIFE—THE BIRTH OF THE SPIRIT

The blood-red dress Tashi insisted she must wear and the heat that would be generated by the blaze of weapons trained upon her, signaled completion of a process and triumph of a soul. It was not incidental that Tashi was executed on a soccer field. A sport esteemed by most of the world, soccer is said to mirror a society and to be an indicator of political and cultural attitudes. "Soccer is never just soccer: it helps make wars and revolutions, and it fascinates mafias and dictators."[40] On this field, Tashi was once again "in the territory of men," in the din of codified language that silenced women's songs.[41]

But the women had begun to decipher patriarchal codes and had created their own. The inner fire of Tashi's life transformed the color symbolism of the banner of the Olinka nation—the vivid yellow and blue, bleeding into the vivid red of the flag that Tashi had once saluted in blind patriotism. The colors now resonated the completion and confirmation of her Work. "Our Leader," who clamored for her death louder than anyone, was no longer her Christ. Having recognized "her own blood power," Tashi had christened the "territory of men" anew and baptized the red-beribboned babies that lined the path she walked.[42]

Through her careful portrayal of the physical, psychic, and spiritual anguish of Tashi Evelyn, Alice Walker makes it clear that black people do not joyfully "survive the suffering and humiliation inflicted upon them." Neither are women, contrary to Old Torabe's blind belief, "indestructible down there."[43] As there is "no happy community in which there [is] one unhappy child," Walker's novel crystallizes the fact that there is no happy tribe, people, nation, or world in which women are enslaved, dominated, repressed, or forced to leave the child within them on a mat, bloodied and screaming.[44]

As such human suffering demands acknowledgment and requires healing balm, Walker's novel initiates the reader into The Great Work that is to be done. Through Tashi's journey to psychic wholeness, Walker leads the reader through the process of individuation which makes possible the attainment of wholeness and the totality of the Self. Importantly, she demonstrates that the process is an essential one, for it is the individual thusly transformed who can contribute to a regenerated society. It is this individual, restored to wholeness and personal dignity, that is the best hope of a free, equal, and humanistic society. Such a society requires that one faithfully answer the question: *Why is the child crying?*

SEVENTEEN

Sub Rosa No Longer: Our Daughters Have Mothers

As though they too had stepped out from M'Lissa's shadow, actual African women and girls had found their tongues to speak about the cutting away of the tongue and lips between their thighs. They have spoken of the unspeakable losses they have suffered in relation to the rite of female circumcision. Alice Walker refers to this ritual as "female genital mutilation" ("FGM"). Pratibha Parmar calls it "ritualized violence."[1] The two women spoke out about this ritual in the documentary film *Warrior Marks* and the companion book *Warrior Marks: Female Genital Mutilation and the Sexual Blinding of Women.*[2]

Walker estimates the practice of FGM to be at least 6,000 years old. Upwards of one hundred million women and girls in Africa, Asia, and the Middle East have been subjected to this ancient practice of female genital mutilation.[3] Language is deceptive, however, as the descriptive "ancient" renders the thing described as remote, outdated, "past history." But, as James Baldwin contended, history "does not refer merely, or even principally to the past." For, we carry history within us and are unconsciously controlled by it; thus, "history is literally *present* in all that we do." Because it is history that informs our identities, "it is with great pain and terror that one begins to assess the history which has placed one where one is, and formed one's point of view. In great pain and terror because, thereafter, one enters into battle with that historical creation, Oneself, and attempts to re-create oneself according to a principle more humane and more liberating."

Achieving personal maturity and freedom, says Baldwin, "robs history of its tyrannical power, and also changes history."[4] The tyranny of history is also the tyranny of tradition and taboo. In *Warrior Marks*, Walker and Parmar "enter into battle" with the historical conception of women as profane and unnatural. They join their voices and efforts with those presented in the film and the book, on behalf of "the female child of Africa" to whom Walker dedicated the book. They enter into battle, too, on behalf of human personality, struggling to rouse itself from the weight of history and waken to its true nature as *Anthropos*.

For, as Walker and Parmar noted, "Any definitive and irremediable removal of a healthy organ is a mutilation. The female external genital organ normally is constituted by the vulva, which comprises the labia majora, the labia minora or nymphae, and the clitoris, covered by its prepuce, in front of the vestibule to the urinary meatus and the vaginal orifice. Their constitution in female humans is genetically programmed and is identically produced *in all embryos in all races*. The vulva is an integral part of the natural inheritance of humanity."[5] (Emphasis mine.) Thus, Walker and Parmar also enter battle on behalf of a future that supports the human species, extricated from repetitive cycles of unconscious and absurd self-destructive violence.

In spite of its antiquity and ubiquity, the ancient tradition of FGM remained relatively unknown beyond the societies in which it was practiced. Even within these societies, the origins and history of FGM remained obscured, as the topic was taboo. Some females are initiated as infants, so they are not likely to consciously recall the experience of initiation. "But of course they don't forget," says Walker, "The body does not forget pain."[6]

Older girls, four to eleven years of age, were cowed into silence by both taboo and intimidation. When refugee Aminata Diop told her story of escape from FGM in Mali, she had to tell it in a foreign tongue as "there are no words in her language with which to discuss female genital mutilation."[7]

In the years preceding her work on *Warrior Marks*, Alice Walker had committed herself to telling this "herstory." She committed herself to answering the question: Why is the female child of Africa crying? She had learned about female circumcision when working in Kenya, while still a student. Like the African American therapist Raye in *Possessing*, Walker professed she knew nothing about this practice. "[I]t was so completely beyond my experience at the time," said Walker, "I literally didn't understand what they meant."[8]

Communicating the enormity of the meaning of FGM through the novel *Possessing* proved to be whelming. "First of all," stated Walker, "it took a lot, twenty years or more, for me to decide to write it, because I wanted to be sure that it would be in a form that people could feel and not really get away from, and also in a form that . . . wouldn't intimidate anyone either." Walker had also anticipated a backlash to her daring in addressing the subject. So, in the parlance of Zora Neale Hurston, she said, "I dragged my feet for a long time."[9]

She knew that her whole life would change once the book was published. More compelling for Walker, however, were the heartrending screams of little girls that would go unheard. "I don't really care where the child is who's suffering," declared Walker. "I really don't. I just know that the child is suffering. That she's been held down and cut open. That she will never forget it. You know, you don't forget anything. You may not remember, but you don't forget."[10]

Also compelling for Walker was the unacknowledged suffering of females during the trafficking and enslavement of Africans. "As far as I'm concerned," she asserted, "I am speaking for my great-great-great-great grandmother who came here with all this pain in her body. Think about it. In addition to having been captured, put in the hull of a ship, packed like sardines, put on the auction block, in addition to her children being sold, she being raped, in addition to all of this, she might have been genitally mutilated. I can't stand it!" Walker channeled her grief for African women and girls in the past and present into her work. "I would go nuts if this part of her story weren't factored in. Imagine if men came from Africa with their penises removed. Believe me, we would have many a tale about it."[11]

In *Possessing*, Walker acknowledged and thanked a cadre of writers and activists for their work on FGM. She had envisioned *Possessing* as an invitation to collective organization around the subject, and had hoped the novel would strengthen the burgeoning anti-FGM movement. She was confident that "together we may be able to do something."[12] Walker and Parmar's *Warrior Marks* would serve to amplify the cause of African women and children in relation to FGM and the attending scourge of AIDS.

Even so, they were met with hostility. Some African women were categorically antithetical toward interventions into African affairs by Westerners. Parmar related that women across cultures and races demanded, "Have you thought about questions of cultural transference and cultural imperialism?" During the Decade for Women Conference in Nairobi, Kenya, African women attendees were indignant that Western feminists addressed the subject of FGM: "Stop groping about in our panties," was the collective outcry.[13]

Pratibha Parmar, a Hindu woman born in Kenya and living in London, was not insensible to the outcries. "Clearly," she wrote, "female genital mutilation is a painful, complex, and difficult issue, which involves questions of cultural and national identities, sexuality, human rights, and the rights of women and girls to live safe and healthy lives. But this complexity is not an excuse to sit by and do nothing. Who cares if African women and children are subjected to violence? *We should all care.*"[14] Even as some African women pushed back, others, like FORWARD International director Efua Dorkenoo, were receptive to Walker and Parmar and the support that their venture might generate.

Dorkenoo invited Walker to become matron of FORWARD (Foundation for Women's Health, Research and Development), the organization Dorkenoo founded in 1983. Its mission was the eradication of harmful traditional practices, including, and specifically, FGM. Malian political activist and author

Awa Thiam had also responded positively. Thiam had written *Speak Out, Black Sisters: Feminism and Oppression in Black Africa* (1978), one of the first books that expressed African women's concerns about FGM. Thiam agreed with Parmar that "what was happening to women in Africa should concern *all* women across the world."[15]

In *Speak Out*, Thiam spoke to the disingenuousness of female and male African intellectuals regarding FGM:

> They have the tendency to say that struggling for women's rights is something specifically for Western civilization and has nothing to do with Africa, the real Africa, traditional and traditionalist Africa. I find that very wrong. Liberty concerns all of us, and fighting for universal rights is also fighting a universal struggle. One cannot be an intellectually honest man and not recognize the fair struggle of women to have their rights respected.[16]

Egyptian dissident, physician, and author-activist Nawal El Saadawi was also receptive. Saadawi had undergone a clitoridectomy at six years of age. She wrote about her experience and the suffering of women under patriarchy in *The Hidden Face of Eve: Women in the Arab World* (2007). Saadawi's voice accorded with the collective voices of women and a number of honest men in *Warrior Marks* who testified that the violence endured by females in mutilating societies was and is inexcusable and indefensible.

In *Warrior Marks*, Parmar references a narrative collected in Thiam's work that exemplifies what millions of females have endured. The narrative tells the story of P. K., who was initiated at twelve years of age. Her mother was too upset to participate in the ceremony, so P. K.'s aunts delivered her to the "*old woman.*" She was assured by her elders that the procedure would not hurt. Inside the hut, nevertheless, she was overcome with terror:

> "*Lie down there,*" *the excisor suddenly said to me, pointing to a mat stretched out on the ground. No sooner had I lain down than I felt my thin frail legs tightly grasped by heavy hands and pulled wide apart. I lifted my head. Two women on each side of me pinned me to the ground. My arms were also immobilized. Suddenly I felt some strange substance being spread over my genital organs. I only learned later that it was sand. It was supposed to facilitate the excision, it seems. The sensation I felt was most unpleasant. A hand had grasped a part of my genital organs. My heart seemed to miss a beat . . . , then a shooting pain brought me back to reality from my thoughts of flight. I was already being excised: first of all I underwent the ablation of the labia minora and then of the clitoris. . . . I was in the throes of endless agony, torn apart both physically and psychologically.*[17]

It was against the rules for girls of her age group to cry, but, "*I broke the rule. . . . Never had I felt such excruciating pain!*" Like captives, from the hold of a "slave ship," brought up to dance for exercise and for the entertainment of their captors, P. K. and the other initiates were ordered up from their mats to partake in the ritual dance that followed the operations. "*There was a burning*

sensation between my legs. Bathed in tears, I hopped about, rather than danced. . . .
I suddenly felt everything swimming around me. Then I knew nothing more. I had
fainted."[18]

Walker and Parmar found the consequences of FGM to be as dreadful as they were legion. In addition to psychological and physical trauma, death was not uncommon. Aminata Diop's bid for asylum in France was precipitated by the death of her friend: "She was excised on a Thursday, and the following Monday she died. That's when I decided it would never happen to me."[19] The conditions under which "operations" were performed contributed to the spread of infection and disease. And the terror to which initiates were subjected engendered in them a psychic predisposition to submissiveness and the acceptance of domination.

A girl's initiation into womanhood initiated a cycle of pain for the duration of her life. If she survives to marry, she has cause for trepidation. In order to engage in marital sex, writes Parmar, "some men go to the mid-wife and have their wives opened up, while others do it themselves using razors or knives." Referencing an interview in Hanny Lightfoot-Klein's *Prisoners of Ritual* (1989), Parmar presents the issue of intercourse from a male point of view. Though men boast among themselves about having sex on their wedding night, one male shared, "*I know for a fact that this is virtually impossible. You are dealing with heavy scar tissue that is overgrown, and you are using flesh to penetrate it, and not iron. You could not penetrate a wall with flesh, and this is like a wall. Actually most men are afraid.*" There are those who "*get very drunk so they will not feel what they are doing, because they know they are doing something wrong. When they are drunk, they do not care what their partners are suffering.*"[20]

Childbearing, too, was excruciating, said Senegalese gynecologist and activist Dr. Henriette Kouyate. "An area which is normally elastic has become a cicatrix area. As a result, many women tear, at the top and at the bottom." The delivery can be less traumatic in a hospital. But women who give birth at home "are just left with a tear at the top, . . . causing massive hemorrhaging, at the bottom even worse." The inflexibility of the vaginal opening and the prolonged process can cause problems for the baby as well, says Dr. Kouyate.[21]

Interviews Walker and Parmar conducted revealed that the justifications for the practice of FGM were consistent with the reasons for its continuation. They were told that the primary purpose for circumcision was to "make the girls marriageable."[22] This purpose was supported by a list of reasons attributed to "*They*": "They say it's in the religion. . . . They say the clitoris is dirty and has to be destroyed. . . . They say the clitoris would grow like a penis and hang between the legs if it is not removed. . . . They say a woman will remain childless if she is not excised. . . . The clitoris is an evil, which makes men impotent and kills children at birth"; "the unmutilated female vulva frightens men and destroys crops."[23]

Walker put the question to Awa Thiam: "*Why is it still practiced?*" "I think," responded Thiam, "the answer is in the questions "Why is it that everywhere women are dominated? Why do they continue to be submissive?" Regardless of culture and location, women, says Thiam, "are always subordinate to men. The subordination we're speaking about exists everywhere."[24]

As subordination was common among women, so was violence against women a common occurrence. Yet some Western women sensationalized the issue of FGM as "something outside the realm of Western civilization," a practice that was "something 'other,' 'remote,' 'barbaric.' " Those in the West who held such views could then disidentify from cultural "others" and express precious little empathy for their plight.[25] Walker pointed out that in the purportedly "'enlightened' West, it is as if genital mutilation has been spread over the entire body, as women (primarily) rush to change their breasts, their noses, their weight and shape—i.e., by removal of ribs and fat, and by such things as deliberate starvation."[26]

"In fact," added Parmar, "the psychic and physical mutilations that women in the West undergo are equally devastating: unwanted hysterectomies, endless face-lifts, liposuction, bulimia, anorexia, silicone breast implants."[27] In the article "The International Crime of Genital Mutilation," to which Parmar alludes, Robin Morgan and Gloria Steinem disclose the fact that Western doctors had also performed FGM on Western women. Medical practitioners of the nineteenth century accepted genital mutilation as treatment "for 'nymphomania,' 'hysteria,' masturbation, and other nonconforming behavior." And Sigmund Freud had written that "elimination of clitoral sexuality is a necessary precondition for the development of femininity." There are women alive today, wrote Morgan and Steinem, who have suffered "gynophobic, medically unnecessary, mutilating surgery."[28]

Morgan and Steinem's article also underscored the perspective that FGM is a patriarchal practice and clitoridectomy and infibulation are patriarchal wounds. The article highlighted the distinction between male circumcision and "female circumcision"—which the authors declared to be a misnomer. Whereas male circumcision "does not destroy its victim's capacity for sexual pleasure," female "circumcision" destroys a female's full capacity for both sexual pleasure and self-pleasure. Given that "the clitoris has as many nerve endings as the penis," the authors state that a clitoridectomy is more analogous to a penisectomy.[29]

Warrior Marks unmasks FGM as an exercise of patriarchal politics and an expression of sexual colonialism. "I think of sexuality," says Walker, "as something that, like spirit, has been colonized."[30] Woman has suffered domination by man just as the earth has been subjugated to his dominion. The body of a woman suffers the same kind of scarring, mutilation, and control that the earth does, states Walker: "You know, 'If you're gonna have a crop, it's gonna be my crop. This is what you're gonna have. It's gonna be cotton, it's gonna be corn, it's gonna be soybeans.'" In the same attitude, a woman is cut and sewn up and told, "If you're gonna have children, it's gonna be my child, it's gonna be a boy."[31]

That the cutting or tearing into and sewing up of a woman was typically done by a woman only spoke to the extent to which women had been mentally and emotionally colonized. Walker and Parmar found that the lyrics of certain ritual songs of female circumcision were codifications of patriarchal power. In the call of one song Walker came across, "the bond between grandmother and mother, mother and daughter" is eradicated. The mothers sing to their daughters the dissolution of their friendship. They proclaim themselves the master who holds the knife and who will cut off the daughter's clitoris and throw it away, "*for today I am a man.*"[32]

After the daughters sing their response of fear, the impossibility of escape, and professions of bravery, other women join the mothers to mock the girls' erstwhile pride, vitality, independence, sexuality, and personal power. The girls then sing their concession: "*Today the knife has killed the guardian. Now he is dead. My village is unguarded. It used to be dirty, but now the guardian is gone. It will be clean.*"[33]

The call-and-response indoctrination is tantamount to an induction into female servitude. The huts wherein girls are initiated are comparable to the "breaking grounds" to which Africans were taken in "the new world" before being sold into bondage. The girls' initiation into womanhood only empowered the male principle, both within the women and within the men who dominated them. But the women elders, having taken on the persona of the male elders, were only empowered to do the will of their "masters." Walker and Parmar show that behind the hand of the woman circumciser is an established patriarchy that is sanctioned by androcentric cultural tradition.

The Islamic scholar Baba Lee shared with Parmar that female circumcision existed "long before Islam came to this continent. It has nothing to do with Islam. It is not mentioned in the Holy Koran it is not mentioned in any hadith." It is neither *sunna* nor *faridah*, nor is it obligatory, he said. It is propaganda, Baba Lee stated clearly. "It is a means of suppressing women. During the occasion of the circumcision they have their own school to teach women how to be obedient, how to be subdued with men, how to carry on traditions that matter."[34] Awa Thiam offered a similarly unvarnished view: "Circumcision and infibulation constitute for me the most eloquent expression of oppression of women by men."[35]

Male suppression of the female betrays a fear and envy of women, their bodies, and their bodily functions. "The controlling, curbing, and problematizing of women's sexuality have always been cross-cultural," writes Parmar. "Freud's concept of 'vagina dentata'" compares with folklore and legends recounted in Thiam's work. "The myth of the toothed vagina is found . . . among the Ben-Lulua people in Congo, in Gran Chaco among the Toba, and among the Aino of Japan. It is surprising to note that the Bambara concept of the clitoris as a dagger is almost identical to that of the Toba, who view it as a residual tooth, presumably all that remains of the toothed vagina."[36]

Alice Walker's writings tell the tales of women who are mutilated by men desperate to control them—a theme that is as ancient as it is mythic. "To murder a woman by cutting is a theme of many tales," writes Clarissa Pinkola Estés.[37] And as her rendition of the "The Handless Maiden" indicates, the mutilation

of a woman is often related to male ambition. In this story, the father, a beleaguered miller, strikes a deal with the Devil that results in the sacrifice of his
daughter. The negotiations require the father to chop off his daughter's hands.
Unless the father meets his demands, the Devil bellows, "Everything here will
die, including you, your wife, and all the fields for as far as you can see." The
devil in the tale symbolizes the predator who is "more than a murderer, he is a
mutilator. He requires mutilation, not decorative or simple initiatory scarification, but the kind that intends to disable a woman forever." Estés writes further that "the unredeemed aspect of the psyche does not feel, and in its insane
envy of those who do, it is driven to a cutting hatred."[38]

Warrior Marks reveals the sleight of hand performed by male elders and by
leaders who attribute their violence against women to the invisible hand of
God or tradition. Or they attribute it to the visible hands of God's helpmeets—
"Grandmothers of the Race" who wield the "'crown' of authority" ("a stick of
wood with a silver band around its middle, which looked remarkably like a
penis") in the name of man.[39] Importantly, Walker and Parmar make visible
the hand of woman in exposing deceptions and lies, while also revealing the
power symbolized in hands to heal, comfort, and do "the Work" of transformation. For, as Estés asserts, there is no such thing as a work-free transformation.
One must release the tragic story and embrace the heroic story. Mourning and
tears are essential to the healing process.

In chronicling their journey, Walker and Parmar both speak of moments
of being moved to tears, of weeping quietly or openly for the young girls who
had been circumcised and for those who would be. In "The Handless Maiden,"
the daughter kept the Devil at bay with her tears. For women, tears are the
beginning of initiation into the Scar Clan said Estés. "There are oceans of tears
women have never cried," she observed, "for they have been trained to carry
mother's and father's secrets, men's secrets, society's secrets, and their own
secrets, to the grave."[40] "Circumciser #1" boasted to Walker that the girls she
had circumcised would never tell their secrets, "even if you put a knife on their
throat, they would never tell you what was done to them. It's—it's painful, but
they would never say it. It's—it's their tradition."[41]

The problem with secrets "surrounded by shame," Estés explains, "is that
they cut a woman off from her instinctive nature, which is in the main, joyous
and free."[42] But it is this joy and this freedom that the mutilator would deny
the female. "Jung said," quotes Estés, "keeping secrets cuts us off from the
unconscious. Where there is a shaming secret, there is always a dead zone in
the woman's psyche, a place that does not feel or respond properly to her own
continuing emotional life events or to the emotional life events of others."[43]
Therefore "Circumciser #3" can matter-of-factly state, "I pay for my home and
my clothes. Everything comes from this knife."[44]

A woman's psyche is enthralled by the taboo or the secret; for "she is encouraged to believe that the secret must never be revealed, and further, she must
believe that if she does reveal it all decent persons who come across her shall
revile her in perpetuity." Only those "inhabiting a small and black space in

their hearts," says Estés would subject another human being to such psychic manipulation and intimidation. "Among persons of warmth and love for the human condition, quite the opposite is true. They would help to draw out the secret, for they know it makes a wound that will not heal until the matter is given words and witness."[45]

Walker and Parmar's work has assisted those who have suffered mutilation and those who campaign against it to "draw out the secret" of FGM. The book and the film are the "words and witness" that heal. Having survived the secret shame of an injury sustained during her childhood, Alice Walker identified with the girls and women who suffered FGM and was sensitive to their stories and how their stories would be told. In an early letter to Pratibha Parmar, Walker explained that she wanted to be a part of the film as subject "not just an observer." Her intention was "to stand with the mutilated women, not beyond them. I know how painful exposure is," she confided, "it is something I've had to face every day of my life, beginning with my own first look in the mirror in the morning!"[46]

Walker writes that it was her own visual mutilation that helped her to "'see' the subject of genital mutilation." As one cannot see her own reflection in the eyes of another when the pupil of one's own eye is destroyed, "a woman can never see herself reflected in the healthy, intact body of another" when the clitoris and other sexual organs are destroyed.[47] Having been visually blinded, Walker could see that circumcised girls had been sexually blinded.

Walker's letters to Parmar speak of the difficulty of adjusting to life with impaired vision, learning to walk again without walking into objects she could not see. She speaks of enduring pain from the initial injury itself and the surgeries that followed. She speaks of the scar tissue that had her look down for six years. When Walker saw little girls who had been "set aside" to recover from the wounding, she recalled her own banishment and the silence about what had happened to her. The shuffling walk and downcast eyes of circumcised girls were her own.

The dimming of the light in the eyes or the cast that concealed the eyes of mutilated girls ensured that those who injured them would not see their own image reflected back. The perpetrators, then, would also not have access to the reflection that is necessary for self-knowledge, growth, and redemption. As the mutilators cut little girls off from their physical and psychic wholeness, they cut themselves off from the feeling, seeing, and healing aspects of human nature. The sexual blinding of the little girls was the self-blinding of a society.

Walker was delighted to learn from her investigations that sexually mutilated women still retained a capacity to experience sexual pleasure and enjoy making love. Her talks with Efua Dorkenoo confirmed that even as there were women that "*fall by the wayside, women who do crack up, women who don't make it,*" there are many women who do. It is "within this stream of survivors," says Dorkenoo, "where things are going to change and happen."[48]

Pratibha Parmar writes that the spirit of resistance she witnessed in the women who told her and Walker their stories, reminded her of something

James Baldwin had said: "The victim who articulates the situation of the victim is no longer a victim; he or she is a threat."[49] Such women number among the initiates of Estés's Scar Clan, "that timeless tribe of women of all colors, all nations, all languages, who down through the ages have lived through a great something, and yet who stood proud, still stand proud."[50] Where Estés describes their wounds as "Battle Scars," Walker and Parmar describe them as *Warrior Marks*.

EIGHTEEN

Absolute Goodness

"Was woman herself not the tree of life?" Tashi Evelyn Johnson queried. She had been crucified, but her husband Adam said he couldn't preach even one sermon about it because he was too embarrassed to do so. In any case, Tashi Evelyn recognized her identity as "the tree of life."[1] In *The Color Purple*, Shug Avery's first step from the deified image of "the old white man was trees. Then air. Then birds. Then other people." In her solitude, she had awakened to "that feeling of being part of everything, not separate at all. I knew that if I cut a tree, my arm would bleed."[2] Celie's first step from Mister was also the trees. Mister had damned Celie as "nothing at all": "You black, you pore, you ugly, you a woman. Goddam, he say, you nothing at all." But Celie, strengthened by a growing sense of self, cursed Mister. "Until you do right by me, I say, everything you even dream about will fail. I give it to him straight, just like it come to me. And it seem to come to me from the trees."[3] In *Meridian*, Meridian Hill enjoyed the mystery of The Sojourner, the sheltering tree that gave safe harbor. Though it had been cut down, it bloomed anew.

In Walker's fiction, trees reflect the psychic life of her female characters. These women symbolize Earth and Earth's creative essence. And they sometimes function as the Cosmic Tree or the archetypal *axis mundi*. The Cosmic Tree represents the center or navel of the world. This primordial feminine principle is reproduced in the female body of the human species. Walker's writing, both fiction and nonfiction, illustrates how, under patriarchy, females are not perceived as the embodiments of the primordial feminine principle that they are. Rather, they have been crucified, demonized, and cut down. Adam, who refuses to publicly recognize Tashi's suffering, reflects the unconsciousness of a humanity that also refuses to recognize the suffering of the Dark Mother—as woman, as continent, as planet Earth. Yet they are all one.

Human beings "have an African mother," says Walker. "That is the common mother. And we have been taught to be so different and separate. And that's an illusion. . . . So I'm hopeful that now that geneticists have actually done the work of linking us by DNA to our African mother that at some point that is going to sink into human consciousness and lead to an understanding of who the Mother is. Hopefully, the human Mother and then of course the Earth Mother." The illusion of difference and separation, Walker states further, has had murderous consequences. "Because you can only do those terrible things that people do when you have that illusion of separation."[4] Walker's work shows patriarchal ideology to be at the root of much human suffering. Masculo-centric mythologies and patriarchal religious systems have undermined the sovereignty of women, specifically, and have demonized the feminine principle, generally. Upon realizing what female genital mutilation meant, Tashi's therapist Raye exclaimed, "Religion is an elaborate excuse for what man has done to women and to the earth."[5]

The illusion of separation evident in patriarchal religion was also evident in Eurocentrism. Among the reasons Alice Walker greatly respected Carl Jung was his willingness to tell the truth—about everything. Europe had much to account for, was his attitude. "What we from our point of view call colonization, missions to the heathen, spread of civilization, etc., has another face—the face of a bird of prey seeking with cruel intentness for distant quarry—a face worthy of a race of pirates and highwaymen."[6] The character Mzee in *Possessing the Secret of Joy*, who is based on Carl Jung, manages to see past the illusion of ethnicity and color to know his oneness with Adam and Tashi. In embracing them, he feels his totality, "A truly universal self. That is the essence of healing that in my European, 'professional' life I frequently lost."[7]

Though of European heritage, Jung was not afraid to critique Europe. Though male, he could see the problem of excessive masculinity. Through his practice and in his own life he wrestled with these issues. What endeared Jung further still to Walker was that he did not separate human nature from Nature, and he recognized Nature's divinity. Creation, for Jung, was "the essence of God," and "God," to Jung, "was everything." Jung saw plants as "a kind of direct communication from" Divinity. Human beings and other animals "were bits of God that had become independent. That was why they could move about on their own and choose their abodes. Plants were bound for good or ill to their places. They expressed not only beauty but also the thoughts of God's world, with an intent of their own and without deviation. . . . Trees in particular were mysterious and seemed to me direct embodiments of the incomprehensible meaning of life."[8]

As Jung decried the European man's "masculinization of the white woman," he decried man's attempt to dominate nature.[9] To achieve this would be a pyrrhic victory. "In spite of our proud domination of nature," states Jung, "we are still her victims as much as ever and have not even learnt to control our own nature, which slowly and inevitably courts disaster."[10] Walker interrogated this improvident inclination in *By the Light of My Father's Smile*. In this novel, The Mundo could hear the story of man's dominion over earth and woman only as a lie, one that would—as Jung, also, warned—unravel the world. And when Señor Robinson said that "God had said man had dominion over all the earth," the Mundo men were confounded because they knew the impossibility of the pronouncement. "Perhaps, they had said, stroking their bearded chins, it is the one lie that has unraveled your world."[11]

They received with even greater consternation Señor Robinson's story about women being evil. "They had never understood how woman could be considered evil, either, since they considered her the mother of corn. When hearing of her original sin of eating the forbidden fruit, they scratched their chins again and said, even more gravely, perhaps this is the one biggest lie that has unraveled your world." The Mundo men questioned this accusation and implored Señor Robinson to keep such stories to himself. But the Mundo women learned of the charge against them and were hurt. "That they could be considered not good had never entered their minds."[12] Perhaps the reason the Mundo perceived the story of woman's sinful nature as "the biggest lie" is because the lie involved heaven and earth and the universe entire. Was woman not, through her body "part of everything, even something so distant as the moon."[13] Was she not, as Tashi had understood, the cosmic tree?

Señor Robinson and his visiting associates considered the Mundo "as unsophisticated as children[.] Just because they didn't lie."[14] The Mundo saw the whole of life and they saw that on earth the whole of life was bound up in woman. This belief was at the center of their cosmology and the basis of their socio-religious philosophy. They had not, like Señor Robinson and those he symbolized, become "sophisticated"—that is, in the original sense of the term, they had not become sophists. They had not become deceitful, corrupted, or capable of developing specious arguments.

Señor Robinson had become "a man whose voice was separated from his mind." The sense of separation Robinson experienced within himself was projected onto the world. In such a projection, it was conceivable that woman was separate from earth, that flesh was separate from Holy Spirit. This confusion distracted Robinson from his belief. "His belief in woman. In the woman he made love to, the woman-to-be who was his own child." The Mundo feared men who did not like women. "We knew those men would lead us straight off the face of the earth."[15] Belief in the illusion of separation, as Walker contended, would attain to such consequences.

The notion of man's dominion over the Dark Mother brought humanity dangerously close to the precipice. In his work, Carl Jung continuously sounded the alarm that the intellect of modern man, separated from his soul had created another kind of "new world." One populated with "monstrous machines," catastrophic weaponry, and compelled by "a war instinct."[16] He urged that modern man be aware of this propensity, to be aware "that there is a terrible demon in man that blindfolds him, that prepares awful destruction."[17] In "Why the War You Have in Mind (Yours and Mind) Is Obsolete," Alice Walker reminds us that there is but one mind, and movement of the mind of anyone affects all. That one mind conceives of dropping a bomb on one or a million heads, is not so clever, as it signals the end for all.

Blindfolded, modern humanity does not see itself as an integral part of the whole of creation. Estranged from that part of its nature that is emotional and empathic, humanity, says Jung, has become estranged from the numinous qualities of nature and has thus lost the ability to participate in natural events in ways that are inspiring and meaningful: "No river contains a spirit, no tree means a man's life, no snake is the embodiment of wisdom, and no mountain still harbors a great demon. Neither do things speak to him nor can he speak to things, like stones, springs, plants, and animals. . . ." He no longer has a familiar, he has lost direct communication with nature, "and the emotional energy it generated has sunk into the unconscious."[18] Jung's work shows that the resulting separation between humanity and nature mirrors the disconnect between the conscious and unconscious mind. For, says Jung, "[T]he collective unconscious is simply Nature."[19] The security of the earth and the sanity of humanity are indeed one, and both require that human beings recognize and reconnect with the sanctity of Nature.

Alice Walker's work and life suggest that the experience of the sacred in nature remains available to us. That snakes do embody wisdom, and not only can one speak to the earth, but that the whole universe will respond to one's prayer. In *Absolute Trust in the Goodness of the Earth,* Walker shares the delight of being alive, the mystery of being in a body, and the joy of being in love with life, which is "the Award" that we have all already won—because we exist.[20] There is no contest to be engaged in to receive this award; for Life doesn't compete with us—It is us, and we are Life Itself. If there is a struggle at all, it is the struggle to wake up to this reality. And even then, Walker's poems and essays and novels offer evidence that everything needed to fit us for the struggle is given to us—by Life. On the journey to the realization of oneness with all creation and the divinity of all life, Walker writes that through glorious days and star-filled nights, through sacred medicinal-spiritual herbs and plants, through the infinitude of its bounty, and the run of horses that beautify the landscape, as well as the numinosity of chickens crossing a road, Earth has provided for our sustenance, peace of mind, and restoration to balanced living.

The poems collected in *Absolute Trust* reflect the year Walker experienced as "apprentice elder" in Mexico and the Amazon. They are signposts that point to pathways of understanding, of knowledge and wisdom, and, ultimately, pathways of return—to nature, to spirit, to Self. For a year, Walker inquired into the means of "insightful living."[21] She sought understanding of what compels humankind to addictions of drugs, food, alcohol, sex, and thinness. Written in the wake of the attacks on the World Trade Towers and the Pentagon, she wanted to know "how humans might live peacefully and more lovingly upon the earth." Three times during the year she sat in a circle with other women seekers and shamans and drank *ayuascha*—"the vine of the soul"—"a healing medicine used for thousands of years by indigenous peoples."[22] Other times she sat with women and men seekers and shamans to eat the healing mushrooms revered as "the flesh of the gods." Walker writes that her apprenticeship continued in the Amazon, "home of 'Grandmother' Ayuascha, where she herself instructed me I need look no further in her mirror; what she'd shown me already was enough."[23]

She had seen that the perceived separation from The Mother, from Earth, and from other individuals and society expresses as a sensation of emptiness, a feeling of something lacking, something missing. Addictions distract from the existential angst while they simultaneously promise to fill the void. "Our children take addictive drugs," she imparted, "partly to allay their fears about what begins to look like a severely compromised future, one filled with hatred and with war. They take drugs to feel less lonely in a world that consistently chooses 'profit' over community." More fundamentally, states Walker, their indulgence in addictive substances and behaviors is indicative of their "desire to have a religious or spiritual or ecstatic and transformative experience, a need hardwired into our being."[24]

For thousands of years, sacred plants have been used in rituals of healing and in ceremonies that connect the individual with the Infinite, says Walker. But modern laws and ethics that support a system invented "to make money off of making others intoxicated," disrupt the communion between humans and Divinity and interrupt the communication inherent in rituals and ceremonies that engender community.[25] In her poem, "The Tree," The shaman José discloses that he and his people no longer dream the common dream of the World Tree that "reached from / Heaven to earth / Earth to heaven," and sang.[26] The cutting down of the rainforest, a consequence of modern man's "dominion" of the earth, has scattered his people who are sick and dying. But the Tree they no longer see appeared in the speaker's dream-vision. Though large and awesome, it did not sing. The World Tree, that contained the world and sky, was afraid to sing aloud, and was seeking shelter in the dream of one dreamer.

When a tree seeks shelter, one might take it as a sign that a great deal in the world has gone wrong. What does it mean that a tree, whose body is used for human shelter, seeks shelter in the body of a human? That it seeks shelter implies the possibility of protection. That it appears in the dream of a human being implies its identity with humankind and its faith in humanity to protect and save it. That it manifests as dream communicates that it is message. As archetypal World Tree, it is a message from the unconscious to the conscious mind; it is a message from Nature to human nature. That the dream-vision comes to one dreamer, alone, indicates that each individual human being is called to wake up to the personal and collective responsibility of protecting the planet.

Alice Walker's "The Tree" affirms the possibility of direct communication with Nature. This poem and the volume from which it comes reflect Walker's lifelong communion with Earth. Her heartfelt compassion for the companion of her youth, a tree of "old growth pine nobility" that was cut down, is present in her concern for the arthritic limbs and poisoned and tired "feet" of the "middle-aged to old conifers" in California with whom she converses as an adult. In the essay "Everything Is a Human Being," Walker's "intense dialogue with the trees" yields this revelation: "The Earth holds us responsible for our crimes against it, not as individuals, but as a species." "Just as human beings perceive all trees as one, . . . all human beings, to the trees, are one." Earth does not entertain "exceptions." "But the Earth is wise," Walker intuits, "It has given itself into the keeping of all, and all are therefore accountable."[27]

In the poem "Though We May Feel Alone," the speaker conveys that the ancestors, "The one called / God / & / The One Called / Death," allow that humanity makes missteps and loses its way. "What matters to them / Is that / We right ourselves / Keep a better watch."[28] Walker's contribution to the collective responsibility of righting ourselves and keeping better watch is evident in her writing and activism. *Horses Make the Landscape More Beautiful* captures the splendor of nature. *A Poem Traveled Down My Arm* offers epiphanies and recipes to walk or return to the path that recognizes the equality of all life. *Now Is the Time to Open Your Heart* is an illustration of absolute trust. Characteristic of Walker's fiction, it reveals what has been concealed. Focusing on the historical and contemporary politics relevant to the peoples of Hawaii, the novel gives voice to stories of earth and peoples long silenced, and it details The Great Work that is required to create the beloved community.

In *Anything You Love Can Be Saved* and *We Are the Ones We Have Been Waiting For*, Walker's activism on behalf of the planet and all creation manifests a concern and commitment, rooted in her own mother's garden. Her animal rights activism, promotion of vegetarianism, and paganist orientation all express an ecofeminist politics. Her commitment to the politics, philosophy, and vision at the core of ecofeminism and its various branches or complementary movements—such as vegetarianism, environmentalism, spiritual ecofeminism, and deep ecology—are longstanding and are rooted in a love of Mother Earth that is an integral part of her African American and Native American ancestral and cultural heritage.

Walker's maternal great-grandmother, Tallulah Calloway, was of Cherokee heritage. Walker fully claims her maternal ancestral lines. She officially changed her middle name from Malsenior to Tallulah-Kate, in 1994, in honor of her maternal great-grandmother and mother Tallulah, and her paternal grandmother Kate. "Whatever the word Tallulah means in itself, to me it means 'restored' in me. . . . The word Kate means 'remembered' in me."[29] And in poems and essays and political activities, she salutes her "three heritages." In works like *By the Light of My Father's Smile*, she honors a band of African-Amerindians whose cosmology reflects her own ancestry.

It wasn't so long ago, Walker recalled, that only Indigenous peoples honored earth and sought to live in rhythm with her cycles. "And then this man—Lovelock, I think it was—found the Greek word 'Gaia' for the Earth

Mother/Goddess Mother, and was just astonished that, you know, hey—it's alive. Now everybody knew it was alive. All of the people who have lived on this planet for thousands of years, praying to the earth and thanking the earth, they completely knew—of course it's alive!"[30]

Walker recognizes Native Americans as the guardians of the land, those who for centuries, "lived on the land, making love to it through worship and praise, without once raping or defiling it."[31] Ancestors like Black Elk, says Walker, told the story that was good to tell, a story that traced the origin of the "two-leggeds," the "four-leggeds," the winged, and all things green, back to "one mother and their father is one 'Spirit.'" "It is their light step upon the Earth that I admire and would have us emulate," contemplates Walker, "The new way to exist on the Earth may well be the ancient way of the steadfast lovers of this particular land."[32]

We are earthlings after all and are therefore behooved to learn and implement the way of the guardian-parents of the land "before it is too late."[33] In doing so, there is an identity of Oneness that recognizes no ideology that separates, no illusion that enslaves; and in this, she says, is a radical freedom to be had. Important to Walker's vision of radical freedom is the spirit of Maria Sabina, legendary shaman-healer-priest of Oxaco, Mexico. Maria Sabina also knew intimate communion with The Mother and sacred communication with herbs and plants. An embodiment of ancient wisdom, Maria Sabina left "a legacy of an amazing freedom, the foundation of which is absolute trust in the goodness of the earth; in its magic, in its love of us humans, in its ever-present assistance the moment we give ourselves, unconditionally, into its wonder."[34]

Maria Sabina reminds us of the centrality of woman in the balance of the world. Her healing powers speak to her stature as the tree of life that connects earth with the heavens and the regions below. The unraveling of the world by the biggest lie ever told can be halted, writes Walker: "[N]othing / Stops a lie / Like being / Yourself."[35]

NINETEEN

Why War Is Never a Good Idea

Only War thinks war is a good idea. If War had to drink the water from the well that was poisoned by the leaching of "leftover gunk" from exploded missiles that took huge bites out of a village, War might change its mind. Because it has one—a mind, and eyes, nose and ears, tongue and teeth.[1] *Why War Is Never a Good Idea* is a children's book that is drawn from the picture poem of the same title, collected in Alice Walker's *Absolute Trust in the Goodness of the Earth*. The book is dedicated "to my global grandchildren," and the picture poem is written "for Children Blinded in War."[2] The narrative-poem depicts war with the features and attributes of a human being. The personification of war emphasizes the fact that war and the disaster that trails it is not some puzzling phenomenon that mysteriously occurs in nature separate from human will. It emphasizes the fact that the thoughts, feelings, and emotions that combine to erupt into war are embodied in the attitudes and actions of actual human beings. As the narrator observes, becoming belligerent and destructive and careless of consequences and careless of life is something that happens within even the nicest people on the planet.

The book illustrates that human beings make the treacherous decision to camouflage as The Mother, and in fatigues of green and brown that are indistinguishable from the fields just beyond the doors and windows of nursing mothers and suckling babes, they steal close enough to strike. Although War can see what it wants—oil, gas, minerals, and metals beneath the earth—it is blind to everything else. And although War is old and it has been around a long time and has traveled to many places, the narrative voice tells us, it is witless. The only wisdom for War—"the War You Have in Mind (Yours and Mine)"—writes Walker in *Absolute Trust* is obsolescence.[3] This wisdom requires recognition of what Jung described as "the war instinct" and what Albert Camus referred to as the "death-instinct."[4]

The image Alice Walker uses for these deadly inclinations is "the dogs of war" because sometimes War does not roam in search of things, but is spurred on by an inveterate and ravenous nihilism that feeds on life, destroying what it could never create, its appetite never quenched.[5] The image of the dogs of war, says Walker, is ancient. However, what astonishes her "is how accurately and irresistibly it has arisen in the psyche. And the psyche recognizes this image, not because it is external. But because some part of it is internal as well. Which means we must all look inside and get to know our own dogs of war."[6]

Walker urges humanity to this recognition; for, as Tashi Johnson deliberates in *Possessing the Secret of Joy*, "World wars have been fought and lost; for every war is against the world and every war against the world is lost."[7] Thus, in *Overcoming Speechlessness* and *Sent by Earth: A Message from the Grandmother Spirit*, Walker reiterates what is apparent, but what those who are blind to the war and death instinct within themselves have not yet learned to acknowledge: That war is never the answer to whatever questions arise with life events. That the issue of War is a resentment seethed in hatred that stills itself for retaliation. That, unidentified, this human instinct continues to move through humanity unabated, with our willful, if unconscious, collusion. And that as injustice anywhere is a threat to justice everywhere, so the war instinct in us all fuels wars everywhere.

War, in its guise of genocide, raged in Rwanda. Alice Walker journeyed to Rwanda and the Congo to pay respects to those whose lives were decimated. At Kigali, the capital city of Rwanda, she visited the museum which exhibited the "open smiles or wise and consoling eyes" that had belonged to the bodies in the nearby burial sites. Among the hacked bodies of adults and elders buried in the mass graves, were those of infants, toddlers, teenagers, and adolescents "who had been hacked into sometimes quite small pieces by armed strangers, or by neighbors, or by acquaintances and 'friends' they knew."[8] The survivors told Walker their unspeakable stories. Gruesome and chilling, the effect of hearing them left her speechless. Yet Walker, like the survivors who shared their stories, knew the importance of speaking the unspeakable, of exposing to the light of awareness the unconscionable human acts that transpire under cover of darkness.

The historical background of the genocide in Rwanda is ensnared in the long shadow cast, on the one hand by German colonialists—whose nation would generate the twentieth century's prototype for "ethnic cleansing"—and on the other by Belgian colonialists. Both colonies settled into the region in the 1800s. Walker considered this history while regarding the, perhaps, surprised smiling faces and incredulous but consoling eyes she regarded there on exhibit. She had written a college paper on the Belgian Congo, the account of which was also on display at the museum. The history chronicled the colonization of the people and the exploitation of their resources. The Belgian colonialists robbed the land of its mineral wealth and the trees of their rubber for the profit of the Firestone Corporation. "King Leopold of Belgium introduced the policy of cutting off the hands of enslaved Africans who didn't or couldn't fulfill their rubber quota."[9]

In addition, the colonialists robbed the native people—the Tutsi and Hutu—of their longstanding love for and trust in one another and the social harmony they enjoyed prior to colonization. They were indoctrinated with hatred, and the seeds of resentment were planted along with those of social strife. On their leaving the region, the colonialists left in place a social structure designed to collapse into a bitter and murderous chaos. What transpired became another tragic example reifying the truism that "if a house be divided against itself, that house cannot stand."[10] Likewise, a mind divided against itself functions in every way but sane. And attack on any part of humanity, of life, is injury to the sacred whole.

Compelled by the suffering of the people and the earth in Palestine/Israel, Walker traveled there, too. Gaza had been bombarded by Israeli rocket fire for 22 days, "a missile landing every twenty-seven seconds."[11] Once again, the rage of War expresses itself, and, once again, Walker spies the long and shapeshifting shadow of European colonialism. She recounts that in 1948, when she was four years old, Jewish people who survived the holocaust orchestrated by Nazi Germany had been "settled in a land that belonged to people already living there, which did not seem to bother the British who, as with India, had occupied Palestine and then, on leaving it, helped put in place a partitioning of the land they thought would work fine for the people, strangers, Palestinians and European Jews, now forced to live together."[12]

Though distant and not so distant familial or cultural kin, Israelis in government gradually claimed the majority of Palestine for Jewish people. While awaiting the processing of paperwork that would allow her group to take the bus to Rafah, Egypt, in order to cross the border into Gaza, Walker perused a postcard. The card illustrated the diminishing landmass of the Palestinians who by 2008 had become "refugees (in their own country) living in camps in the West Bank and Gaza, with the whole land now called Israel."[13] The card conveyed the promise of Ariel Sharon, the former Israeli president, to make "a pastrami sandwich of the Palestinian people, riddling their lands with Jewish settlements until no one would be able to imagine a whole Palestine. Or would know Palestine ever existed."[14]

The destruction Walker looked upon portrayed "the failure, and heartlessness, of the 'partition' plan." The same failure, writes Walker that was mirrored in the partitioning of India and Pakistan. And it also portrayed the attitude of hatred directed against the Palestinian people by the Israeli government in its attempt "to turn Palestinians into the 'new Jews,' patterned on Jews of the Holocaust era, as if someone must hold that place in order for Jews to avoid it."[15]

Walker worked in concert with Women for Women International in Rwanda and the Congo. She had joined forces with CODEPINK in Palestine/Israel in response to the 2008–2009 bombing of Gaza. Walker and her companion and associates walked through the rubble of demolished houses, schools, hospitals, mosques, police stations, parliament buildings, and factories. After the bombardment, the military "had taken pains to pulverize what they had destroyed."[16] Children who hadn't been killed and buried in the rubble weeks ago, were "playing in the white phosphorous-laden rubble that, after twenty-two days of bombing, is everywhere in Gaza[.] White phosphorus, once on the skin, never stops burning."[17]

As in Rwanda and the Congo, Walker listened to women narrate the details of the ruthless and deliberate destruction of Palestinian homes and surrounding gardens and orchards. "An old, old man, leaning on a stick," spoke to her in English. "Come look at my house! . . . They broke my house, he said, by bombing it, and then they came with bulldozers and they broke my lemon and olive trees." "The Israeli military has destroyed over two and a half million olive and fruit trees alone since 1948," Walker observes. "Having planted many trees myself, I shared his sorrow about the fate of these ones."[18]

Walker went to Palestine/Israel to witness the spectacle that inevitably occurs when "the dogs of war," sniffing and scratching in the dark corners of the collective unconscious, are unleashed. She had come to learn this truth also: "that humans are an amazing lot. That to willfully harm any one of us is to damage us all. That hatred of ourselves is the root cause of any harm done to others, others so like us! And that we are lucky to live at a time when all lies will be exposed, along with the relief of not having to serve them any longer."[19] War is the answer, is one of those lies. Contemplating the destruction of life and the war-generated pollution that hastens globe-threatening climate change, Walker entertains this scenario: "How doofus humans are going to look, . . . still firing rockets into apartment buildings full of families, and dropping bombs on school children and their pets, when the ice melts completely in the Arctic and puts an end to our regressive, greed-sourced rage forever?"[20]

Walker traveled to Rwanda, the Congo, Palestine/Israel to bear witness, to offer comfort and support, to listen, and also to stand in solidarity with those who struggle for security and freedom and human dignity. She chose to stand with others as others had stood with African Americans, long abused and dehumanized and subjugated to the tyranny of a feudal, political and social structure. She traveled there to let suffering people know that their cries and screams and wails were not falling on deaf ears, but that they had been heard. She traveled there to inspire hope in those like the woman she met in Gaza who had come to a place of despair.

"We don't hate Israelis, Alice, she says, quietly. What we hate is being bombed, watching our little ones live in fear, burying them, being starved to death, and being driven from our land. We hate this eternal crying out to the world to open its eyes and ears to the truth of what is happening, and being ignored. Israelis, no."[21] In traveling to these places, Walker put her own life at risk. Though repeatedly warned against this, she pressed forward in her journeys to be with others in their suffering and their exquisite joy.

"This is one of the most beautiful passages for human beings," Walker explains. "It is as if we enter a different door of our reality, when someone gives her or his life for us. Why this should be is a mystery, but it is the mystery, I think, behind all the great myths in which there is human sacrifice—not on an altar but on the road, in the street—for the common good."[22] The mystery to which Walker alludes is the knowing—rising from the depths of the human collective unconscious—that there is but one Life. In this realm, the memory of the totality of Self is retained. This realm inspires Walker's selfless "risk" and her resolve.

From this realm, too, comes the poem "Projection," that describes the image of a child who sits "at the back / Of each human's eyeballs."[23] This child, explains the narrator, is the World Child, and it looks out from the eyes of everyone, waiting for everyone to clearly see and understand the projected image. What the World Child waits for us to understand and to share with the World Child without and within is this: "All the children of the Earth / Are perfect." The narrator informs that it is the work of all of us to liberate, "across the planet," the World Child, imprisoned in the image just behind our eyes, that we can sometimes see.[24]

From this realm, too, arises Walker's questions: Where are the World Parents and Caretakers? For there is the work of the Mother and the Daughter to do, as greed and brutality "will grow wherever it is unchecked, in any society." There is also the work of vigilance, of holding one another to account.[25] And yet, interjects Walker, "I firmly believe the only punishment that works is love. Or, as the Buddha said: Hatred will never cease by hatred. By love alone is it healed."[26]

Walker draws inspiration from a poem written by Thich Nhat Hanh to the young people who risked their lives during the Vietnam War. "Remember that war?" she asks. "The napalmed naked children fleeing down a flaming road?"[27] Though they had experienced so much devastation and violence, Hanh urged forgiveness and compassion: "Our enemy is our anger, hatred, greed, fanaticism, and discrimination against (each other). If you die because of violence, you must meditate on compassion in order to forgive those who kill you. When you die realizing this state of compassion, you are truly a child of The Awakened One." If you can meet circumstances of oppression, shame, or violence with forgiveness, Hanh counsels, "you have great power." For a disposition of compassion and forgiveness is the mark of "a mature relationship between people."[28]

We are called upon, says Walker, to develop mature relationships. We are called upon to cultivate awareness in the mind and love in the heart. "Every thought, every act, every gesture, must be in the direction of developing and maintaining a mature relationship with the peoples of the planet; all thought of domination, control, force and violence must be abandoned."[29] To nurture the spirit of peace, love, and equality among all life-forms, Walker's literature for children and adolescents is written to speak to the One World Child that exists in adults and children alike.

To Hell with Dying (1988) is based on a short story Walker wrote that impressed Langston Hughes. Hughes published the story in *The Best Short Stories by Black Writers, 1899–1967* (1967). *To Hell with Dying* exemplifies the magic of unconditional love. Walker regarded Langston Hughes as a literary forefather and loving mentor. In *Langston Hughes, American Poet* (1974), she honors Hughes as an ancestral spirit. The biography addresses the topics of history and cultural heritage and speaks to the importance of embracing one's creative spirit and being true to one's authentic self. *Finding the Green Stone* (1991) demonstrates that even as one is personally responsible for one's emotional state, a loving community is important in helping everyone in the community to maintain or return to a healthy and balanced state of mind. In *There Is a Flower at the Tip of My Nose Smelling Me* (2006) every life-form has subjectivity and agency. The story advances the understanding that existence is the foundation of equality among all life-forms and that the notion of separation is illusion.

Why War Is Never a Good Idea reminds us of our responsibility in becoming acquainted with our own "dogs of war." "Some of our war dogs, we have to own, are paying taxes that will be used to destroy people almost identical to us," writes Walker. "Many of our war dogs are connected to heating our homes and driving cars."[30] Whatever the provocation, whatever the purported benefit or profit, Walker writes that "War is no / Creative response."[31] *Why War Is Never a Good Idea* depicts War's utter lack of imagination as it cannot conceive of the Oneness of all life, and therefore cannot acknowledge that there is no such thing as collateral damage. War can neither imagine the World Child nor hear its cries—nor the bray of a donkey or the croak of a frog. Contrary to its exaggerated self-importance, War is the only thing To leave / Behind / Crying / Lonely / In / The dust.[32]

TWENTY

We Are the Ones

Alice Walker describes her 2006 collection of nonfiction as "medita-tions." They are written and presented in a manner that invites the reader to pause. They inspire a kind of settling in, an inner stillness, that draws the reader into contemplation—about the world in which we live, the planet upon which we walk, and our responsibility to both. In the carry-ing out of the responsibility of turning the world "right side up again," the collection informs us that "we are the ones we have been waiting for."[1] This proclamation also figures as the collection's title.

Between the words of this statement, in the resonance the words make in the mind, in the images conjured by the words and the peace the words inspire in the heart, are voices of wisdom, visions of wholeness, and traditions of resis-tance. The title is a link, connecting the reader to its source, a poem by June Jordan titled "Poem for South African Women." Jordan's poem commemorates *"the 40,000 women and children who, August 9, 1956, presented themselves in bodily protest against the 'dompass' in the capital of apartheid."*[2]

The *"dompass"* or "dumb pass" was a passport that the Dutch Afrikaner officials of apartheid South Africa required native Africans and "coloureds" to carry when traveling beyond their government-established homelands. The Pass Law was designed to reinforce racial segregation, restrict movement of Africans, and control and manipulate the African migrant labor force. Such laws also had the effect of engendering self-hate and humiliation as they were constant reminders of Africans' state of unfreedom in their own land, and they forced African peoples to identify themselves in accordance with a classificatory system that denied both their freedom and their humanity.

Initially, the Pass Law applied to men only. When the government enacted legislation to make the law applicable to women, enforcement of the law was met with resistance. "The early struggles of women against the pass laws (1913), resulted in a more than thirty-year delay in control of their labor via this system." The women continued their resistance to the Pass Law until it was repealed in 1986.[3]

"*We are the ones we have been waiting for*" is the refrain sung by the women of South Africa documented in Jordan's poem, who, with no other voices accompanying theirs, were "standing up" for themselves, their children's future, and for freedom's own sake.[4] The refrain was taken up by Sweet Honey in the Rock, an African American women's ensemble. Founded in 1973 by Bernice Johnson Reagon, the group's repertoire reflects, in content and form, the ancestral and modern musical heritage of African Americans. Prior to founding the group, Reagon was a member of the SNCC Freedom Singers who were noted for their performance of "Movement songs."

Reagon perceived this music as "a unifying, communal force against oppression of all types—racial oppression being just the starting point." Her philosophical perspective is that "music is first a means of communicating to and about one's community, then a method of historical documentation, and only lastly a mode of entertainment." The spirit of the freedom songs is the foundation of Sweet Honey in the Rock, which Reagon conceptualizes as a "woman born of a struggling union of Black Women Singers."[5]

The name, Sweet Honey in the Rock, is inspired by Psalm 81:16: "He should have fed them also with the finest wheat: and with honey out of the rock should I have satisfied thee."[6] The image, said Reagon, "provided a suitable metaphor of African-American women: strong as a rock, sweet as honey." "We Are the Ones We Have Been Waiting For," sung as a congregational chant, opened the group's 25-year anniversary album. The song "asserts the sense of self-empowerment and personal responsibility that defines the creative force called Sweet Honey In The Rock."[7] The refrain has been echoed across countries and cultures and has been taken up by those who remember or are reminded that authentic power is personal and internal.

In the process of healing from the dissolution of her "Movement marriage" and missing the South and having left Mississippi for New York, Alice Walker experienced the music of Sweet Honey in the Rock, as restorative balm. "The absence of *this* sound in my life is why it was so hard of late to remember who I am, or what, indeed the struggle now is." *This* sound, reflected Walker, was soul nurture, inoculation, and immunization against all that threatened the sanctity of the self. In linking all oppressions, *this* sound also highlighted all connections. "I heard all the connectedness that racist oppression and colonial destruction tried to keep hidden. I heard the African beat, yes, and all the African tones. But I also heard the native American 'off-the-note' harmony that used to raise the hair at the back of my neck when my grandmother moaned in church. I heard the white words of the old, nearly forgotten hymns, and felt how the irresistible need of black people to give contemporary witness to struggle infuses them with life."[8]

With Sweet Honey in the Rock, as with Martin Luther King, Jr., Sisyphus, Meridian, Carl Jung, Tashi Evelyn Johnson, Pierre, and Johnny (in Finding the Green Stone), we come upon our rock again. And we are made aware again of The Work to be done, the work required to transform a mountain of despair into a stone of hope, the work required to crack the rock and release the honey.

In *We Are the Ones*, Walker states that we are living in the worst and best of times, and that we need to ready ourselves to meet essentially spiritual trials with practical, life-affirming responses. War is ongoing and everywhere, writes Walker, and "the very Earth is being stolen from us, *by us*: the land and air poisoned, the water polluted, the animals disappeared, humans degraded and misguided."[9] The counterpoint to the dissonance or what makes this "*the best of times*," says Walker, is that "ancient graves, hidden deep in the shadows of the psyche and the earth, are breaking open of their own accord. Unwilling to be silent any longer. Incapable of silence."[10]

In addition to libraries, books, bookstores, and teachers, Walker writes, "99 percent of us have television or the Internet," which she refers to as "*the spider's web*."[11] All the sources of information allow us to see what had been obscured and to know what had been shrouded in secrecy. Information is readily available, facilitating our ability to divine the cause-and-effect of our situatedness. No matter the extent to which news stories are managed and the voice of truth is repressed, deception and hypocrisy will be revealed.

"No leader or people of any country will be safe from these upheavals that lead to exposure," states Walker, "We will know at least a bit of the truth about what is going on, and that will set us free" to understand that the oppression and domination under which we suffer and against which we struggle "is not a comment on our worth."[12]

We are required, she tells us, "to open our eyes, and awaken to our predicament." Moreover, we are required to search out the erstwhile hidden regions of our own hearts and minds, for we have been complicit in our collective problem. Nevertheless, Walker emphasizes, "We *live in a time of a global enlightenment*."[13] We must reclaim our attention in order to open to it. We must pay attention. That is, we must become aware of our own awareness, and notice on what it is that we allow our attention to focus; for whatever it is that we place our attention on, expands.

The dire condition of people around the planet and the ruthless handling of the planet compel us to withdraw our attention from the mind-dulling forces of those social institutions, political factions, corporate entities, and commercial enterprises that dehumanize, objectify, divide, and exploit us all. "Human beings may well be unable to break free of the dictatorship of greed that spreads like a miasma over the world," Walker speculates, "but no longer will we be an inarticulate and ignorant humanity, confused by our enslavement to superior cruelty and weaponry."[14] In the freedom of the truth is clarity.

"We have slumbered a long time believing the lies of those in power. Sending our children to fight those who might have been their playmates. And we know that those in power must spend a lot of their time laughing at us." Walker advocates that we pause, "Take a moment to think about how gullible, how innocent, we must seem to them. Moved about the world to do their bidding, like pieces of a chessboard."[15]

Given the repressive tactics of governmental and corporate entities and their ability to have the efforts of those "who believe in freedom" appear to be insignificant and futile, it may seem easier to accept the absurd hostility of the world as inevitable and to submit to a suicidal despair and resignation. But Walker offers her own life-journey as a mirror for the possibility that lies within each human breast and as encouragement to shout a resounding "Yes" to life and to resistance. As she asserts in *Anything We Love Can Be Saved: A Writer's Activism*, "I have a story to tell."[16]

Having participated in "the dismantling of American apartheid," Walker bore witness to the effects of intimidation and the trauma that causes the radiance of a human being to contract and shrink. Confronted with the socially constructed walls of racial discrimination, reinforced with hatred and violence, Alice Walker knew bleakness. But her activism renewed her hope: "During my years of being close to people engaged in changing the world I have seen fear turn into courage. Sorrow into joy. Funerals into celebrations. Because whatever the consequences, people, standing side by side, have expressed who they really are, and that ultimately they believe in the love of the world and each other enough *to be that*—which is the foundation of activism." She learned during this time, too, that "the daily news of disaster" numbs the spirit, but that one's activism, "however modest," runs counter to the "tide of death," and generates a "'news' that empowers rather than defeats."[17]

To withdraw into the slumbering, to settle even more deeply into the miasma of greed and indifference, Walker cautions, would be "the tragedy of the world." Walker's story testifies to the capability of the individual and the collective to trump the fear engendered by those who traffic in the politics of despair. "It has become a common feeling, I believe, as we have watched our heroes falling over the years, that our own small stone of activism, which might not seem to measure up to the rugged boulders of heroism we have so admired, is a paltry offering toward the building of an edifice of hope. Many who believe this choose to withhold their offerings out of shame."[18]

Walker's work, however, encourages the introspection and the cultivation of an enlightened awareness. It encourages The Work that facilitates the evolvement of the individuated Self. For even as social change requires collective effort, "we can't really do it from being a collective before we are actually self-collected," states Walker.[19] "For we can do nothing substantial toward changing our course on the planet, a destructive one, without rousing ourselves, individual by individual, and bringing our small, imperfect stones to the pile"—not to cast, but to build the "edifice of hope."[20] Walker points out that there is always something that one can do because you can always work with yourself. It is not necessary to try to do what others are doing or try to initiate something; "you can start ever so much in yourself. And that will evolve outwardly."[21]

Walker holds the inner work with the self to be imperative. For it is there that one's own spark abides. And it is that spark that sources one's personal fire, one's creative intelligence, and one's radiance. "Inner Light in a Time of Darkness," is the subtitle of We Are the Ones. Since the outer world reflects one's inner world, the focus of awareness needs to turn within. "It has to be there," Walker advises, because we carry our own inner light. We have, however, been distracted from it and indoctrinated to believe some leader or elected official or celebrity is the source of the light that guides us. So we forget our own small, flickering flame. "And so what we need to do, I think," ponders Walker, "is to be still enough to let that light shine, and illuminate our inner landscape and our dreams—especially our dreams. And then our dreams will lead us to the right way."[22]

Activism is a kind of currency for Walker: "it pays the rent on being alive and being on the planet."[23] And that activism was inspired by her great-great-great-great grandmother May Poole whose attitude and courage made it possible for her to endure a century of enslavement and outlive almost everyone who held her in bondage. Alice Walker was motivated to change the world she inherited—one of "master and slave," limitation and restriction, suppression and separation. She learned from the example of her parents and her community that they were their own best hope to survive an inimical world. At the same time, Walker had to cultivate her own light against the darkness and be the change she wanted to see in the world. Her continuing legacy is a light illuminating the path each one of us must take, the path that leads to the inner light which clarifies that "We are the ones."

SECTION V

Aether

Spark of cosmic intelligence. Aether is the subtlest vibratory element in the manifest world. Its other name is Akasha, "or space."[1] "Nature first gives rise to the intelligent vibratory ether, the subtle background on which all vibrations interplay. Ether in turn gives rise to intelligent cosmic energy, prana or lifetrons." The conscious fabric of the universe, aether is the medium through which Divine Intelligence speaks and listens, through which it moves and plays.[2] The expanse in which all arises, exists, and returns, aether is at the center of everything. It is an incandescent, glowing clarity.[3]

Aether is Essence. It is the vast "nothingness" pregnant with every possibility, potentiality, intentionality. It is the unfathomable "emptiness" containing all conceivable emanations. Aether is the element in which whatever arises becomes perceptible: "Space gives dimension to objects; ether separates the images." It is the matrix wherein vibratory earth, vibratory fire, vibratory air, vibratory water combine to form the macrocosm of universe and microcosm of human being.[4] The field between the material world and the astral dimension, Aether is Gateway.[5]

The element that enables perceptivity, aether teaches awareness. Accommodating all things, aether is spaciousness itself. The presence in which objects appear and disappear, aether teaches nonjudgment and nonattachment; containing all, it identifies with none. The ground of all experience, aether is effortless in its allowing. Everywhere and in all time, aether merges with the infinite internal world of Human, expressing its nature as Being.

"Little Girls"
by Phyllis McEwen

Little girls must be trained away from themselves.
Taught to think boy man at a hairpin turn.
Notice the difference as lack, deformity;
"This is a man's world."
And someone is always there to nod,
"Yes it is chile. Yes it is."
But don't they know this is your world?

That untrained unbridled little girl thing.
Who you are is this:
Short snake—braids that swell in the rain.
Thought machine whose thought is the only parallel to the ideal.
Legs stronger / longer than any pony. Your fantasies
Are the smoothest racket in town.

Little girls have to be trained away from their pleasure.
It must be turned against them.
If they are caught delighted with the sweet
Tomato slice of the self
the honey-bruise plum, like the sound of summer coming;
Little girls have to be taught against their strength.
Because they are the flat, magic chest willing to bubble out
Into a round brave memory of itself.
The rock body strong to suck another out from there:
The tiny, mean witch. Her ovaries are the future's eyes.

So you can dress her in the watered down version of red.
Tell her to be good, gently, fluffy, stuff like that.
But little girls are the tight buds

The hot pants
The pyramids of power
Pregnant when they first arrive.

If they can escape the training, the pruning, the moans,
They deliver, deliver, deliver.

TWENTY-ONE

The Cathedral of the Future

The nature of "God" and the purpose of creation—like "who am I," "what is this place in which I find myself," and "where, in this place, do I belong"—are among the prominent subjects of philosophical inquiry. Examination of such matters gives rise to philosophies, religions, ideologies, and social and political systems. Throughout her lifetime, Alice Walker has investigated these questions and has endeavored to live a life in accordance with the truths she has extrapolated from her observations and experimentations. Her writings reflect and document her search, and her discoveries form the narrative rhythm of her novels and the life-force that animates her characters. "In my novel *The Color Purple*," Walker writes, for example, "Celie and Shug discuss, as all thoughtful humans must, the meaning of God."[1]

However, Walker relates that in a society that cherished the master-slave dynamic, not only were African Americans denied their birthright as "thoughtful humans," but their very ability to believe in their own thinking was severely circumscribed or compromised. "There is a special grief felt by the children and grandchildren of those who were forbidden to read, forbidden to explore, forbidden to question or to know. Looking back on my parents' and grandparents' lives," says Walker, "I have often felt overwhelmed, helpless, as I've examined history and society, and especially religion, with them in mind, and have seen how they were manipulated away from a belief in their own judgment and faith in themselves."[2]

If, as Mzee says to Tashi and Adam in *Possessing the Secret of Joy*, "You, yourselves are your last hope," what becomes of those individuals or peoples who have been socialized into perceiving themselves as hopeless?[3] What happens when one's lifetime or whole generations are spent trying to correct a "flaw"—"of being black, female, human"—a flaw that never existed except as invented by men cloaked in the raiment of "God." The Mundo, in *By the Light of My Father's Smile*, could not bear to hear such lies and Magdalena, in spite of knowing the truth, was undone by them. In her work, Walker analyzes religious doctrine and follows deceptive and enslaving interpretations back to their sources. She then enters into dialogue with relatives and ancestors, while also communicating to readers the boon of her investigations:

> I speak to my parents and to my most distant ancestors about what I myself have found as an Earthling growing naturally out of the Universe. I create characters who sometimes speak in the language of immediate ancestors, characters who are not passive but active in the discovery of what is vital and real in this world. Characters who explore what it would feel like not to be imprisoned by the hatred of women, the love of violence, and the destructiveness of greed taught to human beings as the "religion" by which they must guide their lives.[4]

Masses of people have been taught by destructive religious systems to look to heaven as a reward for the trials they suffer in earthly life. But Walker discovered this: "The Only Reason You Want to Go to Heaven Is That You Have Been Driven Out of Your Mind (Off Your Land and Out of Your Lover's Arms)."[5] What she discovered forms the title of an essay in which she presents insights into the mandate of a patriarchal religion that distracts masses of people from their own best interest. Walker's family labored six days a week as sharecroppers. An inherently criminal system, sharecropping proved to be worse than slavery, writes Walker, as white supremacists resented black people their freedom. "It is no wonder that under such complete subjugation and outright terrorism, which included rape, beatings, burnings, and being thrown off the land, along with the entrenched Southern custom of lynching, people like my parents sought succor from any God they were forced to have." The idea that her family—descendants of Africans, Native Americans and Scotch and Irish Europeans—might have had ancient Gods of their own to inspire them or that they were free to choose a god unique to their own vision, "never entered their minds, except negatively."[6]

They had been told that they were cursed, by God. They were taught that their only hope of redemption and their only possibility for a better existence lay in being like Jesus—whose father owned heaven. Jesus might allow them entry if they managed to be "extra good, obedient, trusting," and acquiescent to "a lifetime of crushing toil and persistent abuse." "Where is heaven?" a young Walker asked her parents. She wanted to know what heaven was like and who was going to be there. "I was told what they sincerely believed: that heaven was in the sky"; "only the best people on earth would go there when they died"; and once there, one could lounge and feast while angels played their harps. The presence of whites was felt to be a disturbing probability—given racial segregation. And there was faith that Christ would be there and speak up for them. "After all, these were black people who were raised never to look a white person directly in the face."[7]

Yet, even as a child, Walker could not concede the notion that her parents were sinners. They were not easy to be around sometimes, she allowed, but she could not see that a white woman, a long time ago, who had eaten and shared with her husband an apple that was given to her by a snake, justified her parents' onerous existence and very possible damnation. "I had a problem with this doctrine at a very early age," writes Walker. "I could not see how my parents had sinned. . . . They were as innocent as trees." She resented both the minister who had condemned them and his Bible that granted him authority to do so. "But what could I do?" she despaired, "I was three years old." The truth as Walker saw it was that heaven or paradise was on earth. But her folks "were worked too hard by the land-grabbers to enjoy it."[8]

Nevertheless, her family's connection to the land was undeniable. They lived in the country where they farmed, planted, and harvested crops. They were peasants, "of the land," meaning they were pagan, Walker explains. "Pagan" also describes someone "whose primary spiritual relationship is with Nature and the Earth. And this, I could see, day to day, was true not only of me but of my parents." However, there was no way for her family to ritualistically express their magical and intimate relationship with creation without being perceived as "indulging in 'heathenism,' that other word for paganism." Moreover, the whole purpose of orthodox Christianity was to deliver them from "*that*."[9] The Bible she would "reverently dust" on Saturdays when she helped her mother clean the church had instructed its adherents to murder those who were unfaithful to the God of Israel. If believers discovered anyone among them, "man or woman," who had "gone and served other gods, and worshipped them either the sun, or moon, or any of the host of heaven, which I had not commanded," these believers were obligated to "stone them with stones, till they die."[10]

Likewise, if a woman or a man had "a familiar spirit" or was a "wizard," followers of the patriarchal, Judaic God were required to kill them. They were directed to "stone them with stones: their blood shall be upon them."[11] "In fact," writes Walker, "millions of people were broken, physically and spiritually, literally destroyed, for nearly two millennia, as the orthodox Christian Church 'saved' them from their traditional worship of the Great Mystery they perceived in Nature."[12] Intrinsic to Alice Walker's spiritual activism is a salvific energy that seeks to wake us up from the enthrallment of contrived religious orthodoxy and to the realization that freedom and spirit are synonymous.

In *Temple of My Familiar*, Miss Lissie's dream about her familiar was a kind of parable that demonstrated the relationship between spirit and freedom, which Miss Lissie had learned, was essentially the same. If one's spirit is colonized, one's instinct for survival as a free being is imperiled. Part of Walker's work as spiritual activist was to see past the mud and "bullfrog spoors" that covered her baptized face, to the ominous fact of spiritual colonization.[13]

The subtitle of the essay "The Only Reason You Want to Go to Heaven," suggests a path to one's spiritual freedom: "Clear Seeing Inherited Religion and Reclaiming the Pagan Self." It was necessary, as Shug Avery counseled Miss Celie, "to git man off your eyeball."[14] Perhaps then one could see the World Child who sat right behind the eyeball. It was necessary to see through repressive dogma and men who refused to be what they were. It was necessary to question a doctrine of casting stones rather than sharing bread, a doctrine that undermined the collective One Spirit that reveals Itself in the axiom we are "Each other's / Own."[15] Once Shug Avery stepped away from the image of "the little fat white man" with which she was indoctrinated, she could see that "God is everything that is, ever was or ever will be." "I agree also," seconded Walker. Only years after she had penned the lines Shug Avery uttered did Walker learn Shug's words were echoes from the ancient Goddess Isis, "who, as an African, can be said to be a spiritual mother of us all."[16]

Although her inclination as a child was to be suspicious of an inglorious religious heritage, Alice Walker also had to engage in the research and discovery of her own ancient gods; for she, too, had been indoctrinated away for her self. Just as the mothers of little girls subjected them to the tradition of female genital mutilation, Walker's mother had her baptized at seven years of age into an inherited religion that avowed she was cursed, promised she would suffer, and demanded that she submit. Apprenticed to her mother, who was the mother of the church, Walker, in retrospect saw that she was "kind of a little church mother in training," taught to clean a pulpit wherein the sacred feminine was not welcome and to dust a sacred book which forbade her to speak.[17] On reflection, she considered the irony. How is it, she wanted to know,

> that the very woman out of whose body I came, whose pillowy arms still held me, willingly indoctrinated me away from herself and the earth from which both of us received sustenance, and toward a frightful, jealous, cruel, murderous "God" of another race and tribe of people, and expected me to forget the very breasts that had fed me and that I still leaned against. But such is the power of centuries-old indoctrination.[18]

Celie was adamant about chasing the old white man out of her head. "But this hard work, let me tell you. He been there so long, he don't want to budge." Though he had never listened "to poor colored women," he demanded their reverence and obedience. "But it ain't easy trying to do without God," acknowledged Celie. "Even if you know he ain't there, trying to do without him is a strain."[19] Because the human psyche expresses a religious instinct, Celie's dilemma is the dilemma of humanity. Carl Jung saw that "the psyche spontaneously produces images with a religious content, that it is 'by nature religious.' It also became apparent to him that numerous neuroses spring from a disregard for this fundamental characteristic of the psyche."[20]

Without proper regard for and vigilance of this religious faculty of the psyche, one is not only subject to neurosis, but one is also vulnerable to spiritual colonialism. That is, one is subject to the willful manipulation of one's religious faculty by deceitful others. Whether or no one believes in a "God," one's innate capacity for belief remains. Whether or no one professes faith in a "God," one's innate capacity for faith remains. Both will manifest, somehow—consciously or unconsciously. As Alice Walker's sociopolitical activism exhorts mindfulness about where we place the focus of our awareness, her spiritual activism emphasizes the importance of assuming personal responsibility for one's soul.

"It is fatal to love a God who does not love you," explicates Walker.[21]It is unconscionable, she argues, that a "God would be so cruel as to curse women and men forever for eating a piece of fruit; no matter how forbidden."[22] People of color, and women across the spectrum of culture and class and throughout the reign of patriarchy, "have been so successfully brainwashed to believe that white orthodox Christianity has given us something we didn't already have that we rarely think of what it has taken away."[23] This sentiment compels Tashi, in *Possessing*, to lash out at Olivia, her Christian missionary friend: "You don't even know what you've lost! And the nerve of you, to bring us a God someone else chose for you!"[24] In Walker's poem "When You Look," is a counter-narrative to the fear engendered by the threatening voice of orthodox Christian patriarchs. It is a liberating thought in the psyche, whispering: It is unnecessary to believe someone who tells you heaven is in the sky. It is unwise to follow those who conceal one's true identity with God. Heaven, the poem whispers, is not a matter of inventing but of recognizing Glory.[25]

Walker recognizes this Glory, to which the poem alludes, as "the God of nonjudgmental Nature." Unconditional in its love for and support of human life, It doesn't require that human beings be other than they are; there's no need "to deny your shadow side" and live a hypocritical life.[26] "I don't believe there is a God beyond nature," states Walker. Without nature, she shrugs, she could not live. "The earth is my God, and nature is its spirit." Walker proclaims herself "a born-again pagan and quite happy in nature."[27]

Her arrival at this understanding of herself is the outcome of The Work in which she has engaged, the *magnum opus* of the scientific and the philosophical alchemist. Walker embraced the perspectives of Christian Gnostics who believed in The Great Work—the alchemical process—that would lead to transcendent wisdom. This process, of both alchemists and alchemical Gnostics, entailed experimentation. Throughout her life, Walker has searched out pathways to individual freedom and societal transformation. As an elder, she sees it as her responsibility "to travel to those realms from which might come new (or ancient) visions of how humans might live peacefully and more lovingly upon the earth."[28]

As a writer, she has experimented with form, stylistics, and content—across genres and across media. Her art is expressed through recitation and lecture, in print and illustrative drawings, via film, and on website blogs. Walker's novels *The Temple of My Familiar* and *By the Light of My Father's Smile* can be considered as mystical literature, for they reflect and extend the spiritual and literary tradition of Christian Gnosticism, a sect of Christianity that encouraged originality and creative expression. The novels exemplify the kind of imaginative literature that emanates from divinely inspired, mystical experience.

"Like circles of artists today," writes Elaine Pagels in *The Gnostic Gospels*, "gnostics considered original creative invention to be the mark of anyone who becomes spiritually alive. Each one, like students of a painter or writer, expected to express his own perceptions by revising and transforming what he was taught. Whoever merely repeated his teacher's words was considered immature"; for, the initiated or mature Gnostic "[comes] to believe from the truth itself."[29] The truth that is revealed to them is understood in accordance with "their own intuition" and their feelings accord with "the harmony that can be seen in creation." What is revealed to them constitutes "their own insight—their own *gnosis*," writes Pagels. And that insight is then expressed "by creating new myths, poems, rituals, 'dialogues' with Christ, revelations, and accounts of their vision."[30]

Walker fully embraced her identity as a creative soul, a visionary artist who is compelled to "experiment": "The writer—like the musician or painter—must be free to explore, otherwise she or he will never discover what is needed (by everyone) to be known. This means, very often, finding oneself considered 'unacceptable' by masses of people who think that the writer's obligation is not to explore or to challenge, but to second the masses' motions, whatever they are."[31] Despite sometimes fierce opposition to her activism, the banning of her books, and hostile adversaries who have directly threatened her life, Alice Walker continued in her pursuit of *gnosis* and in her artistic expression of the knowledge which is revealed to her as the knowledge that is needed to be known by everyone. "I accept all the criticism," states Walker, "I am so thankful that my ancestors made me really strong. You know, I'm really strong, and I understand that strength, having suffered a lot, but I am strong enough to take it, because we are worth it. We are *worth* it."[32]

In *The Temple of My Familiar*, Walker explores insights that resonate with Christian Gnosticism. She creates the character Fanny who sometimes assumes the identity of Christ. "She was, for about a year and a half, really into being Christ. Or, as she would put it, '*a* Christ,' which she said anyone could be."[33] For the Gnostics held, "Whoever achieves *gnosis* becomes 'no longer a Christian, but a Christ.'"[34] And Fanny is the granddaughter of Shug Avery, who like Christ, founds her own church. The tenets of her faith are documented in "The Gospel According to Shug."

In content and style, Shug's "Gospel" recalls the Beatitude sermons recounted in the books of Matthew and Luke in the New Testament. But Shug's gospel does not merely imitate Christ's enumeration of blessings for the multitudes. Her gospel interrogates certain teachings within Christ's sermon, while it revises others and presents new perspectives. In doing so, Shug follows the example of Christ, who, in a mode similar to the signifying tradition in African American folk culture, repeats, then revises the teachings of Moses and the Jewish priests. As Christ's sermons stood in a signifying relationship to the teachings of the Old Testament, so Shug Avery's gospel stands in relation to the teachings of the New Testament.

That Walker titles the pamphlet that contains Shug's writing a "gospel" rather than a sermon, is significant. The gospel, *according to Shug*, envisions Shug as an apostle. Christian Gnostics were among the repressed factions of Christians who embraced those disciples who were not numbered among the twelve recognized by the orthodox church. And, as Pagels writes, "Attributing a writing to a specific apostle" suggests a symbolic meaning. For, according to biblical scholars, gospels were often written by persons other than those to which the gospels were ascribed. Therefore, the titles of such works, states Pagels, "indicate that they were written 'in the spirit' of John, Mary, Magdalene, Philip, or Peter."[35] Thus, Walker writes this gospel "in the spirit" of Shug. What distinguishes Shug Avery's spirit would be evidenced not only in the interrogations or revisions of particular verses, but also in the additional knowledge or perspectives presented.

Carlotta, a character in *Temple* who is in search of her identity and sense of belonging like many of the characters in the novel, discusses Shug's pamphlet with Arveyda, the husband from whom she is separated. Their discussion highlights some of the distinguishing aspects of Shug's revelations. "I like parts of Shug's gospel," she tells Arveyda, "at least she doesn't go on about blessed are the poor. And I love the next to the last line, where she talks about blessed are those who love and support diversity because, in their differentness, they shall be secure." Like Christ's sermon, Shug's gospel addresses societal issues. As Christ revised and reinterpreted traditional teachings in context of a contemporary framework, Shug addresses the social issues of her day—among them racism, heterosexism, cultural hegemony, and the tyranny of tradition. "But the last line baffles me," says Carlotta. "Blessed are those who *know*. Know *what*, I ask myself. And then I think of how I don't, in fact, *know*; and wonder if I ever will."[36]

Arveyda assured Carlotta that she would: "'You *are* beginning to *know*, Carlotta,' he said, with such tenderness that both of them blushed. And then: 'How it becomes you.'"[37] Arveyda's latter comment evokes Fanny's favorite saying of the Goddess Nut: "Whatever I embrace, becomes." The saying recalls the need to be aware and mindful of our inclinations and desires: "we must, all of us, turn toward whatever it is that we do want, in our lives, in our loves, on the planet, and whatever we don't want, just have sense enough to leave alone."[38]

Carlotta wants to *know*, and by questioning her own knowledge—by inquiring into *gnosis*—she has ignited the process of awakening. Shug's gospel, however, doesn't speak of blessings, but of assistance. "HELPED are those who *know*."[39] The emphasis on helping implies that only the individual can initiate the process of self-realization. And as an initiate might listen to a teacher or read a book or pamphlet, ultimately, she must find her own truth, just as Christian Gnostics "derived their *gnosis* from their own experience."[40] Unique also to "The Gospel According to Shug" is the teaching that *gnosis* or truth is grounded in the awe of the cosmos and the love of Earth: "Helped are those who love the Earth, their mother, and who willingly suffer that she may not die; in their grief over her pain they will weep rivers of blood, and in their joy in her lively response to love, they will converse with trees."[41]

The front and back of Shug's pamphlet is illustrated "by several large, serenely alert elephants."[42] In Hindu cosmology, "elephants are related to clouds and rain and hence fertility." They represent antiquity, generosity, perseverance, royalty, and sovereignty. The elephant figures in the pantheon of Hindu deities as Gaṇeśa, the "elephant-headed deity," who assists devotees with the removal of obstacles, and does so with grace and gentleness. Gaṇeśa also symbolizes both intelligence and faith, for both are needed to progress on one's path. With the head of an elephant and the body of a human, Gaṇeśa is a reminder of the oneness of all life and that humans are not separate from nature.[43]

The church Shug founded was encoded in the words and images enfolded in a pamphlet, "not a building or any kind of monument, but simply a few words gleaned, like spiritual rice grains, from her earthly passage."[44] Christ did not deliver his Beatitudes in a synagogue, a temple, or church, but on the mount and on the open plains. Likewise, Shug, who never "found God in church," but did find It in herself and in nature, expressed her gospel in a pamphlet that could be picked up and carried like a leaf on the wind. Shug's notion of divinity and worship resonated with that of Manuelito, the twin of Emmanuel, in *By the Light*: "The cathedral of the future will be nature. . . . In the end, people will be driven back to trees. To streams. To rocks that do not have anything built on them."[45]

TWENTY-TWO

Caritas: The Greatest of These

The church of her childhood formed Alice Walker's *"beloved community."* In this church—the building and the people—she felt embraced by life. The small, simple structure made of "silver-gray lumber" and *"the warmth of the human relationships fashioned within its walls and yard, have influenced every aspect of my life,"* reflects Walker.[1] The teachings of Jesus Christ were integral to the ethos of her beloved community. But as Walker would come to reject inherited religions that were hostile to humanity and Earth, she would also resist Christianity.

Like Miss Celie who battled with the white patriarch emblazoned on her mind's eye, Walker resisted the received image of Jesus Christ. She had "struggled for many years trying to deny him, get rid of him, or ignore him, because he is a captive of the church and they use him for absolutely everything."[2] Yet, he would not be denied and she would eventually open to Jesus's unconditional love and his teachings. For, unlike Miss Celie's apoplectic patriarch who never listened to "poor colored women," Jesus did.

"And I feel a great love for Jesus as a teacher and as a very feminine soul," says Walker, "especially during that time. His tenderness, his caring quality always makes me think of someone who was raised by his mother. I mean, he's the son of a feminist." Such men, observes Walker, love and respect women and are at ease in their company. "You don't have to tell them that women don't like to be called 'bitch' or 'witch' or whatever in a negative way: they know this."[3] In the poem "You Will Never Know," Walker expresses appreciation for Christ's efforts to end violence against women. The poem depicts a community's stoning of a woman. A long-established practice, the stoning was executed with perfect barbarity: this stone is best for crushing a skull, this one for bashing the bridge of a nose, and the other for bruising the eyes shut. Christ tried to stop this practice. His love for woman, Earth, and the feminine within himself endeared him to Walker.[4]

The patriarchal orientation of orthodox Christianity notwithstanding, Walker found Christ's love and loving-kindness irresistible: "I think we should just kidnap Christ and go off with him; he's the best of the whole bunch."[5] The paganistic aspects of Christ's ministry coincided with Walker's own pagan sensibilities and resonated with those aspects of other religious, spiritual, and philosophical traditions which formed her spiritual foundation. Walker believed a spiritual foundation to be essential; for as one moved through life, it was important to be centered.

Her spirituality was eclectic. She absorbed and practiced the gospel of love and nonviolence. She imbibed the social philosophy of liberalism and humanism. She learned Transcendental Meditation. She prayed through her art. She sat in drumming and healing circles with Indigenous peoples of the Americas and among the Aborigines of Australia. She studied with shamans. She practiced ancient Tibetan Buddhist Lojong and Tonglen teachings. Buddhism, Walker states, "makes so much sense."[6]

She has sat in conversation with Tibetan Buddhist nun Pema Chödrön and with the Dalai Lama, Tenzin Gyatso. In the praise poem "What Makes the Dalai Lama Loveable?" Walker describes his effortless beauty and profound influence, and calls him "my teacher."[7] She has incorporated the wisdom teachings of Thich Nhat Hanh into her activism and writings. And in the opening of her 2013 collection of essays, *The Cushion in the Road*, she proclaims, "I have learned much from Taoist thought." The title of the book is also an apt image that reflects the spirit of an Elder whose compassion for people and Earth continue to lure her "out into the world to see how it is doing."[8]

Walker believes that "for many of us, what has happened is that we have perhaps taken some parts of the religions we were raised in, and we have incorporated them into our belief systems—with gratitude. . . . But we're making a new religion."[9] Her spiritual philosophy is also eclectic, with this central thought: "There is / no God / but love."[10] Walker stresses the importance of having "some kind of practice so that when we do go out into the world to confront these more and more horrible situations, we can do that with a feeling of knowing that we are in the right place in ourselves."[11]

A spiritual practice is equally important in keeping one centered when challenging situations arise in the intimate space of one's private and personal life. Throughout her work, Walker has shared difficult and challenging aspects of her personal life. And she has done so even regarding the complexities and emotional pain that attend motherhood and the stark reality that she had "lost" her daughter.

In "Sunniness and Shade," Walker contemplated her "twenty-five years with the woman who made me a mother"—daughter Rebecca. In this essay, in *Anything We Love Can Be Saved*, she looks at "the bittersweet struggle involved in mothering a child."[12] She was taken aback by the realization that she and her daughter had reproduced the same psycho-emotional dynamic that had characterized Walker's childhood relationship with her own mother: the dutiful daughter who, out of love for and protectiveness of the mother who leaves home to slay all sorts of dragons on a daily basis, hides her own loneliness, insecurities, and sense of abandonment.

"I have loved being Rebecca's mom," writes Walker. "There's no one I'd rather hear from, talk with, listen to. Except," hesitates Walker, "for those times when I've had to face the ways in which my being her mother made life harder for her."[13] Except when the hurt and depression hidden behind Rebecca's fundamentally "sunny" disposition erupt. As what lies in the subconscious mind oftentimes wills itself into the conscious realm, Walker witnessed her daughter's other "faces of sorrow, anger, cloud, and storm." Remembering the "valiant solidarity" she felt for her overworked mother, as well as the anger and suicidal depression she experienced, consequent to her own self-denial, Walker's heart broke for her daughter's anguished suffering.[14]

"One of my longest relationships, and the most important," Walker is still astonished that her daughter is "so tall." "This completely separate person came out of my body; I have the stretch marks to prove it." She was still awed by the miracle that is life, that is birth, that is magic women do in peopling the earth. She was equally awed by the inconceivable fact of having found that her

Alice Walker at a Q & A on *Beauty in Truth* in Atlanta. (Gloria Jean Plant-Gilbert)

relationship with her daughter had become estranged. Thirteen years later, the poem "Lost," in *Hard Times Require Furious Dancing*, would inform the reader, "My daughter / is lost / to me."[15] Three years later, in the 2013 film documentary, *Beauty in Truth*, Walker would honor the difficult and speak openly about her relationship with Rebecca.

During the Q & A that followed the world premiere of *Beauty in Truth*, at Queen Elizabeth Hall, London, Walker shared her thoughts and feelings with her audience. "It's the last thing that I would have thought would happen in my life, that I would lose my daughter. It's just this one thing I never even imagined, that I would lose my daughter. And not only that, that I would lose her, not to death, but to a kind of death in life situation."

Yet Walker's faith, nourished in the regenerative power of nature, spiritual practice, and a lifetime of embracing and dancing with struggle, allowed her to open to a philosophical appreciation of her familial circumstances. "I was brought up in a culture where to be a mother was never thought of as just being the mother of your child, just your child. That's totally not my culture. . . . We always thought that to be a mother was to be a mother in the old, old, old sense where you were the mother of everyone in your village, everyone in your community, and everyone . . . everywhere. And I feel this very deeply."[16]

In "Sunniness and Shade," Walker conveys a discovery that "the world is full of mothers who've done their best and still hurt their daughters: that we have daughters everywhere."[17] Inspired by the mothering spirit of Amma, "the hugging saint from Kerala," Walker's heart breaks only to open wider and embrace all daughters as her daughter.[18] And because she had not yet experienced the joy of hugging her grandson, Tenzin Rangdrol, her arms would open even wider to embrace all her grandchildren.

Kaleo Larson, Valery Boyd, Alice Walker, Walker's dog Charlie, Beverly Guy-Sheftall, and Kathleen Bertrand at the Atlanta premier of the film documentary *Alice Walker: Beauty in Truth*. (Gloria Jean Plant-Gilbert)

The optimism she had grown into as one who had overcome despairing and depressing situations and seemingly insurmountable challenges allowed Walker to also anticipate hugging her grandson, as she does in "Meeting You." In this poem she expresses the sentiment that only Life knows the reason it has kept them apart, but what she *knows*, is that, ultimately, nothing can separate them. In *Beauty in Truth*, Walker imagines a possible scenario of their meeting: "One day he will get on his bicycle and come over, I'm sure. But until he does, there are millions of grandsons and millions of granddaughters."[19]

Whether one experiences a sense of loss or sorrow in relation to one's personal family or the world family, Walker attests that we all suffer; for suffering is intrinsic to the human condition. Nevertheless, she relates that not only is suffering useful, but that it is also, ultimately transformative—though in the midst of suffering, the transformative value may not be apparent.

Walker chanced upon this view of suffering while reading Elaine Pagels's *The Gnostic Gospels*, "and there was a quote from Jesus in the Gospels that didn't make it into the Bible (it seems to me his best stuff was censored). He said if you learn to suffer, if you learn *how* to suffer you will not suffer."[20] Given that suffering is inevitable and inescapable, acceptance of it might be deemed a reasonable response. Walker believes, then, that one's task is "to get to know it, and to learn it, and learn how to do it." One can practice the acceptance of suffering by engaging it rather than denying it. Becoming familiar with it rather than surprised by it. And being mindful against projecting it rather than inflicting it onto others. "And true enough," testifies Walker, "I learned how to suffer, which was mainly a matter of *accepting* that I was and that it was not to be escaped. I suffered much less! It was amazing—I felt an instant lightening of spirit."[21]

Walker also references the practice of Tonglen as instrumental in her process of becoming familiar with suffering. Tonglen, as Walker describes it, "is basically a practice of breathing in pain, fear, and darkness, and breathing out what you'd rather the world had." This practice, says Walker, has the effect of releasing dense and heavy emotions that are trapped in a tight and constricted heart. "We need help from the ancient teachings to show us how to stretch and open our hearts." This Tibetan Buddhist practice, which Walker learned through the teachings of Pema Chödrön, "encourages people to accept life in its totality, not just the good parts," says Walker. [22] The perceptions of Westerners tend toward polarizing paradigms such as right-wrong and good-bad, and they feel guilty or at fault when things go "wrong" or an outcome is perceived as "bad." "But sometimes," explains Walker, "things go wrong to teach you what is right." Difficult times, harsh circumstances, and unspeakable loss, she concludes, can yield crucial lessons.[23]

Walker, however, does not dismiss how absurd, difficult, and injurious life events can be: "I am the youngest of eight siblings. Five of us have died. I share losses, health concerns, and other challenges common to the human condition, especially in these times of war, poverty, environmental devastation, and greed that are quite beyond the most creative imagination. Sometimes it all feels a bit too much to bear."[24] At such times, Walker concedes that it may feel impossible to sit, be still, be silent, and meditate. At such times there may be no words to articulate what is unutterable. At such times, there is nothing left to say or do, says Walker—but dance!

Walker expresses this wisdom in the poetry volume titled *Hard Times Require Furious Dancing*. There are poems that register pain, fear, despair, and disaster. But they are met with poems that are touching in their compassion, fierce in their resolve to love, and committed to the Dance of Life. "Suffering is not the end-all in life," Walker announces, "It is a part of it, and then we rise above it, we work through it, we transform it. Jesus did that." And so Walker advocates for accounts of Jesus that encompass "his dancing quality and his joyfulness."[25] Walker's allusion to a dancing Christ is drawn from The Acts of John in the Gnostic Gospels wherein Christ, while teaching his disciples how not to suffer, instructs them on how to dance and chant:

> "To the Universe belongs the dancer."—"Amen."
> "He who does not dance does not know what happens."—
>   "Amen." . . .
> "Now if you follow my dance, see yourself in Me who am
>   speaking . . .
> You who dance, consider what I do, for yours is
> This passion of Man which I am to suffer. For you could by
>   no means have understood what you suffer
> unless to you as Logos I had been sent by the Father . . .
> Learn how to suffer and you shall be able not to suffer."[26]

Christ's words are presented as a call-and-response chant. Implied in the format is the spirit of community which shatters the illusion of separation and alienation, as the individual voice of caller and responder harmonize into a Unified Oneness. According to John, after Christ danced with them, "he went out [to suffer]" the passions of the crucifixion. However, Christ revealed himself to John in a vision, saying, "I have suffered none of the things which they will say of me; even that suffering which I showed to you and to the rest in my dance, I will that it be called a mystery."[27]

Walker's appreciation of dance and its relationship to suffering, celebration, and transcendence reflects ideas set forth in the Gnostic Gospels. For Walker, dance expresses grief *and* joy. It is both balm and stimulant. It steadies and it readies one for the Dance of Life. From the conga lines in Helsinki, Finland, that celebrated the Cuban Revolution, and the dancing Yoruba Priestess in London whose dance blessed Walker and Parmar's work against female genital mutilation, and the dancing celebrants in the common room surrounded by the rubble of demolished homes in Palestine, to the "spirited line dance" created by relatives of Walker at a family gathering in California, Walker acknowledges and participates in dance, the Universal movement of life.[28]

In *Hard Times Require Furious Dancing*, Walker honors "the role of dance in the healing of families, communities, and nations."[29] In *The World Will Follow*

Joy and *The Cushion in the Road*, along with *Hard Times*, she pays homage to *"the notion of song"* that was "kept alive, in so many of our ancestors" and embodied in the form and genius of singers like Phillis Wheatley.[30] Walker's poems and essays encourage readers to "Lift Every Voice and Sing"—which is the first song Walker learned to sing as a child. And at age sixty-five, it is the first song she learned to play on piano, finally realizing her childhood dream of pianist.[31]

As Dance and Song enjoins us to the Circle of Life, Alice Walker invites us to create circles of healing that affirm and nurture life. She encourages the creation of women's and elders' councils about the land; for children "need to know that there are adults *somewhere* sitting together and discussing, at least, what it's going to take for us to survive this brave new world."[32] Circles and councils, says Walker, are ways to "share consciousness," as well as create community. She observes that most people are aware of our perilous condition as earthlings and that "there is no trustworthy leadership. It's important to comfort and be with each other during this time because so many people are alone. That really shouldn't be, but that's where this culture has brought us, to loneliness and isolation."[33]

Perceiving oneself as outside the circle of life, states Walker, is fatal. "You have to feel, I think, more or less equal and valid in order for the whole organism to feel healthy."[34] As Walker envisions them, circles connote connection, cooperation, and confidence; and democracy, equanimity, and inclusivity. They allow for easy circulation of the radical energy of love that recognizes, as Thich Nhat Hanh states, "man is not our enemy."[35] The unconditional quality of love transforms consciousness and allows one the capacity to salute "our friends the enemy." The elucidating power of love that emboldens us to see the "other," the "enemy" as the "same shadowy parts of ourselves" is what compels us to do the Work that brings about change.[36] "In Buddhist thought," Walker writes, "one's enemy is likely to teach so much we otherwise would not learn, is so helpful in strengthening us in ways we might never have imagined, and is so likely to be a primary reason for our growth, that it is wise to recognize him or her as a friend."[37]

Love is the true gold which has the mysterious capacity to "turn our madness into flowers." Walker's poem "Even So" suggests that one can trust in this kind of omnipotent and abiding Love which is "embedded in us, / like seams of gold in the Earth."[38]

TWENTY-THREE

Ouroboros

In *Now Is the Time to Open Your Heart*, Alice Walker comes full circle. She addresses all the major preoccupations to which she devoted herself at the beginning of her enfoldment as writer-activist, along with those she had come to embrace: the lives of black women, the spiritual survival, *whole*, of black people; Spirit, elders and ancestors, her triple identities as African-Amerindian; Earth, humanity and all life-forms; transformation and change, joy and love. In *Now Is the Time*, she addresses these subjects in context of her contemplations on the Circle of Life. And she does so from the vantage point of a seasoned Elder imbued with Grandmother wisdom and the sharp introspection of one who wrote in her college essay on Cicero, "I would not feel that I should be anything but the philosopher."

As Elder and sage, Alice Walker understood that all species of life are interdependent and equally important. Thus, Walker stated, "Just in the natural course of existence my focus has moved to include more than people."[1] She recognized Earth as humanity's most ancient ancestor and the serpent as a symbol of Earth's sacred spirit. The serpent moves almost imperceptibly through the body of Walker's work. In the chapter "Indians and Ecstasy" in *Meridian*, Walker explores the Sacred Serpent of Native American myth and lore and reflects on its association with immortality, enlightenment, and spiritual mysticism.

In *Temple of My Familiar*, the snake is an animal familiar. It is also discussed in relation to the Great Mother of Africa in the form of Medusa, the goddess whom Perseus decapitates. Fanny's sister Nzingha describes Perseus with "the severed head of Medusa, her snakelike locks of hair presented as real snakes—everywhere in Africa a symbol of fertility and wisdom—and there were even two snakes floating about the corners of her mouth."[2] Here, Walker interrogates Greco-European epics whose narratives progress only as a consequence of the destruction of the Dark Mother and the serpent that embodies her spirit.

In her childhood years, Walker was one with nature and had no fear of the outdoors. But in her adult life, she had developed an attitude similar to the elderly woman in *Now Is The Time* who had "learned to live without picking up any snakes" because she "killed everyone she saw."[3] In the essay "Everything Is a Human Being," in *Living by the Word*, Walker relates that she would either chase snakes away from her garden or call someone who would kill them. She confesses to having succumbed to religious indoctrination and of having played the role of the frightened lady in need of the rescuing knight.

"Everything I was ever taught about snakes—that they are dangerous, frightful, repulsive, sinister—went into the murder of this snake person" who was only trying to remain in its home, wrote Walker. Her fear of the snake, and her "ladylike 'nervousness'" upon seeing the snake was all learned behavior. "I knew at once that killing the snake was not the first act that should have occurred in my new garden, and I grieved that I had apparently learned nothing, as a human being, since the days of Adam and Eve."[4] Having opened to the wisdom of her Native American kin, she learned to respect the snake as a relative—her Grandfather no less.

In the collection of drawings and poetry in *A Poem Traveled Down My Arm*, there is a drawing of two snakes undulating in a northeasterly direction. The first is longer and is an outline in black. Nearby and to the right of it is a smaller snake whose shape is filled in black. There seems to be a protective, parent-child dynamic in play. But as they are two, the snakes may well represent the twin nature of the Cosmic Serpent who is androgynous or bisexual and, in many ancient mythologies, is the creatrix-god of the human species. On the opposite page is, "Snake / they / separated / us."[5]

Kate Nelson, the protagonist in *Now Is the Time*, contemplates this separation: "*What does it mean to be completely outside the circle of goodwill?*"[6] It is a question that resonates with her, for it is a question entertained, at some point, by groups of people who find themselves outside the goodwill of a society. And it is entertained, at some point, by individuals who experience a sense of alienation within the private sphere of their individual lives. This is the point wherein we meet Kate in the novel. Like the anaconda in her dreams that is alive though frozen, Kate's life-force is frozen. She had lived the conventional life of marriage, family, and career. At middle age, however, rather than feeling fulfilled, she felt robbed, usurped, and separated from her own good. She had awakened from the spellbinding societal narrative of domesticity. But no longer attached to the narrative, she felt herself adrift.

Kate was a woman who was "no longer sure there was a path through life or how, indeed, to follow one if there was." Nonetheless, she concluded, "I need more of my own life." She had recurrent dreams of a dry riverbed within herself. Intuitively she knew that her dry river had to be connected to a wet river "somewhere on earth."[7] Compelled by an internal force, Kate found herself waiting for the boats that would move her downriver from the Colorado in North America to the Amazon in South America, to somewhere better.

The serpentine flow of these rivers as described in the novel evokes the imagery and symbolism of the sacred serpent and they writhe with its initiatory power. Kate's travels downriver—with rapids to ride, boulders to skirt, and crocodiles and piranhas to avoid—symbolize the nature of the work before her. Yet even as life brings "many deep rivers / To cross," It brings "as many sturdy / Boats."[8] So as the Colorado and the Amazon carry Kate on a journey to the interior of her self, the Cosmic Serpent calls all humanity back to its origins, back to the power of the Heart, back to its oneness with all Creation, back to the Circle of Life.

Like the sloughing off of skin that allows the snake to emerge from its old self, reborn and renewed, Kate's frequent regurgitation and diarrhea while on her journeys release the stagnant energy of her past lives. During her three weeks on the Colorado, she frees herself from a "massive accumulation of words . . . collected over a lifetime." They filled her throat and spewed forth. "Words she had said or had imagined saying or had swallowed before saying to her father, dead these many years. All the words to her mother. To her husbands. Children. Lovers. The words shouted back at the television set, spreading its virus of mental confusion."[9] Toward the end of her three weeks on the Colorado, Kate found that her dry river was indeed connected to this wet one. It had flowed into and stirred the dry river of Kate's dreams. Her life-force had begun to writhe, and she had to decipher its meaning and her response to it.

It was in her dream of emptying her freezer that she had discovered the inert anaconda. She had run about seeking help to destroy it. "She felt she must kill it before it thawed." But she was unsuccessful in communicating her distress. Upon awakening, she realized that "dealing with the anaconda was an inside job. Whether to kill it or let it thaw and live was entirely up to her." Making sense of her waking life-force was also an inside job. In the midst of her consternation, Kate recalled the teachings of Grandmother Yagé: "We are all on the back of a giant anaconda. It is slithering and sliding, darting and diving, like anacondas do. That is the reality of the world."[10]

Kate had come to the teachings of Grandmother through Anunu, an African-Amerindian shaman. Anunu had assisted Kate with her sessions with "Grandmother," the name given to the sacred plant, Ayahuasca, which meant "vine of the soul."[11] Grandmother's name speaks to her antiquity and her relationship with humans. Drinking of the vine initiated Kate into a journeying of a kind that moves through subtle psychic and spiritual dimensions. In her journeying, Kate experiences Grandmother as primeval teacher: "The oldest Being who ever lived. Her essence that of Primordial Female Human Being As Tree."[12] Within the space of her expanded consciousness, Kate found the "brick" or what was "more like a scale on the side of a very large reptile, and gotten inside the world where Grandmother lived. It was as if Grandmother had been waiting thousands of years to take her onto her lap. The teaching had begun immediately."[13]

Guided by Grandmother to ride the giant anaconda, Kate kissed her lover Yolo good-bye to continue her river-run down the Amazon and into the rainforest to embrace Grandmother once more. Yolo, a gifted visionary artist, was not a "seeker" as such, yet a hobbit-like spirit being informs him otherwise, telling him, "You are lost, my boy." Desperately crying out, "Which way to the river?" Yolo wakes from his dream.[14] While Kate meanders down the Amazon, Yolo finds his way to a beach in Hawaii.

Yolo is mistaken for a "bradda" by Jerry, a resident of the island, who asks him to sit with the body of a young man who has overdosed. Sitting with the body, Yolo, in effect, sits with death. His agreement to do so initiates him into The Work, transforming his tourist's vacation into a journey of awakening which parallels that of Kate. In the Amazon jungle, Kate sits in a healing circle of seekers, three women and two men, taught by Grandmother and guided by the shaman Armando and Cosmi, his apprentice. Yolo's willingness to let go of his postcard image of Hawaii and Hawaiians and sit with "incredibly beautiful" death, gains him entry into a healing circle of men who are guided by Aunty Perlau and Aunty Alma.

Aunty Perlau is a Mahu, one who is born male but lives as woman. This is a "very special charge" given to them by their ancestors, she states, a charge that has planetary reverberations. For Mother rule was not only the principal way of life in Hawaii, but all over the world. Mahus, says Aunty Perlau, continue to carry out their charge of safeguarding the sovereignty of woman and protecting her children. They had memories of their subjugated Queen Lili'uokalani, and they had witnessed the domination and enslavement of woman and the suffering of her children. Therefore, Aunty Perlau proclaimed "that until woman was restored to her rightful place," they would live her part in the world, as women. "That is to say, we would live openly the feminine part of our nature, which, as we know, is sometimes the dominant nature with which we are born, whether as 'men' or as 'women.'"[15] She asked the gathering of men to make choices that honored children and to be the examples that would create a future wherein children had hope and life-sustaining options.

Yolo describes Aunty Alma as old, gorgeous, youthful, and radiant. "She was dressed in a long green dress that made her seem part of the ocean that had walked up on the shore" and her thick, silver hair seemed part of the moon. Aunty Alma's appearance and energy was that of the winged serpent, the dragon, a personification of Grandmother Yagé. As Grandmother was teaching Kate and her circle, Aunty instructed her "children," the men gathered in the circle at her feet. "Between us, she said to the circle, my sister Aunty Perlua and I have kept something real about our culture alive. She has taught generations of Hawaiian women the true hula, the dance of the traditions and of the soul; and I have worked to teach cleanliness of the earth temple, the human body."[16]

Administering Grandmother to Kate and her sister and fellow seekers, Armando had explained, "You could never put a sacred medicine into a polluted body." A cleansed body and an undistracted mind are more conducive to an opening of the heart and "an experience of the soul."[17] Integral to their spiritual journey were visions of serpents and dragons. Hugh had seen "*humongous* dragons. Breathing fire.*" Rick exclaimed that the dragon he saw "breathed fire for a while and then water for a while, and then people. Streams of people just poured out of its mouth. . . . We were being vomited up, our species, out of the depths of our own unconscious, is what it felt like."

Missy had seen "really big snakes. A couple of them, she added. Wrapped around each other."[18] The serpent or dragon Kate had first encountered while journeying with Anunu was a huge beaded or bejeweled creature. "You have now experienced what humans thousands of years ago, to their great amazement I'm sure, also experienced," Armando told them. "It is what humans have been experiencing for thousands of years since. Grandmother Yagé is a medicine of origins and endings, yes, Armando concluded, softly. That is why Grandfather reptile always appears."[19]

Armando's summary statement complemented Kate's discussion with Anunu about ethnobotany and confirmed her instinctive understanding about *"People and their plants. Plants and their people."* And although Anunu withheld telling Kate that "their first image, after fully receiving the medicine, would in all likelihood be of two gigantic entwined, perhaps copulating snakes," Kate had nevertheless experienced the reptilian aspect of Grandmother. But for all of her experience with Grandmother and her group's discussion of their visions, Kate remained fearful of snakes.[20]

While in the Amazon, a small serpent made periodic visits to Kate's hut. Although she was informed of its harmlessness, "It still scared her." Upon entering her hut sometimes, Kate would see the snake nearby and feel anxious. "It seemed to be testing her."[21] Some reactionary element of Kate's earlier dream of the frozen anaconda remained with her—should she kill the snake or let it live?

In any case, no one in the healing circle was allowed to harm anything. And in spite of her fear, Kate had no desire to harm the serpent. Thus her contemplation: "*What does it mean to be completely outside the circle of goodwill?*" Kate's question invites deliberation given that not so very long ago, the serpent was held in high esteem above all animals. It was perceived as sacred, revered as a deity, and worshipped as the creator of human beings. The worship of snakes, or ophiolatreia, was the basis of humanity's first developed religious systems.[22] Philip Gardner states in *Legend of the Serpent: The Biggest Religious Cover Up in History* that serpent religions originated in Africa more that 70,000 years ago and spread across the world as the dominant form of religious worship. The imagery and the symbolism of the snake was ubiquitous.[23]

Laird Scranton writes, in *The Science of the Dogon: Decoding the African Mystery Tradition*, "One predominant symbol of these ancient religions—the serpent—crosses virtually all known borders and boundaries and serves to tie divergent societies together."[24] Importantly, in many ancient mythologies and cosmologies, serpent deities were recognized as the embodiments of the divine feminine, creative force. As Monica Sjöö and Barbara Mor write, "Everywhere in world myth and imagery, the Goddess-Creatrix was coupled with the sacred serpent."[25]

Humankind was captivated by the mystery of the serpent and considered it a great gift from Nature. The shedding of its skin symbolized the cycle of birth and death, rebirth and immortality, and eternity and infinity. It was valued for its health benefit to humans, as its skin, blood, bile, flesh, as well as its venom, contained medicinal properties. But as Laird Scranton points out, the serpent "was most commonly associated with the acquisition of wisdom": "One of the best-known attributes of the serpent is WISDOM. The Hebrew tradition of the fall speaks of that animal as the most subtle of the beasts of the field; and the founder of Christianity tells his disciples to be as wise as serpents, though as harmless as doves."[26]

The ubiquity of serpent reverence may be explained by human biology and psychology. According to Philip Gardner, in certain altered states of consciousness, human beings have found themselves on different planes of existence. "In that state are archetypes that all will see—the serpent form, they see the spiral, they see waves, wave forms or DNA."[27] In *Now Is the Time*, Anunu anticipated Kate's encounter with serpents as Armando had expected the visions among his circle of seekers. Ayahuasca was the sacred plant that facilitated the journeys among the characters in Walker's novel. In Jeremy Narby's book *The Cosmic Serpent: DNA and the Origins of Knowledge*, Narby recounts the experiences of those who utilized "the vine of the soul" to reach altered states of consciousness and enter different planes of existence in order to gain knowledge and acquire wisdom. Narby also discusses the relationship and the correlation between serpents, the brain, and the spiral ladders of DNA that lie coiled, like a snake, within the cell nucleus.[28]

Where plants are used as a means of accessing serpent wisdom, the venom of the snake itself, say Sjöö and Mor, was also a means to reach mystical realms within the psyche. "According to Merlin Stone," they write, "snake venom . . . has highly hallucinogenic qualities; some venom is chemically similar to mescaline (peyote) or the psilocybin of mushrooms. Reported effects were clairvoyance, extraordinary mental powers, enhanced creativity, prophetic visions, and illumination about the primal processes of existence." Thus, the live snakes within the temples of goddesses "were perhaps not merely the symbols but actually the instruments through which the experiences of divine revelation were reached."[29]

Reverence, respect, and gratitude for the serpent notwithstanding, serpent worship met with a decided turning point. "Because of religious indoctrination," says Kate in *Now Is the Time*, "almost everyone feared and loathed the serpent."[30] As Scranton explains, The serpent was transformed in the minds of people "from deified ancestors to vilified fallen gods."[31] Sjöö and Mor elaborate further that when we consider "this worldwide occurrence of the Goddess and her Serpent, and then recall the ancient African Black Goddess, the Black Witch, imaged with the snake in her belly," we appreciate the profound power, universality, and endurance of this cosmological symbol. Then we can also begin to understand the demonization of "the goddess/serpent" by patriarchal religions. To the extent that they have succeeded in their crusade to destroy the world's primordial religion, "Western biblicized peoples have lost their original concept, and memory, of what the Goddess and her Serpent really meant—to all people, and all time."[32]

Throughout *Now Is the Time*, Kate Nelson's attitude about serpents changes. Toward the end of the novel, she begins to identify with the serpent in a way that flouts her former indoctrination. She becomes interested in its well-being: "What damage had such hatred done to it; a magical expression of Creation? Was this, the banning of the serpent from the circle, the beginning of separation? Was this the model for all the other banishments? Hunted and killed, or killed instantly, on sight, forced to hide at all times, what did the serpent think of humanity?"[33] Blacks had been cast outside the circle of goodwill as women had been despised, desecrated, and destroyed when societies had been indoctrinated against them. Perhaps Kate's own knowledge of being outcast was at the root of her feeling of kinship with the serpent. And perhaps her feeling of kinship was deeper than her own knowledge and more ancient than the illusion of separation.

In her dream, the serpent talked with her: "*It will be a long time before humans lose their terror of me, said the serpent. Though this serpent shape, this slithery form, is buried deep in every cell of every person on earth. It is the fundamental shape that is common to all. It is the shape of your DNA.*" Given the reactive mentality of human beings, Kate asked the serpent, "*How are we to deal with fear?*" The serpent responded, "*Make friends with it.*"[34] For fear drove humans to cast one another and other life-forms outside the circle of life. Armando had explained to his group that circles were sacred. What made "a circle sacred is that those who show up for it are the ones who belong in it. Casting anyone out, no matter how bizarre their behavior, drained the energy of the circle."[35] Kate was beginning to understand that everything around her, having shown up, belonged in the circle.

Ironically, the very animal that had been cast out of the sphere of human goodwill was the animal who had reconnected her to her own good. It was the serpent, coiled in the DNA molecules in the nuclei of her cells, the serpent asleep between the hemispheres of her brain, and the *kundalini* energy coiled at the base of her spine that Grandmother, through the snaking vine of the soul, had awakened in her. And, it was to Kate that Armando and other shamans had gone to seek assistance in safeguarding the sacred plants. "*Necesito ayuda! Puedo?*"[36] Grandmother had helped Kate, now Kate, renewed and reborn, was in a position to help Grandmother.

By virtue of their experiences, both Kate and Yolo had grown into greater personal and spiritual maturity. The journeys they each took in search of wholeness were two tributaries that meandered, found meaning, then merged anew. On the literal level of the narrative, Kate and Yolo had become stronger and were therefore even more capable of enjoying a mutually supportive and satisfying relationship.

On the symbolic level of the narrative, each one's journeying represents a strand of the DNA molecule, reflecting one face of the twin aspects of Creation: primal feminine, masculine principle; female, male; mind, body; spiritual, physical; river, reed; space, atom; wave, particle. Each strand engages in a spiraling dance reflecting the double-helix structure of the DNA molecule. The wisdom each journey acquired constitutes the rungs of the spiraling rails, containing genetic information, the basic building blocks of a joyful life—love, freedom, beauty, and compassion and their various expressions and recombinations.

The bliss Kate and Yolo experienced in the wake of what they had come to know inspired them to "marry." But as Yolo stated, they had "outgrown actual marriage."[37] They were more inclined toward "The Feast!" "Feast" means joyous. It described the energy they would share with those who would join them in beloved community. The perfect environment for the feast was an idyllic campground with a fire pit and a perfect "languidly flowing river," just beyond. All the elements that constitute life—earth, fire, water, air, aether— were honored in the choices Kate and Yolo were making. And, apparent in the clear waters of the river, were "rust-red salmon."[38]

Fish are a "world-wide symbol of the Great Mother," writes Barbara Walker, and in some myths they are associated with "the clots of 'wise blood'" that emanate from the Great Mother in her form as Cosmic Tree. The "blood-red nuts" of this tree were eaten by "salmon of knowledge." Those who ate these fish were gifted with the power to articulate their *gnosis.* "Poets and story-tellers, speaking of any subject difficult to deal with, often say, 'Unless I had eaten the salmon of knowledge I could not describe it.'"[39] The "rust-red" salmon in the river near the campground reflects a mystical knowledge of sacred and eternal union between humanity and Divinity. The setting Kate and Yolo found was perfect. "It was paradise."[40] It was the Garden of Eden Revisited. The snake was no longer under the heel of man and woman was no longer under man's thumb.

In *Mending the Past and Healing the Future with Soul Retrieval*, Alberto Villoldo avers that what orthodox Judeo-Christian religion describes as "original sin" constitutes, an "original wounding." The notion that the first humans were living in paradise, in the Garden of Eden, then cast out because they ate of a forbidden tree had the effect of engendering in human beings a grave psychic and spiritual trauma. Villoldo asserts that this story of expulsion, for which the serpent and Eve were blamed was experienced as a fall from grace and as "our *collective* soul loss as human beings."[41] He perceives permanent banishment to a life of suffering and unrewarding work as another figuration of the never-healing Amfortas wound. But as heroes and heroines have ventured beyond walls of all kind and traveled all manner of serpentine labyrinths, Villoldo posits, and Walker's novel demonstrates, that humanity's birthright of value, well-being, and wholeness can be restored through liberatory knowledge and wisdom. Villoldo informs us that this "original wounding" can be healed by "making our lives a spiritual journey, an inner quest."[42]

In those myths, legends, and stories that inspire vision, it is conceivable that destiny will triumph over fate. But in the West, however, are creation stories wherein humanity is born into iniquity, and is, *ipso facto*, separated from the goodwill of its Creator. "In contrast to the Judeo-Christian belief that we were born into a perfect state and then banished from it, shamanic mythology says that our perfect nature always remains intact. In fact," says Villoldo, "other belief systems don't embrace this Judeo-Christian idea of being cast out of Eden." The Aboriginal peoples of Australia, sub-Saharan peoples, Native Americans, rain forest-dwelling tribes in Brazil, and Pacific Islanders "still perceive themselves as continuing to live in Eden as they speak to the rivers, the trees, and God. In fact, native mythologies go so far as to state that we humans were created to serve and be the stewards of the garden."[43]

Now Is the Time to Open Your Heart questions whether it is even possible to be outside the circle of divine goodwill. Separation, Alice Walker has stated, is illusion. Yet, in one's attempt to reify an impossible idea, much suffering is generated. Therefore, Kate wondered "what did the serpent think of humanity?"[44] In the world that unfolds in the narrative of *Now Is the Time*, we see what the serpent thinks. For even from a despised and absurd place, the serpent continued to teach humanity and always would. Kate signals her understanding of this as she places her serpent clock in the lap of the Buddha. "The serpent was an anaconda that carried the world, with the face of a clock, on its back."[45]

It behooved humanity to open its heart and mind and return the serpent to the fold, for there is no wisdom without it. "Philosophy," is defined as the love of wisdom, that is, the love of Sophia, the Goddess of wisdom. The name "Sophia," Philip Gardner explains, is formed by combining the sibilant letter "S" with "ophia," which is derived from the root "ophis-," which means snake.[46] Like the serpents, goddesses and Gnostics and alchemists alike were pushed outside the Circle of Life. And yet they all knew the power of the alchemical red and white; of blood and venom; of life and wisdom. And all they knew was symbolized in the image of the Ouroboros, the tail-devouring serpent, and inscribed in the motto written within the circle: ONE THE ALL.[47]

TWENTY-FOUR

"Alice" Is Old Greek for Truth

As first names are indicative of one's personal identity and destiny, Alice Walker might be perceived as the embodiment of the will-to-truth and her body of work—her art and activism—might be perceived as an expression of that will. In the essay "A Name Is Sometimes an Ancestor Saying Hi, I'm With You," Alice Walker looks into the meaning of her name, exploring its correlation with the name of her ancestor and spiritual helper—Sojourner Truth: "Even laying aside such obvious resemblances as the fact that we are both as concerned about the rights of women as the rights of men, and that we share a certain 'mystical' bent, Sojourner ('Walker'—in the sense of traveler, journeyer, wanderer) Truth (which 'Alice' means in Old Greek) is also my name."[1]

Like her namesake, Alice Walker was born into a society that would have her believe herself unworthy on account of her race, unworthy on account of her sex, and unworthy on account of her class. And like her namesake, Walker would have the wisdom to see through such lies. She would have the insight to see that those lies are derived from the socially bankrupt ideologies of white supremacy, patriarchy, and elitism. And she would have the ability to penetrate the lies to the deeper reality that by virtue of her very existence she was worthy of and had an inalienable right to freedom, self-determination, security, dignity, and self-expression. Given the inimical and absurd environment into which they were born, both women saw that in order that they and their oppressed kin live in a free and just society, they would have to defy the lies, define themselves, and resist tyranny.

Alice Walker's commitment to civil rights and women's rights continued Truth's activism as an abolitionist and a suffragist. Truth's spirit of defiance would live on in Walker who would journey across the globe on behalf of the unheard and unprotected and in the name of Truth and Freedom: "I get a power from this name that Sojourner Truth and I share," stated Walker. "And when I walk into a room of strangers who are hostile to the words of women, I do so with her/our cloak of authority—as black women and beloved expressions of the Universe (i.e., children of God)—warm about me."[2]

Walker began to experience the power of truth as a child in the affirming embrace of her father. She had accidentally broken a fruit jar one day. Standing before him, she could perhaps deny responsibility and bluff her way out of a whipping, or she could confess. "I've never forgotten my feeling that he really wanted me to tell the truth," Walker writes. "And because he seemed to desire it—and the moments during which he waited for my reply seemed quite out of time, so much so I can still feel them. . . . I was only three, if that— I confessed."[3] It was also as a child that Walker had realized the effects of telling a lie.

The "happy relief" Walker noted on her father's face when she told the truth contrasted sharply with the pangs of self-disappointment she experienced when she was bullied into lying to her parents about the injury to her eye. The anguish she experienced engendered in her the "need to tell the truth, always."[4] She would thenceforth be vigilant against any falsehood within herself and intolerant of dishonesty in others. The lives of oppressed, mutilated, or otherwise abused women in Walker's fiction and nonfiction would always demonstrate this truth: "If you lie to yourself about your own pain, you will be killed by those who will claim you enjoyed it."[5]

The moral compass that directed the lives of Sojourner Truth and Alice Walker was pointed toward truth. They both subscribed to the teaching of Jesus Christ which declared, "And ye shall know the truth, and the truth shall make you free."[6] Truth and freedom were one, and for Alice Walker, the path to both was knowledge. Through her activism in the freedom movement, Alice Walker acquired the gift of knowledge—of herself, of her condition, and of her society. Through her struggles for freedom she awakened to the mystery and meaning of the truth of her own existence.

Her hard-won self-knowledge along with her pursuit of truth and freedom are all aspects of Walker's fundamentally philosophical orientation. Alice Walker's "Yes" to life evolved her path as an activist-writer. And philosophy would become the lamp that would illuminate her path and guide her investigations into critical personal and social inquiries: How does one change a systemically racist and violent society? How does one succeed as a black woman writer? How does one live life on one's own terms? How does one save humanity and Earth? How does one implement Democratic Womanism, Democratic Socialist Womanism, Democratic Motherism? How does one start "The Mother Defend Yourself Party"?[7]

In addition to courage, industry, commitment to struggle, and a refusal to be anything but her authentic self, Alice Walker's life suggests a reclaiming of one's mother's garden and a receptivity to ancestors whose lives were also lanterns, radiating inspiration and instruction: "'Mama, I'm walking to Canada and I'm taking you and a bunch of other slaves with me.' Reply: 'It wouldn't be the first time.'"[8]

The twin paths of truth and the beauty inherent in Alice Walker's heroic and continuing effort to relieve the suffering of humanity and the planet are presented in Pratibha Parmar's documentary film *Alice Walker: Beauty in Truth*. The film recounts Walker's life from her humble beginnings as a daughter of sharecroppers to her renown as a celebrated literary artist and extraordinary activist. Pratibha Parmar articulates her rationale for selecting Walker as subject for a documentary film:

> Alice's story and Alice's writing, and everything, as a public intellectual and as a writer, she has shaped so many cultural discourses, not just within America, but internationally. And I think that part of my agenda, very clearly, as a feminist and as a filmmaker is to make sure that women's stories, inspirational stories are heard and seen because too often . . . there's a kind of historical amnesia about women's stories. It is my obligation, as a filmmaker, to ensure that actually we fill those gaps so that there are stories that younger women can say well, I too can do that.[9]

Parmar's documentary sounds the truth of Walker's journey in the world. It captures in film what truth looks like when uncompromised and expressed beautifully, from one generation to the next.

TWENTY-FIVE

Lapis Philosophorum

The objective of the *magnum opus*, The Great Work, of ancient alchemists was the discovery of the *lapis philosophorum* or the philosophers' stone. This stone, the "stone which is no stone," was the transmuting agent that would purify material imperfection, improve health, and achieve immortality, or transmute base metal into silver or gold.[1] For the philosopher, the transmuting agent would transform the unconscious mind or unenlightened soul and facilitate *gnosis* or spiritual transcendence.

In her lifelong struggle for justice, peace, and dignity for all humans and Earth, Walker's work, on many levels, manifested as the work of an alchemist. Much of her effort involved the alchemical process of "turning madness into flowers."[2] In the process of The Great Work, Walker discovered her transmuting agent, her philosophers' stone, to be Love. As she perceived peace to always be a better idea than war, so love was the only response to hate and devastation. And for Alice Walker, love, if it were love at all, was unconditional. Loving "my friend the enemy" was imperative; for "compassion does not stop at who was right or wrong, does not stop at feeling loving kindness for the miserable and oppressed, does not stop at feeling the pain of the victim while ignoring the pain of the victimizer."[3]

Walker had come to understand that people could be loved and were lovable in spite of their perceived imperfections. As she would write in *Hard Times*, even leaders whose policies court the instinct of war and death can be perceived more perfect for their imperfections and be unconditionally loved. A belief in Oneness and her absolute trust in the goodness and unconditional love of Earth for all creation inspire Walker to embody the sensibilities she divines in Mother Earth. In embodying these sensibilities, she witnesses her own metamorphosis into Love, Itself, the Ultimate.

Always of the perspective that life is the award, Walker sees abundant love as the award for living a long life full of work. She asks in one poem, "What do I get for getting old?"[4] Among the perks she lists is an ever-deepening, ever-expanding love. Love, she says, permeates everything as she feels everything to be made of it. She experiences this numinous quality of love as awakening; for she has come to the awareness that love is enough. It is both what we need, and because it is pervasive, it is what we have.

Like aether, love is essence and everywhere. It is the matrix out of which schools materialize, orphanages are built, children are fed, and little girls wear brilliant smiles. The love of which Walker speaks is healing, tender, and knowing. It is a witness to the unconscionable violations so many have suffered and continue to suffer. Torture, rape, genocide, rabid dogs of war are not new. But what is new, writes Walker, is her immense and far-reaching love. And with it an ability to reach sufferers on the waves of "ether" and comfort them with the knowledge that they are innocent and are not alone, and to urge them to remember, "Alice *loves* me."[5]

As the embodiment of unconditional love, Walker radiates as "human sunrise." The breadth of her thought, the body of her work, and an activism that spans decades and continents testify that love is the quintessential transmuting agent. She might have engaged in other work, but her mind was being trained in other things: "Poetry, Philosophy, Literature / Survival, for a girl."[6]

Notes

INTRODUCTION

1. Alice Walker, *The World Has Changed: Conversations with Alice Walker*, edited by Rudolph P. Byrd (New York: The New Press, 2010), 204.
2. Alice Walker, *We Are the Ones We Have Been Waiting For: Inner Light in a Time of Darkness* (New York: The New Press, 2006), 13, 14.
3. Ibid., 3.
4. Ray Monk, "Philosophical Biography: The Very Idea," in *Wittgenstein, Biography and Philosophy*, edited by James C. Klagge (Cambridge: Cambridge University Press, 2001), 3.
5. Alice Walker, *By the Light of My Father's Smile* (New York: Random House, 1998), 219.

SECTION I. EARTH

1. Paramahansa Yogananda, *God Talks with Arjuna: The Bhagavad Gita*, Volume 1 (Los Angeles: Self-Realization Fellowship, 1995), 368; Paramahansa Yogananda, *God Talks with Arjuna: The Bhagavad Gita*, Volume 2 (Los Angeles: Self-Realization Fellowship, 1995), 882.
2. Tenzin Wangyal Rinpoche, *Healing with Form, Energy and Light* (Ithaca, NY: Snow Lion Publications, 2002), 13, 72; Starhawk, *Truth or Dare: Encounters with Power, Authority, and Mystery* (New York: Harper and Row, 1987), 267.
3. Starhawk, *The Earth Path: Grounding Your Spirit in the Rhythms of Nature* (New York: HarperSanFrancisco, 2004), 158.
4. Cait Johnson, *Earth, Water, Fire, & Air: Essential Ways of Connecting to Spirit* (Woodstock, VT: SkyLight Paths Publishing, 2003), 3, 4.
5. (The *kshetra* is the objective dream body or "field" of the human soul in which wisdom and ignorance operates): Yogananda, *God Talks with Arjuna*, Volume 2, 883, 861; Yogananda, *God Talks with Arjuna*, Volume 1, 190.
6. Yogananda, *God Talks with Arjuna*, Volume 2, 883.

CHAPTER ONE. I AM THE EARTH. . . .

1. Alice Walker, *The World Has Changed: Conversations with Alice Walker*, edited by Rudolph P. Byrd (New York: The New Press, 2010), 173.
2. Evelyn C. White, *Alice Walker, A Life* (New York: Norton, 2004), 101.

3. Betty Wood, "James Edward Oglethorpe, Race, and Slavery, A Reassessment," in *Oglethorpe in Perspective, Georgia's Founder after Two Hundred Years*, edited by Phinizy Spalding and Harvey H. Jackson (Tuscaloosa: University of Alabama 1989), 67, 71.

4. Ibid., 67.

5. White, *Alice Walker*, 12.

6. Alice Walker, *Anything We Love Can Be Saved: A Writer's Activism* (New York: Ballantine, 1997), xiii.

7. Alice Walker, *Revolutionary Petunias & Other Poems* (New York: Harcourt, Brace, Jovanovich, 1971), 6.

8. White, *Alice Walker*, 13–14.

9. Walker, *The World Has Changed*, 233.

10. White, *Alice Walker*, 15.

11. Ibid.

12. Ibid., 17.

13. Walker, *The World Has Changed*, 245.

14. Ibid., 124.

15. Kimberly N. Ruffin, *Black on Earth: African American Ecoliterary Traditions* (Athens, GA: University of Georgia, 2010), 42.

16. Ibid., 2–3.

17. Kibibi Tyehimba, Cochair of National Coalition of Blacks for Reparations in America, quoted in *Black on Earth*, 28.

18. Ruffin, *Black on Earth*, 59, 3.

19. Walker, *The World Has Changed*, 236.

20. Alice Walker, "In Search of Our Mothers' Gardens," in *In Search of Our Mothers' Gardens: Womanist Prose* (New York: Harcourt, Brace, Jovanovich, 1983), 241.

21. Walker, *The World Has Changed*, 236.

CHAPTER TWO. FOR SIX YEARS I DO NOT LOOK UP

1. Alice Walker, *Her Blue Body Everything We Know: Earthling Poems, 1965–1990 Complete* (Orlando, FL: Harcourt, 1991), 412.

2. Evelyn C. White, *Alice Walker, A Life* (New York: Norton, 2004), 30, 31.

3. Walker, *Her Blue Body*, 412–415.

4. Alice Walker, *The World Has Changed: Conversations with Alice Walker*, edited by Rudolph P. Byrd (New York: The New Press, 2010), 124.

5. Ibid., 56, 233.

6. Alice Walker, *Revolutionary Petunias & Other Poems* (New York: Harcourt, Brace, Jovanovich, 1971), 19.

7. Alice Walker, *The World Has Changed*, 244, 245.

8. Ibid., 233–234.

9. Alice Walker, "Beauty," in *In Search of Our Mothers' Gardens: Womanist Prose* (New York: Harcourt, Brace, and Jovanovich, 1983), 386, 387.

10. White, *Alice Walker*, 7.

11. Walker, "Beauty," 387.

12. Ibid., 387, 388.

13. Ibid., 387.

14. Ibid., 388–389.

15. White, *Alice Walker*, 39, 40.

16. Walker, "Beauty," 387.

17. Ibid., 391.

18. Walker, *The World Has Changed*, 35.

CHAPTER THREE. EVERYTHING CHANGED

1. Alice Walker, *The World Has Changed: Conversations with Alice Walker*, edited by Rudolph P. Byrd (New York: The New Press, 2010), 35.

2. Ibid., 233.

3. Alice Walker, "Beauty," in *In Search of Our Mothers' Gardens: Womanist Prose* (New York: Harcourt, Brace, and Jovanovich, 1983), 389.

4. Evelyn C. White, *Alice Walker, A Life* (New York: Norton, 2004), 44.

5. Ibid., 45.

6. Walker, "Beauty," 389–390.

7. Ibid., 390; White, *Alice Walker,* 52, 53.

8. White, *Alice Walker,* 53, 52.

9. Alice Walker, *Revolutionary Petunias & Other Poems* (New York: Harcourt, Brace, Jovanovich, 1971), 20, 21, 22.

10. Walker, "Beauty," 390.

11. White, *Alice Walker*, 61.

12. White, *Alice Walker,* 58.

13. Alice Walker, "Choosing to Stay at Home," in *In Search of Our Mothers' Gardens: Womanist Prose* (New York: Harcourt, Brace, and Jovanovich, 1983), 162.

14. White, *Alice Walker,* 61.

15. Walker, *The World Has Changed*, 232.

16. Alice Walker, "The Civil Rights Movement: What Good Was It?" in *In Search of Our Mothers' Gardens: Womanist Prose* (New York: Harcourt, Brace, and Jovanovich, 1983), 124; Alice Walker, "Choice: A Tribute to Martin Luther King, Jr." in *In Search of Our Mothers' Gardens: Womanist Prose* (New York: Harcourt, Brace, and Jovanovich, 1983), 144.

17. Walker, "Choice: A Tribute to Dr. Martin Luther King, Jr." 143.

18. Alice Walker, "Choosing to Stay Home: Ten Years after the March on Washington," in *In Search of Our Mothers' Gardens: Womanist Prose* (New York: Harcourt, Brace, and Jovanovich, 1983), 162.

19. White, *Alice Walker*, 64.

20. Ibid., 64–65.

CHAPTER FOUR. A SPELMAN GIRL

1. Howard Zinn, *You Can't Be Neutral on a Moving Train, A Personal History of Our Times* (Boston, MA: Beacon Press, 1994), 21–22; Harry G. Lefever, *Undaunted by the Fight: Spelman College and the Civil Rights Movement, 1957–1967* (Macon, GA: Mercer University Press, 2005), 9.

2. Lefever, *Undaunted, by the Fight*, 15. See also Zinn, *You Can't Be Neutral on a Moving Train,* 18–19.

3. Lefever, *Undaunted*, ix.

4. Ibid., 22.

5. Ibid., 148.

6. Alice Walker, "My Father's Country Is the Poor," in *In Search of Our Mothers' Gardens: Womanist Prose* (New York: Harcourt, Brace, Jovanovich, 1983), 200–201.

7. Anglela Y. Davis, 1974, *Angela Davis, An Autobiography*, reprint (New York: International Publishers, 1988), 123.

8. Walker, "My Father's Country Is the Poor," 201–202.

9. Evelyn C. White, *Alice Walker, A Life* (New York: Norton, 2004), 71, 72.

10. Walker, "My Father's Country Is the Poor," 201.

11. Ibid.

12. Alice Walker, *The World Has Changed: Conversations with Alice Walker*, edited by Rudolph P. Byrd (New York: The New Press, 2010), 45.

13. White, *Alice Walker*, 72.

14. Zinn, *You Can't Be Neutral*, 44.

15. Walker, *The World Has Changed*, 42–43.

16. Walker, "My Father's Country Is the Poor," 201.

17. White, *Alice Walker*, 74.

18. Ibid., 76.

19. Martin Luther King, Jr., *I Have a Dream: Writing and Speeches That Changed the World* (New York: HarperOne, 1992), 103, 102.

20. Zinn, *You Can't Be Neutral*, 40.

21. White, *Alice Walker*, 86.

22. Ibid., 90.

23. Ibid., 89.

24. Ibid., 88.

25. Zinn, *You Can't Be Neutral*, 45.

CHAPTER FIVE. ON MY OWN TERMS

1. History and institutional profile of Sarah Lawrence College is drawn from "Setting a New Ship A'Sail: The Founding of Sarah Lawrence College," by Elizabeth Sargent (Bronxville Historical Conservancy: *The Bronxville Journal*, Vol. 2, 2002–2003), 62, accessed April 13, 2012; and from "Make Yourself Useful," in *Alice Walker, A Life*, by Evelyn C. White (New York: Norton, 2004), 99–107.

2. Sargent, "Setting a New Ship A'Sail," 77, n7, 63.

3. Ibid., 67.

4. Ibid., 74, 75.

5. White, *Alice Walker*, 100.

6. Ibid., 101.

7. White, *Alice Walker*, 104.

8. Alice Walker, "Suicide of an American Girl," Emory University Archives, Alice Walker Papers, Box 73, Folder 1, 28.

9. White, *Alice Walker*, 105, 104.

10. Ibid., 109.

11. Alice Walker, "A Talk: Convocation 1972," in *In Search of Our Mother's Gardens: Womanist Prose* (New York: Harcourt, Brace, Jovanovich, 1983), 38.

12. White, *Alice Walker*, 109.

13. Alice Walker, "Choosing to Stay at Home: Ten Years after the March on Washington," in *In Search of Our Mothers' Gardens: Womanist Prose* (New York: Harcourt, Brace, Jovanovich, 1983), 159.

14. White, *Alice Walker*, 102.

15. Ibid., 110.

16. Ibid., 111.

17. Ibid., 111–112.

18. Alice Walker, *The World Has Changed: Conversations with Alice Walker*, edited by Rudolph P. Byrd (New York: The New Press, 2010), 35.

SECTION II. FIRE

1. Paramahansa Yogananda, *God Talks with Arjuna: The Bhagavad Gita*, Volume 2 (Los Angeles: Self-Realization Fellowship, 1995), 941–942.

2. Starhawk, *Truth or Dare: Encounters with Power, Authority, and Mystery* (New York: Harper and Row, 1987), 265.

3. Starhawk, *The Earth Path: Grounding Your Spirit in the Rhythms of Nature* (New York: HarperSanFrancisco, 2004), 122.

4. Paramahansa Yogananda, *God Talks with Arjuna: The Bhagavad Gita*, Volume 1 (Los Angeles: Self-Realization Fellowship, 1995), 519.

5. Yogananda, *The Bhagavad Gita*, Volume 2, 776; Starhawk, *The Earth Path*, 122.

6. Yogananda, *The Bhagavad Gita*, Volume 2, 941, 961.

7. Ibid., 776.

CHAPTER SIX. I WOULD ONLY BE THE PHILOSOPHER

1. Evelyn C. White, *Alice Walker, A Life* (New York: Norton, 2004), 112; Alice Walker, *The World Has Changed: Conversations with Alice Walker*, edited by Rudolph P. Byrd (New York: The New Press, 2010), 35.

2. Alice Walker, "Comments On: *The Year of Protest, 1956*," Collection 1061; Box 88; Folder 1, p. 14; Alice Walker Papers; Manuscript, Archives, and Rare Book Library, Emory University.

3. Alice Walker, "The Life of Cicero" Collection 1061; Box 88; Folder 7, p. 1; Alice Walker Papers; Manuscript, Archives, and Rare Book Library, Emory University.

4. Ibid., 9.

5. Ibid., 19.

6. Ibid., 20.

7. Ibid., 11–12.

8. Ibid., 20.

9. Ibid., "Post Script," 1, 3.

10. Alice Walker, "Francis Petrarch: Prototype of the Modern Student," Collection 1061; Box 88; Folder 14, p. 6; Alice Walker Papers; Manuscript, Archives, and Rare Book Library, Emory University.

11. Ibid., 5.

12. Ibid., 7.

13. Ibid., 1

14. Ibid., 9.

15. Alice Walker, "Albert Camus: The Development of His Philosophical Position as Reflected in His Novels and Plays," Collection 1061; Box 88; Folder 19, p. 28; Alice Walker Papers; Manuscript, Archives, and Rare Book Library, Emory University.

16. Ibid., "Post Script," i.

17. Ibid., "Introduction," i.

18. Albert Camus organized his work in the tradition of the triptych of Greek mythology and designated the three phases of his work as Absurd, Revolt, and Love: "I had a precise plan when I began my work. What I wanted to express first was negation. In three ways: in novel form (which produced *The Outsider*); in theatrical form

(which produced *Caligula* and *Cross Purposes*); and in essay form (*The Myth of Sisyphus*). Then I foresaw three more works expressing positive values: in the form of a novel (*The Plague*); as theatre (*State of Siege* and *Les Justes*); and in an essay (*Rebellion and Revolt*). I also dimly projected a third layer of writing, on the theme of love." (Albert Camus, *The Plague, The Fall, Exile and the Kingdom, and Selected Essays* [New York: Everyman's Library, 2004], xiv.) Walker's descriptive for category three differs from Camus's, and her categorization of texts in the latter two categories differs as well. Her effort, however, was not necessarily to repeat Camus's organization. She indicated in the introduction to her work that the organizational structure of her discussion as well as the selection of texts discussed were determined "all by instinct really" (ii).

19. Alice Walker, "Albert Camus," "Introduction," i.
20. Ibid., "Introduction," i; 28.
21. Ibid., 5, 1.
22. Ibid., 2, 3.
23. Ibid., 4.
24. Ibid.
25. Ibid., 22.
26. Ibid.
27. Ibid.
28. Ibid., Epigraph.
29. Ibid., 22.

CHAPTER SEVEN. CHANGING THE WORLD

1. Alice Walker, "A Talk: Convocation 1972," in *In Search of Our Mothers' Gardens: Womanist Prose* (New York: Harper, 1983), 37.
2. Evelyn C. White, *Alice Walker, A Life* (New York: Norton, 2004), 129, 130.
3. Ibid., 134.
4. Ibid., 157.
5. Ibid., 141.
6. Ibid., 150.
7. Ibid., 154.
8. Ibid., 156.
9. Ibid., 157.
10. Ibid., 157.
11. Alice Walker, "Recording the Seasons," in *In Search of Our Mothers' Gardens: Womanist Prose* (New York: Harcourt, Brace, and Jovanovich, 1983), 228.
12. Alice Walker, "Coretta King: Revisited," in *In Search of Our Mothers' Gardens: Womanist Prose* (New York: Harcourt, Brace, and Jovanovich, 1983), 148.
13. Walker, "Recording the Seasons," 225.
14. Walker, "Coretta King: Revisited," 148.
15. Ibid., 148.
16. Alice Walker, "But Yet and Still the Cotton Gin Kept on Working," in *In Search of Our Mothers' Gardens: Womanist Prose* (New York: Harcourt, Brace, and Jovanovich, 1983), 32.
17. Albert Camus, *The Myth of Sisyphus* in *The Plague, the Fall, Exile and the Kingdom, and Selected Essays* (New York: Everyman's Library, 2004), 495.
18. Alice Walker, *The Third Life of Grange Copeland* (New York: Harcourt, Brace, Jovanovich, 1970), 20.

19. Camus, *The Myth of Sisyphus*, 497.

20. Walker, *Third Life*, 21.

21. Ibid., 31.

22. Ibid., 53.

23. Camus, *The Myth of Sisyphus*, 563, 503.

24. Albert Camus, *Caligula*, in *Caligula and Three Other Plays* (New York: Vintage, 1958), 8.

25. Walker, *Third Life*, 107.

26. Ibid., 122.

27. Camus, *Caligula*, 73.

28. Walker, *Third Life*, 227.

29. Camus, *Caligula*, vi.

30. Ibid., 72.

31. Walker, *Third Life*, 152, 153.

32. Ibid., 153.

33. Walker, *The World Has Changed*, 52.

34. Walker, *Third Life*, 155, 138.

35. Ibid., 175.

36. Leo Tolstoy, *Resurrection*, 1899 (New York: Penguin, 2009), 144.

37. Albert Camus, *The Just Assassins*, in *Caligula and Three Other Plays* (New York: Vintage, 1958), 245.

38. Walker, *Third Life*, 214.

CHAPTER EIGHT. *MERIDIAN*: COMING OF AGE IN MISSISSIPPI

1. Alice Walker, "Recording the Seasons," in *In Search of Our Mothers' Gardens: Womanist Prose* (New York: Harcourt, Brace, Jovanovich, 1983), 223–224; Alice Walker, *The Way Forward Is with a Broken Heart* (New York: Ballantine, 2000), 3.

2. Evelyn C. White, *Alice Walker, A Life* (New York: Norton, 2004), 207.

3. Walker, "Recording the Seasons," 165.

4. Ibid., 166, 224.

5. Walker, "Recording the Seasons," 167.

6. White, *Alice Walker*, 262.

7. Ibid., 286.

8. Alice Walker, *Meridian* (New York: Washington Square Press, 1977), 28.

9. Helen Lynd, *On Shame and the Search for Identity* (New York: Harcourt, Brace, Jovanovich, 1958), 13.

10. Walker, *Meridian*, 69.

11. Ibid., 70, 73.

12. Lynd, *On Shame*, 14–15.

13. Walker, *Meridian*, 90, 91.

14. Ibid., 91.

15. Ibid., 91, 97.

16. Lynd, *On Shame*, 50.

17. Ibid., 34, 26, 31.

18. Walker, *Meridian*, 106.

19. Ibid., 107.

20. Ibid., 108, 109, 107.

21. Lynd, *On Shame*, 49.

22. Ibid., 50.
23. Walker, *Meridian*, 148.
24. Ibid., 130.
25. Ibid., 139.
26. Lynd, *On Shame*, 35.
27. Ibid., 20.
28. Ibid., 50–51.
29. Walker, *Meridian*, 118, 119.
30. Lynd, *On Shame*, 36.
31. Walker, *Meridian*, 52.
32. Joseph Campbell, 1949, *The Hero with a Thousand Faces* (Princeton, NJ: Princeton University Press, 2004), 119 n.46.
33. Walker, *Meridian*, 90.
34. Campbell, *The Hero with a Thousand Faces,* 75.
35. Walker, *Meridian*, 213; Albert Camus, *The Myth of Sisyphus* in *The Plague, the Fall, Exile and the Kingdom, and Selected Essays* (New York: Everyman's Library, 2004), 592.
36. Walker, *Meridian*, 213, 197.
37. Campbell, *The Hero with a Thousand Faces,* 28, 18.
38. Ibid., 15.
39. Ibid., 16.
40. Ibid., 200.
41. Walker, *Meridian*, 201,191.
42. Ibid., 151.

CHAPTER NINE. THOUGHT AT THE MERIDIAN

1. Albert Camus, *The Rebel, An Essay on Man in Revolt* (1951; New York: Vintage Books, 1991), 300, 304, 297.
2. Ibid., 289, 283.
3. Discussion is informed by Stephen R. McKevitt's *Meridian Hill: A History* (Charleston, SC: The History Press, 2014).
4. Camus, *The Rebel,* 290–291.
5. Ibid., 14, 15.
6. Helen Lynd, *On Shame and the Search for Identity* (New York: Harcourt, Brace, Jovanovich 1958), 66.
7. Alice Walker, *Meridian* (New York: Washington Square Press, 1977), 33.
8. Camus, *The Rebel,* 283.
9. Walker, *Meridian*, 42, 44, 43.
10. Ibid., 44.
11. Nell Irvin Painter, *Sojourner Truth, A Life, A Symbol* (New York: Norton, 1996), 25.
12. Ibid., 75.
13. Ibid., 139.
14. Ibid., 11.
15. William Shakespeare, *Titus Andronicus* (c.1588, Oxford: Oxford University Press, 1998), 149.
16. Ibid., 129.
17. Ajit Mookerjee, *Kali, The Feminine Force* (Rochester, VT: Destiny Books, 1988), 8.
18. Ibid., 8, 62; David Kinsley, *Tantric Visions of the Divine Feminine, The Ten Mahavidyas* (Berkeley: University of California Press, 1997), 283.

19. Walker, *Meridian*, 46, 47.

20. Kinsley, *Tantric Visions*, 81, 83.

21. Ibid., 84, 81.

22. Walker, *Meridian*, 48.

23. Ibid., 37.

24. Shakespeare, *Titus Andronicus*, 187.

25. Camus, *The Rebel*, 11.

26. Mookerjee, *Kali*, 8–9.

27. Alice Walker, *The World Has Changed: Conversations with Alice Walker*, edited by Rudolph P. Byrd (New York: The New Press, 2010), 40.

28. Alice Walker, *In Love and Trouble* (New York: Harcourt, Brace, Jovanovich, 1973), 8.

29. Ibid., 15, 18.

30. Ibid., 14.

31. Ibid., 65, 67.

32. Ibid., 107.

33. Ibid., 114.

34. Ibid., 9, 67.

35. Alice Walker, *You Can't Keep a Good Woman Down* (Orlando, FL: Harcourt, 1981), 18.

36. Ibid., 67.

37. Ibid., 42.

38. Ibid., 52.

39. Ibid., 92, 95.

40. Ibid., 94, 92.

41. Ibid., 148, 165.

42. Ibid., 167, 165.

43. Jean Toomer, "The Blue Meridian," in *The Collected Poems of Jean Toomer*, edited by Robert B. Jones and Margery Toomer Latimer (1936; Chapel Hill: University of North Carolina Press, 1988), 50, 642.

44. Ibid., 74.

CHAPTER TEN. TRUTH TELLER, FREEDOM WRITER

1. Plato, *The Trial and Death of Socrates* (New York: Chartwell Books, 2010), 33.

2. Anthony Everitt, *Cicero: The Life and Times of Rome's Greatest Politician* (New York: Random House, 2001), 318–319.

3. Evelyn C. White, *Alice Walker, A Life* (New York: Norton, 2004), 40.

4. Alice Walker, *The World Has Changed, Conversations with Alice Walker*, edited by Rudolph P. Byrd (New York: The New York Press, 2010), 40.

5. Muriel Rukeyser, "Käthe Kollwitz," in *The Collected Poems of Muriel Rukeyser*, edited by Janet E. Kaufman and Anne F. Herzog (Pittsburgh, PA: University of Pittsburgh Press, 2015), 463.

6. Alice Walker, *The Color Purple* (Orlando, FL: Harcourt, 1982), 1.

7. Ibid., 1.

8. Ovid, *The Metamorphoses* (New York: Everyman's Library, 2013), 319.

9. Ibid., 326.

10. Walker, *The Color Purple*, 112.

11. Ovid, *The Metamorphoses*, 193; Walker, *The Color Purple*, 126.

12. Ovid, *The Metamorphoses*, 194.

13. Ibid., 195.

14. Alice Walker, *The Same River Twice: Honoring the Difficult* (New York: Washington Square Press, 1996), 62–63.

15. Ibid., 135–136.

16. Walker, *The Color Purple*, 85, 84.

17. Ibid., 86–87.

18. Ibid., 200.

19. Ibid., 193, 96.

20. *Holman KJV Study Bible* (Nashville, TN: Holman Bible Publishers, 2012), John 15:13, 1791.

21. Walker, *The Color Purple*, 127.

22. Frederick Douglass, *The Portable Frederick Douglass*, edited by John Stauffer and Henry Louis Gates, Jr. (New York: Penguin, 2016), 288. 127.

23. Walker, *The Color Purple*, 126, 21, 22, 20.

24. Ibid., 28.

25. Ibid., 86.

26. Ibid., 282.

27. Ibid., 282–283.

28. Ibid., 253, 254, 284.

29. Rukeyser, "Käthe Kollwitz," 463.

30. Albert Camus, *The Rebel, An Essay on Man in Revolt* (1951; New York: Vintage Books, 1991), 259, 263.

31. Ibid., 258, 262.

32. Ibid., 195.

SECTION III. AIR

1. Paramahansa Yogananda, *God Talks with Arjuna: The Bhagavad Gita*, Volume 2 (Los Angeles: Self-Realization Fellowship, 1995), 868; Starhawk, *Truth or Dare: Encounters with Power, Authority, and Mystery* (New York: Harper and Row, 1987), 265; Tenzin Wangyal Rinpoche, *Healing with Form, Energy and Light* (Ithaca, NY: Snow Lion Publications, 2002), 73.

2. Yogananda, *God Talks with Arjuna*, 798; Rinpoche, *Healing with Form, Energy and Light*, 73.

3. Rinpoche, *Healing with Form, Energy and Light*, 45.

4. Cait Johnson, *Earth, Water, Fire, & Air: Essential Ways of Connecting to Spirit* (Woodstock, VT: SkyLight Paths Publishing, 2003), 146; Yogananda, *God Talks with Arjuna*, 798.

5. Rinpoche, *Healing with Form, Energy and Light*, 17, 18.

6. Ibid., 18.

CHAPTER ELEVEN. APOLOGIA: HONORING THE DIFFICULT

1. Evelyn C. White, *Alice Walker, A Life* (New York: Norton, 2004), 359.

2. Ibid., 363; Alice Walker, *You Can't Keep a Good Woman Down* (Orlando, FL: Harcourt, 1981), 38; White, *Alice Walker*, 359.

3. Alice Walker, *The World Has Changed: Conversations with Alice Walker*, edited by Rudolph P. Byrd (New York: The New Press, 2010), 318; White, *Alice Walker*, 299.

4. Walker, *The World Has Changed*, 318.

5. Doris Lessing, *Prisons We Choose to Live Inside* (New York: Harper Perennial, 1987), 8, 7.

6. Alice Walker, *The Same River Twice: Honoring the Difficult* (New York: Washington Square Press, 1996), 13.

7. White, *Alice Walker,* 359.

8. Walker, *The Same River Twice,* 22.

9. Ibid.

10. Ibid., 23.

11. Calvin Hernton, "Who's Afraid of Alice Walker?," in *The Sexual Mountain and Black Women Writers: Adventures in Sex, Literature, and Real Life* (New York: Anchor Press, 1987), 31.

12. Walker, *The Same River Twice,* 13.

13. Alice Walker, "Zora Neale Hurston, A Cautionary Tale," in *In Search of Our Mothers' Gardens: Womanist Prose* (New York: Harcourt, Brace, and Jovanovich, 1983), 86, 87.

14. Walker, *The Same River Twice,* 223.

15. Ibid., 22.

16. Ibid., 170.

17. Rainer Rilke, *Letters to a Young Poet* (1984; New York: The Modern Library, 2001), 35, 68.

18. Walker, *The Same River Twice,* 38.

19. Ibid., 33.

20. Ibid., 35.

21. Ibid., 30.

22. Ibid., 160, 162.

23. Ibid., 24.

24. Ibid., 24, 27.

25. Ibid., 38.

26. Ibid., 28.

27. Ibid., 27.

28. Jean Shinoda Bolen, *Crossing to Avalon: A Woman's Midlife Pilgrimage* (New York: HarperSanFrancisco, 1994), 34.

29. Walker, *The Same River Twice,* 34.

30. Ibid.

31. Rilke, *Letters to a Young Poet,* 68.

32. Ibid., 33.

33. Ibid., 42.

34. Ibid., 19.

35. Ibid., 171.

36. Ibid.

37. Ibid., 35.

38. Heraclitus, *Heraclitus, Fragments,* translated by Brooks Haxton (New York: Penguin, 2003), 51.

39. Walker, *The Same River Twice,* 21.

40. Ibid., 13, 38.

CHAPTER TWELVE. HELPED ARE THOSE WHO KNOW

1. Alice Walker, *The Same River Twice: Honoring the Difficult* (New York: Washington Square Press, 1996), 280.

2. Ibid., 32.

3. Carl Jung, "Approaching the Unconscious," in *Man and His Symbols,* edited by Carl G. Jung (New York: Doubleday, 1964), 67, 43.

4. Ibid., 102.

5. Walker, *The Temple of My Familiar*, 226.

6. Ibid., 220.

7. Ibid., 229.

8. Ibid., 222–223.

9. Ibid., 231.

10. Alice Walker, *Revolutionary Petunias & Other Poems* (New York: Harcourt, Brace, Jovanovich, 1971), 16.

11. Walker, *The Temple of My Familiar*, 32.

12. Carl Jung, *The Earth Has a Soul: C. G. Jung on Nature, Technology & Modern Life*, edited by Meredith Sabini (Berkeley, CA: North Atlantic Books, 2002), 98.

13. Ibid., 73.

14. Ibid.

15. Adam Hochschild, *King Leopold's Ghost: A Story of Greed, Terror, and Heroism in Colonial Africa* (Boston: Houghton Mifflin, 1998), 39.

16. Walker, *The Temple of My Familiar*, 254.

17. Ibid., 73.

18. Ibid., 48.

19. Ibid., 51.

20. Ibid., 255.

21. Ibid., 260.

22. Ibid., 259.

23. Ibid., 259–260.

24. Carl Jung, *The Portable Jung*, edited by Joseph Campbell (New York: Penguin Books, 1976), 52.

25. Walker, *The Temple of My Familiar*, 130.

26. Ibid., 28, 29.

27. Hochschild, *King Leopold's Ghost*, 295.

28. Walker, *The Temple of My Familiar*, 243.

29. Ibid., 356.

30. Ibid., 52.

31. Ibid., 364.

32. Ibid., 364–365.

33. Jung, "Approaching the Unconscious," 24.

34. Ibid., 120.

CHAPTER THIRTEEN. A WOMAN OF ONE'S OWN: WOMANIST PHILOSOPHY AND REVITALIZATION OF THE SOVEREIGN FEMININE

1. Evelyn C. White, *Alice Walker, A Life* (New York: Norton, 2004), 278, 306.

2. Gloria Steinem, "Alice Walker: Do You Know This Woman? She Knows You," in *Gloria Steinem: Outrageous Acts and Everyday Rebellions* (New York: Holt, Rinehart, and Winston, 1983), 274.

3. Alice Walker, "Saving the Life That Is Your Own: The Importance of Models in the Artist's Life," in *In Search of Our Mothers' Gardens: Womanist Prose* (San Diego, CA: Harcourt, Brace, and Jovanovich, 1983), 4.

4. Ibid., 9.

5. Ibid., 11.

6. Ibid., 9.

7. Ibid., 13.

8. Ibid., 14.

9. Virginia Woolf, *A Room of One's Own* (1929; Orlando, FL: Harcourt Brace, 1991), 26–27.

10. Ibid., 47.

11. Ibid., 45.

12. Ibid., 44, 49.

13. Ibid., 58, 123.

14. Ibid., 48.

15. Ibid., 48–49.

16. Ibid., 60.

17. Alice Walker, "In Search of Our Mothers' Gardens," in *In Search of Our Mothers' Gardens: Womanist Prose* (New York: Harcourt, Brace, and Jovanovich, 1974), 233.

18. Woolf, *A Room of One's Own*, 49.

19. Walker, "In Search," 235.

20. Walker, "But Yet and Still the Cotton Gin Kept on Working . . .," in *In Search of Our Mothers' Gardens: Womanist Prose* (New York: Harcourt, Brace, and Jovanovich, 1974), 34.

21. Walker, "In Search," 239–240.

22. Walker, "The Black Writer and the Southern Experience," in *In Search of Our Mothers' Gardens: Womanist Prose* (New York: Harcourt, Brace, and Jovanovich, 1983), 18.

23. Walter Jackson Bate, *John Keats* (Cambridge, MA: Harvard University Press, 1963), 694.

24. Woolf, *A Room of One's Own*, 87, 71.

25. Ibid., 71.

26. Walker, "Saving the Life That Is Your Own," 5.

27. Thomas Jefferson, *Notes on the State of Virginia* (1785; New York: Penguin, 1999), 147.

28. Walker, "In Search," 237, 243.

29. Woolf, *A Room of One's Own*, 122.

30. Alice Walker, "Womanist," in *In Search of Our Mothers' Gardens: Womanist Prose* (New York: Harcourt, Brace, and Jovanovich, 1983), xi.

31. Ibid., xi–xii.

32. Alice Walker, "Gifts of Power: The Writings of Rebecca Jackson," in *In Search of Our Mothers' Gardens: Womanist Prose* (New York: Harcourt, Brace, and Jovanovich, 1983), 74.

33. Ibid., 79, 81.

34. Ibid., 80, 81.

35. Ibid., 82.

36. Ibid., 240, 241–242.

37. Ibid., 238.

38. Walker, "*One* Child of One's Own: A Meaningful Digression within the Work(s)," in *In Search of Our Mothers' Gardens: Womanist Prose* (New York: Harcourt, Brace, and Jovanovich, 1983), 363, 368.

39. Ibid., 367, 369.

40. Walker, "Beauty: When the Other Dancer Is the Self," in *In Search of Our Mothers' Gardens: Womanist Prose* (New York: Harcourt, Brace, and Jovanovich, 1974), 393.

41. Walker, "In Search," 237.

42. Alice Walker, *The Same River Twice: Honoring the Difficult* (New York: Washington Square Press, 1996), 54.

43. Alice Walker, "Coming in from the Cold," in *Living by the Word* (San Diego, CA: Harcourt, Brace, Jovanovich, 1988), 61.

CHAPTER FOURTEEN. THE SACRED MASCULINE

1. Alice Walker, *Temple of My Familiar* (San Diego, CA: Harcourt, Brace, Jovanovich, 1989), 241.

2. Ibid., 241, 242.

3. Ibid., 243.

4. Ibid., 244, 237.

5. Ibid., 244, 276, 278.

6. Ibid., 279.

7. Ibid., 282, 238.

8. Ibid., 164.

9. Ibid., 166–167.

10. Ibid., 167.

11. Edred Thorsson, *Runelore: The Magic, History, and Hidden Codes of the Runes* (San Francisco, CA: Weiser Books, 1987), 127; Walker, *Temple of My Familiar*, 291.

12. Walker, *Temple of My Familiar*, 291.

13. Carl Jung, *The Portable Jung*, edited by Joseph Campbell (New York: Penguin Books, 1976), 154.

14. Alice Walker, *The Same River Twice: Honoring the Difficult* (New York: Washington Square Press, 1996), 52.

15. Jean Shinoda Bolen, *Crossing to Avalon: A Woman's Midlife Pilgrimage* (New York: HarperSanFrancisco, 1994), 103.

16. Alice Walker, *The Color Purple* (Orlando, FL: Harcourt, 1982), 17.

17. Alice Walker, *Living by the Word* (San Diego, CA: Harcourt, Brace, Jovanovich, 1988), 80.

18. Carl Jung, *Memories, Dreams, Reflections*, edited by Aniela Jaffé (New York: Vintage, 1965), 391.

19. Walker, *The Color Purple*, 269.

20. Jung, *The Portable Jung*, 145; Jung, *Memories, Dreams, Reflections*, 391.

21. Alice Walker and Pratibha Parmar, *Warrior Marks: Female Genital Mutilation and the Sexual Blinding of Women* (New York: Harcourt Brace, 1993), 34.

22. Virginia Woolf, *A Room of One's Own* (1929; Orlando, FL: Harcourt Brace, 1991), 108, 114.

23. Ibid., 106.

24. Ibid., 107.

25. Ibid., 107–108.

26. Ibid., 37.

27. Walker, *The Color Purple*, 24.

28. Woolf, *A Room of One's Own* 38.

29. Walker, *The Color Purple*, 199.

30. Ibid., 206, 207.

31. Woolf, *A Room of One's Own*, 99.

32. Ibid., 38, 99.

33. Walker, *Living by the Word*, 80.

34. Walker, *The Same River Twice: Honoring the Difficult* (New York: Washington Square Press, 1996), 157.

35. Walker, *The Same River Twice*, 157.

36. M.-L. von Franz, "The Process of Individuation," in *Man and His Symbols*, edited by Carl G. Jung (New York: Doubleday, 1964), 196.

37. Alice Walker, *The Temple of My Familiar*, 409.

38. Ibid., 415, 412.

39. Ibid., 415, 413.

40. Ibid., 415.

41. Ibid., 414.

42. Ibid., 416.

CHAPTER FIFTEEN. THE GNOSTIC GOSPEL OF MY FATHER'S SMILE

1. Alice Walker, *By the Light of My Father's Smile* (New York: Random House, 1998), 28.

2. Ibid., 31.

3. Ibid., 26.

4. Ibid., 28.

5. Ibid., 30.

6. Ibid., 19.

7. Ibid., 159.

8. Ibid., 154, 30.

9. Ibid., 155, 18.

10. Elaine Pagels, *The Gnostic Gospels* (New York: Random House, 1979), 65.

11. Walker, *By the Light*, 153.

12. Pagels, *The Gnostic Gospels*, 49, 48.

13. Ibid., 48–49.

14. Ibid., 50–54.

15. Ibid., 57.

16. Carl Jung, *Memories, Dreams, Reflections* (1961; New York: Vintage, 1965), 398.

17. The Nomenology Project, *The Hidden Truth of Your Name, A Complete Guide to First Names and What They Say about the Real You* (New York: Ballantine, 1999), 11.

18. Pagels, *Gnostic Gospels*, 144.

19. Dorothy Astoria, *The Name Book: Over 10,000 Names—Their Meanings, Origins, and Spiritual Significance* (1982; Minneapolis: Bethany House, 1997), 248.

20. *Holman KJV Study Bible* (Nashville, TN: Holman Bible Publishers, 2012), 1708.

21. Barbara G. Walker, *The Woman's Encyclopedia of Myths and Secrets* (New York: HarperSanFrancisco, 1983), 484.

22. Marvin Meyer, editor, *The Nag Hammadi Scriptures, the International Edition* (New York: HarperSanFrancisco, 2007), 738.

23. Ibid., 744, 745.

24. The Nomenology Project, *The Hidden Truth of Your Name*, 500.

25. *Holman KJV Study Bible*, Matthew 1:23, 1577.

26. Ibid., Luke 8:3, 1708–1709.

27. Michael D. Coogan, editor, "Susanna," in *The New Oxford Annotated Apocrypha, New Revised Standard Version*, 4th edition (Oxford: Oxford University Press, 2010), 190–193.

28. Walker, *By the Light*, 55.

29. Ibid., 7.

30. Barbara Walker, *The Woman's Encyclopedia* (New York: HarperCollins, 1983), 543, 541.

31. Catherine Soanes and Angus Stevenson, editors, *Oxford Dictionary of English*, 2nd edition, revised (Oxford, UK: Oxford University Press, 2005), 58.

32. The Nomenology Project, *The Hidden Truth of Your Name*, 344.

33. Barbara Walker, *The Woman's Encyclopedia*, 449, 409.

34. Pagels, *Gnostic Gospels*, 60; Elaine Pagels, *Beyond Belief: The Secret Gospel of Thomas* (New York: Random House, 2003), 81.

35. Véronique Dasen, *Dwarfs in Ancient Egypt and Greece* (1993; Oxford: Oxford University Press, 2013), 29, 48–54, 244.

36. Walker, *By the Light*, 62, 63.

37. Barbara Walker, *The Woman's Encyclopedia*, 283.

38. Walker, *By the Light*, 187.

39. Ibid., 199.

40. Ibid., 201, 200.

41. Lawrence Principe, *The Secrets of Alchemy* (Chicago: University of Chicago Press, 2013), 18.

42. Ibid., 75,77, 78.

43. Ibid., 124.

44. Walker, *By the Light*, 17.

45. Principe, *The Secrets of Alchemy*, 123–124.

46. Walker, *By the Light*, 18.

47. Barbara Walker, *The Woman's Encyclopedia*, 18.

48. Walker, *By the Light*, 17.

49. Astoria, *The Name Book*, 182.

50. Walker, *By the Light*, 4.

51. Barbara Walker, *The Woman's Encyclopedia*, 806.

52. Ibid.

53. Walker, *By the Light*, 211.

54. Barbara Walker, *The Woman's Encyclopedia*, 18, 669.

55. Walker, *By the Light*, 113.

56. Ibid., 141.

57. Ibid., 4, 6.

58. Ibid., 144.

SECTION IV. WATER

1. Paramahansa Yogananda, *God Talks with Arjuna: The Bhagavad Gita*, Volume 2 (Los Angeles: Self-Realization Fellowship, 1995), 786.

2. Starhawk, *Truth or Dare: Encounters with Power, Authority, and Mystery* (New York: Harper and Row, 1987), 266; Tenzin Wangyal Rinpoche, *Healing with Form, Energy and Light* (Ithaca, NY: Snow Lion Publications, 2002), 73.

3. Cait Johnson, *Earth, Water, Fire, & Air: Essential Ways of Connecting to Spirit* (Woodstock, VT: SkyLight Paths Publishing, 2003), 61; Yogananda, *God Talks with Arjuna*, 869.

4. Starhawk, *The Earth Path: Grounding Your Spirit in the Rhythms of Nature* (New York: HarperSanFrancisco, 2004), 134.

5. Rinpoche, *Healing with Form, Energy and Light*, 15.

CHAPTER SIXTEEN. MBELE ACHÉ

1. Alice Walker, *Possessing the Secret of Joy* (Orlando, FL: Harcourt, Brace, Jovanovich, 1992), 147, 159.
2. Albert Camus, *Caligula and Three Other Plays* (1944; New York: Vintage, 1958), 300.
3. Walker, *Possessing*, 249.
4. Ibid., 120.
5. Ibid., 43.
6. Ibid., 22.
7. Ibid., 64.
8. Ibid., 59.
9. Ibid., 59, 60.
10. Ibid., 11.
11. Ibid., 18–19.
12. Ibid., 25.
13. Ibid., 26–27.
14. Carl Jung, *Memories, Dreams, Reflections*, edited by Aniela Jaffé (New York: Vintage, 1965), 215.
15. Walker, *Possessing*, 52.
16. Ibid., 72.
17. Ibid., 78.
18. Ibid., 73.
19. Ibid., 80–81.
20. Ted Andrews, *Animal Speak: The Spiritual and Magical Powers of Creatures Great and Small* (Woodbury, MN: Llewellyn Publications, 2007), 268.
21. Jung, *Memories, Dreams, Reflections*, 206.
22. Walker, *Possessing*, 169.
23. Ibid., 226–227.
24. Ibid., 233–234.
25. Jung, *Memories, Dreams, Reflections*, 214.
26. This discussion of the Fisher King and Parsifal is informed by Alberto Villoldo's analysis of the legend in "Transforming Fate into Destiny," in *Mending the Past and Healing the Future with Soul Retrieval* (Carlsbad, CA: Hayhouse, 2005), 18.
27. Walker, *Possessing*, 161.
28. Elaine Pagels, *The Gnostic Gospels* (New York: Random House, 1979), 123.
29. Ibid., 122, 123.
30. Jung, *Memories, Dreams, Reflections*, 227.
31. Ibid.
32. Gerald D. Hart, *Asclepius, The God of Medicine* (London, UK: Royal Society of Medicine Press, 2000), 33.
33. Walker, *Possessing*, 129, 174, 276, 142.
34. Ibid., 19.
35. Alice Walker, *The Same River Twice: Honoring the Difficult* (New York: Washington Square Press, 1996), 167.
36. Ibid., 277.
37. Ibid., 137, 138.
38. Ibid., 54.
39. Andrews, *Animal Speak*, 294.
40. Simon Kuper, *Soccer: Against the Enemy: How the World's Most Popular Sport Starts and Fuels Revolutions and Keeps Dictators in Power* (1994; New York: Nation Books, 2006), 1.

41. Walker, *Possessing*, 136.
42. Ibid., 104, 203.
43. Ibid., vii, 162.
44. Ibid., 7.

CHAPTER SEVENTEEN. *SUB ROSA* NO LONGER: OUR DAUGHTERS HAVE MOTHERS

1. Alice Walker and Pratibha Parmar, *Warrior Marks: Female Genital Mutilation and the Sexual Blinding of Women* (New York: Harcourt Brace, 1993), 4, 95.
2. Pratibha Parmar, *Warrior Marks* (New York: Women Make Movies, Inc., 1993). Unless otherwise indicated, "*Warrior Marks*" refers to both the book and the film. All quotations are from the book.
3. Ibid., 24, 269; See Hilary Burrage, *Female Mutilation: The Truth behind the Horrifying Global Practice of Female Genital Mutilation* (London: New Holland Publishers, 2015).
4. James Baldwin, "The White Man's Guilt," in *Baldwin, Collected Essays* (1965; New York: The Library of America, 1998), 722–723.
5. Walker and Parmar, *Warrior Marks*, 290.
6. Ibid., 347.
7. Ibid., 30.
8. Alice Walker, *The World Has Changed: Conversations with Alice Walker* (New York: The New Press, 2010), 95.
9. Ibid., 95, 86.
10. Ibid., 87.
11. Ibid.
12. Ibid., 88.
13. Walker and Parmar, *Warrior Marks*, 94, 93–94.
14. Ibid. 94–95.
15. Ibid., 94.
16. Ibid., 289.
17. Ibid., 106–107.
18. Ibid., 107.
19. Ibid., 258.
20. Ibid., 158.
21. Ibid., 296.
22. Ibid., 46.
23. Ibid., 139–140, 18.
24. Ibid., 284–285.
25. Ibid., 109.
26. Ibid., 9–10.
27. Ibid., 109.
28. Robin Morgan and Gloria Steinem, "The International Crime of Genital Mutilation," in *Outrageous Acts and Everyday Rebellions*, by Gloria Steinem (New York: Holt, Rinehart, Winston, 1983), 293.
29. Ibid., 294–295.
30. Walker, *The World Has Changed*, 130.
31. Ibid., 95–96.
32. Ibid., 179, 178.

33. Ibid., 179.
34. Ibid., 325, 326.
35. Ibid., 290.
36. Ibid., 110.
37. Clarissa Pinkola Estés, *Women Who Run with the Wolves: Myths and Stories of the Wild Woman Archetype* (1992; New York: Ballantine, 1995), 409.
38. Ibid., 391, 409.
39. Walker and Parmar, *Warrior Marks*, 46.
40. Estés, *Women Who Run with the Wolves*, 374.
41. Walker and Parmar, *Warrior Marks*, 304.
42. Estés, *Women Who Run with the Wolves*, 375.
43. Ibid., 377–378.
44. Ibid., 319.
45. Ibid., 377.
46. Walker and Parmar, *Warrior Marks*, 13.
47. Ibid., 18, 19.
48. Ibid., 251, 252.
49. Ibid., 207.
50. Estés, *Women Who Run with the Wolves*, 374.

CHAPTER EIGHTEEN. ABSOLUTE GOODNESS

1. Alice Walker, *Possessing the Secret of Joy* (Orlando, FL: Harcourt, Brace, Jovanovich, 1992), 273–274.
2. Alice Walker, *The Color Purple* (Orlando, FL: Harcourt, 1982), 195–196.
3. Ibid., 206.
4. Alice Walker, *The World Has Changed: Conversations with Alice Walker*, edited by Rudolph P. Byrd (New York: The New Press, 2010), 291.
5. Walker, *Possessing the Secret of Joy*, 229.
6. Carl Jung, *The Earth Has a Soul: C. G. Jung on Nature, Technology & Modern Life*, edited by Meredith Sabini (Berkeley: North Atlantic Books, 2002), 43.
7. Walker, *Possessing the Secret of Joy*, 84.
8. Jung, *The Earth Has a Soul*, 28–29.
9. Ibid., 55.
10. Ibid., 122.
11. Alice Walker, *By the Light of My Father's Smile* (New York: Random House, 1998), 81.
12. Ibid., 81, 82.
13. Ibid., 208.
14. Ibid., 81.
15. Ibid., 152, 156, 153.
16. Jung, *The Earth Has a Soul*, 122, 22.
17. Ibid., 166.
18. Ibid., 79–80.
19. Ibid., 82.
20. Alice Walker, *Absolute Trust in the Goodness of the Earth* (New York: Random House, 2003), 165.
21. Ibid., xiii, xii.

22. Ibid.
23. Ibid., xiii.
24. Ibid.
25. Ibid.
26. Ibid., 131.
27. Alice Walker, *Living by the Word* (San Diego, CA: Harcourt, Brace, Jovanovich, 1988), 140, 142.
28. Walker, *Absolute Trust*, 166, 167.
29. Evelyn C. White, *Alice Walker, A Life* (New York: Norton, 2004), 462–463; Alice Walker, *The World Has Changed*, xvi.
30. Walker, *The World Has Changed*, 291–292.
31. Walker, *Living by the Word*, 145.
32. Ibid., 145, 150.
33. Ibid., 146.
34. Walker, *Absolute Trust*, xiv.
35. Ibid., 65.

CHAPTER NINETEEN. WHY WAR IS NEVER A GOOD IDEA

1. Alice Walker, *Why War Is Never a Good Idea* (New York: Random House, 2007), 24.
2. Ibid., 29; Alice Walker, *Absolute Trust in the Goodness of the Earth* (New York: Random House, 2003), 156.
3. Walker, *Why War Is Never a Good Idea*; Walker, *Absolute Trust*, 123.
4. Carl Jung, *The Earth Has a Soul: C. G. Jung on Nature, Technology & Modern Life*, edited by Meredith Sabini (Berkeley: North Atlantic Books, 2002), 166; Albert Camus, *Albert Camus: Speech of Acceptance upon the Award of the Nobel Prize for Literature—December 10, 1957*, xi.
5. Alice Walker, *Sent by Earth: A Message from the Grandmother Spirit* (New York: Seven Stories Press, 2001), 19.
6. Ibid.
7. Alice Walker, *Possessing the Secret of Joy* (Orlando, FL: Harcourt, Brace, Jovanovich, 1992), 152.
8. Alice Walker, *Overcoming Speechlessness, A Poet Encounters the Horror in Rwanda, Eastern Congo, and Palestine/Israel* (New York: Seven Stories Press, 2010), 7–8.
9. Ibid., 8–9.
10. *Holman KJV Study Bible* (Nashville, TN: Holman Bible Publishers, 2012), Mark 3:25, 1647.
11. Walker, *Overcoming Speechlessness*, 46.
12. Ibid., 19.
13. Ibid., 28.
14. Ibid., 29.
15. Ibid., 19, 65.
16. Ibid., 63.
17. Ibid., 58.
18. Ibid., 61–62.
19. Ibid., 60.
20. Ibid., 48.
21. Ibid., 57.
22. Ibid., 39.
23. Walker, *Absolute Trust*, 124.

24. Ibid., 125.
25. Walker, *Overcoming Speechlessness*, 66.
26. Walker, *Sent by Earth*, 29.
27. Ibid., 33.
28. Ibid., 34.
29. Ibid.
30. Ibid., 19–20.
31. Walker, *Absolute Trust*, 151.
32. Ibid., 152.

CHAPTER TWENTY. WE ARE THE ONES

1. Sojourner Truth, "Ar'n't I a Woman?," in *Sojourner Truth, A Life, A Symbol*, edited by Nell Irvin Painter (New York: Norton, 1996), 168; Alice Walker, *We Are the Ones We Have Been Waiting For* (New York: The New Press, 2006), 3.
2. June Jordan, *Passion, New Poems, 1977–1980* (New York: Beacon, 1980), 42.
3. Bernard Magubane and Ibbo Mandaza, editors, *Whither South Africa?* (Trenton, NJ: Africa World Press, 1988), 153.
4. Jordan, *Passion, New Poems*, 43.
5. Jim Bessman, "25," CD Liner Notes, . . . *twenty-five* . . ., Ysaye M. Barnwell, Producer (Salem, MA: RYKODISC USA, 1988), 1, 4.
6. *Holman KJV Study Bible* (Nashville, TN: Holman Bible Publishers, 2012), 983.
7. Bessman, "25," 1, 4.
8. Alice Walker, *Anything We Love Can Be Saved: A Writer's Activism* (New York: Ballantine, 1997), 52, 53, 54.
9. Walker, *We Are the Ones*, 1.
10. Ibid., 1, 2.
11. Ibid., 10, 68.
12. Ibid., 2–3.
13. Ibid., 2.
14. Ibid., 2.
15. Ibid., 13.
16. Walker, *Anything We Love*, xxiii.
17. Ibid.
18. Ibid.
19. Alice Walker, *The World Has Changed: Conversations with Alice Walker*, edited by Rudolph P. Byrd (New York: The New Press, 2010), 287.
20. Walker, *Anything We Love*, xxiii.
21. Walker, *The World Has Changed*, 287.
22. Ibid., 286.
23. Ibid., 80.

SECTION V. AETHER

1. Paramahansa Yogananda, *God Talks with Arjuna: The Bhagavad Gita*, Volume 1 (Los Angeles: Self-Realization Fellowship, 1995), 40; Paramahansa Yogananda, *God Talks with Arjuna: The Bhagavad Gita*, Volume 2 (Los Angeles: Self-Realization Fellowship, 1995), 867.
2. Yogananda, *God Talks with Arjuna*, Volume 2, 867, 868.

3. Tenzin Wangyal Rinpoche, *Healing with Form, Energy and Light* (Ithaca, NY: Snow Lion Publications, 2002), 19, 74.

4. Yogananda, *God Talks with Arjuna*, Volume 2, 867, 868.

5. Yogananda, *God Talks with Arjuna*, Volume 1, 40.

CHAPTER TWENTY-ONE. THE CATHEDRAL OF THE FUTURE

1. Alice Walker, *Anything We Love Can Be Saved: A Writer's Activism* (New York: Ballantine, 1997), 3.

2. Ibid., 4.

3. Alice Walker, *Possessing the Secret of Joy* (New York: Harcourt, Brace, Jovanovich, 1992), 53.

4. Walker, *Anything We Love*, 4.

5. Ibid., 3.

6. Ibid., 16.

7. Ibid., 14, 17.

8. Ibid., 19, 14.

9. Ibid., 17.

10. Ibid., 12, 23.

11. Ibid., 24.

12. Ibid., 17.

13. Ibid., 24.

14. Ibid., 4, 9.

15. Alice Walker, *Absolute Trust in the Goodness of the Earth* (2003; New York: Random House, 2004), 120.

16. Walker, *Anything We Love*, 3, 4.

17. Ibid., 11.

18. Ibid., 20.

19. Ibid., 9, 5.

20. Aniela Jaffé, "Introduction," in *Memories, Dreams, Reflections*, by Carl G. Jung, edited by Aniela Jaffé (New York: Vintage, 1965), x.

21. Walker, *Anything We Love*, 25.

22. Ibid., 13.

23. Ibid., 21.

24. Walker, *Possessing the Secret of Joy*, 23.

25. Walker, *Absolute Trust*, 127–128.

26. Walker, *Anything We Love*, 13, 9.

27. Alice Walker, *The World Has Changed* (New York: The New Press, 2010), 52, 110, 127.

28. Walker, *Absolute Trust*, xiii.

29. Elaine Pagels, *The Gnostic Gospels* (New York: Random House, 1979), 19, 20.

30. Ibid.

31. Walker, *The World Has Changed*, 51.

32. Ibid., 251.

33. Alice Walker, *The Temple of My Familiar* (Orlando, FL: Harcourt, Brace, Jovanovich, 1989), 245.

34. Pagels, *Gnostic Gospels*, 134.

35. Ibid., 18, 17.

36. Walker, *Temple of My Familiar*, 295.

37. Ibid.

38. Ibid., 279.

39. Ibid., 289.

40. Pagels, *The Gnostic Gospels*, 18.

41. Walker, *The Temple of My Familiar*, 288.

42. Ibid., 295.

43. David Kinsley, *Tantric Visions of the Divine Feminine* (Berkeley: University of California Press, 1997), 225–226, 229, 282; Braham Aggarwal, *Significance of Hindu Deities* (Orlando, FL: Hindu University of America, n.d.), 3.

44. Walker, *The Temple of My Familiar*, 295.

45. Alice Walker, *By the Light of My Father's Smile* (New York: Random House, 1998), 193.

CHAPTER TWENTY-TWO. CARITAS: THE GREATEST OF THESE

1. Alice Walker, *Anything We Love Can Be Saved: A Writer's Activism* (New York: Ballantine, 1997), 1, 10.

2. Alice Walker, *The World Has Changed: Conversations with Alice Walker*, edited by Rudolph P. Byrd (New York: The New Press, 2010), 127.

3. Ibid.

4. Alice Walker, *Hard Times Require Furious Dancing* (Novato, CA: New World Library, 2010), 83–86.

5. Walker, *The World Has Changed*, 127.

6. Ibid., 299.

7. Alice Walker, *The World Will Follow Joy* (New York: The New Press, 2013), 6.

8. Alice Walker, *The Cushion in the Road: Meditation and Wandering as the Whole World Awakens to Being in Harm's Way* (New York: The New Press, 2013), 1, 3.

9. Walker, *The World Has Changed*, 301.

10. Walker, *Hard Times*, 43.

11. Walker, *The World Has Changed*, 223.

12. Walker, *Anything We Love*, xxii.

13. Ibid., 76.

14. Ibid., 74, 78.

15. Ibid., 75; Walker, *Hard Times*, 25.

16. Alice Walker, "Q & A," in *Alice Walker: Beauty in Truth*, directed by Pratibha Parmar, Women Make Movies, Kali 8 Productions and Kali Films Limited, 2013.

17. Walker, *Anything We Love*, 78.

18. Walker, *The World Will Follow Joy*, 128.

19. Walker, "Q & A."

20. Walker, *The World Has Changed*, 126.

21. Ibid., 127.

22. Ibid., 205.

23. Ibid., 206.

24. Walker, *Hard Times*, xv.

25. Walker, *The World Has Changed*, 307.

26. Elaine Pagels, *The Gnostic Gospels* (New York: Random House, 2004), 74.

27. Ibid., 74–75.

28. Walker, *Hard Times*, xvi.

29. Ibid., xvi.

30. Alice Walker, *In Search of Our Mothers' Gardens: Womanist Prose* (New York: Harcourt, Brace, Jovanovich, 1974), 237.

31. Walker, *Hard Times*, 163.

32. Walker, *The World Has Changed*, 264.

33. Ibid., 204.

34. Ibid., 85.

35. Alice Walker, *Sent By Earth: A Message from the Grandmother Spirit* (New York: Seven Stories Press, 2001), 30.

36. Walker, *The Cushion in the Road*, 42, 51.

37. Ibid., 42.

38. Walker, *The World Will Follow Joy*, xiv; Walker, *Hard Times*, 150.

CHAPTER TWENTY-THREE. OUROBOROS

1. Alice Walker, *The World Has Changed: Conversations with Alice Walker*, edited by Rudolph P. Byrd (New York: The New Press, 2010), 130.

2. Alice Walker, *The Temple of My Familiar* (San Diego, CA: Harcourt, Brace, Jovanovich, 1989), 267.

3. Alice Walker, *Now Is the Time to Open Your Heart* (New York: Random House, 2004), 9.

4. Alice Walker, *Living by the Word: Selected Writings, 1973–1987* (San Diego, CA: Harcourt Brace, Jovanovich, 1988), 143.

5. Alice Walker, *A Poem Traveled Down My Arm* (New York: Random House, 2003), 27.

6. Walker, *Now Is the Time*, 203.

7. Ibid., 15–16, 33, 22.

8. Alice Walker, *Absolute Trust in the Goodness of the Earth* (New York: Random House, 2003), 221.

9. Walker, *Now Is the Time*, 23.

10. Ibid., 7.

11. Ibid., 214.

12. Ibid., 52.

13. Ibid., 88.

14. Ibid., 17, 18.

15. Ibid., 121, 122.

16. Ibid., 173.

17. Ibid., 52, 50.

18. Ibid., 158.

19. Ibid., 159.

20. Ibid., 69.

21. Ibid., 203.

22. Laird Scranton, *The Science of the Dogon: Decoding the African Mystery Tradition* (2002; Rochester, VT: Inner Traditions, 2006), 143.

23. Philip Gardner, *Legend of the Serpent: The Biggest Cover Up in History*, directed by Philip Gardner and Tim Cowles, Reality Films, 2009.

24. Scranton, *The Science of the Dogon*, 167–168.

25. Monica Sjöö and Barbara Mor, *The Great Cosmic Mother: Rediscovering the Religion of the Earth* (1987; New York: HarperCollins, 1991), 57.

26. Scranton, *The Science of the Dogon*, 168.

27. Gardner, *Legend of the Serpent*.

28. Jeremy Narby, *The Cosmic Serpent: DNA and the Origins of Knowledge* (1998; New York: Putnam, 1999).

29. Sjöö and Mor, *The Great Cosmic Mother*, 60–61.

30. Walker, *Now Is the Time*, 203.

31. Scranton, *The Science of the Dogon*, 179.

32. Sjöö and Mor, *The Great Cosmic Mother*, 58.

33. Walker, *Now Is the Time*, 203–204.

34. Ibid., 211.

35. Ibid., 148.

36. Ibid., 7.

37. Ibid., 195.

38. Ibid., 196.

39. Barbara Walker, *The Woman's Encyclopedia of Myths and Secrets* (New York: Harper-Collins, 1983), 313, 314.

40. Walker, *Now Is the Time*, 196.

41. Alberto Villoldo, *Mending the Past and Healing the Future with Soul Retrieval* (Carlsbad, CA: Hayhouse, 2005), 47, 48.

42. Ibid., 51.

43. Ibid., 52.

44. Walker, *Now is the Time*, 204.

45. Ibid., 198.

46. Gardner, *Legend of the Serpent*.

47. Lawrence Principe, *The Secrets of Alchemy* (Chicago: University of Chicago Press, 2013), 25, 26.

CHAPTER TWENTY-FOUR. "ALICE" IS OLD GREEK FOR TRUTH

1. Alice Walker, *Living by the Word* (San Diego, CA: Harcourt, Brace, Jovanovich, 1988), 97.

2. Ibid., 98.

3. Ibid., 12.

4. Evelyn C. White, *Alice Walker, A Life* (New York: Norton, 2004), 40.

5. Alice Walker, *Possessing the Secret of Joy* (New York: Harcourt, Brace, Jovanovich, 1992), 106.

6. *Holman KJV Study Bible* (Nashville, TN: Holman Bible Publishers, 2012), John 8:32, 1777.

7. Alice Walker addresses these latter questions in "Democratic Womanism" and "Democratic Motherism" in *The World Will Follow Joy*, by Alice Walker (New York: The New Press, 2013), 171–183.

8. Walker, "Womanist," in *In Search of Our Mothers' Gardens: Womanist Prose* (New York: Harcourt, Brace, Jovanovich, 1983), xi.

9. Pratibha Parmar, *Alice Walker: Beauty in Truth*, directed by Pratibha Parmar, Women Make Movies, Kali 8 Productions and Kali Films Limited, 2013.

CHAPTER TWENTY-FIVE. *LAPIS PHILOSOPHORUM*

1. Lawrence M. Principe, *The Secrets of Alchemy* (Chicago: University of Chicago Press, 2013), 26.

2. Alice Walker, *The World Will Follow Joy* (New York: The New Press, 2013), xiii.

3. Alice Walker, *The Cushion in the Road: Meditation and Wandering as the Whole World Awakens to Being in Harm's Way* (New York: The New Press, 2013), 51.

4. Walker, *The World Will Follow Joy*, 72.

5. Alice Walker, *Hard Times Require Furious Dancing* (Novato, CA: New World Library, 2010), 156, 158.

6. Walker, *The World Will Follow Joy*, 24.

Index